The Changing Worlds of
Older Women
In Japan

Anne O. Freed, M.S.W.

With the assistance of
Yukiko Kurokawa, M.A.,
and Hiroshi Kawai, M.D.

KNOWLEDGE, IDEAS & TRENDS, INC.
THE POSITIVE PUBLISHER

First Published in 1993 by:
    Knowledge, Ideas & Trends, Inc.
    1131-0 Tolland Turnpike, Suite 175
    Manchester, CT 06040
    1-800-826-0529

Library of Congress Cataloging-in-Publication Data

CIP: 92-14990
ISBN 1-879198-10-X

1. Aged Women - Japan - Biography.
2. Women - Japan - Biography. 3. Life cycle, Human. I. Kurokawa, Yukiko. II. Kawai, Hiroshi.

10 9 8 7 6 5 4 3 2 1

First Edition
Printed in the United States of America

Cover Design and Art by Gil Fahey
Cover Photo by Pamela Quayle Hasegawa
Editorial Design by Cindy Parker

To my husband Roy
and my colleague and friend
Yuki Kurokawa
both of whom made this book possible

Table of Contents

Preface

In present day Japan, one sees many elderly Japanese women scurrying along the streets, mostly in western dress but occasionally in kimono and geta, whose lifetime extends from the Madame Butterfly era to the modern age. We can learn much from these women. They lived through at least three Japanese eras, especially the Sino-Japanese War that grew into World War II, in which Japan almost conquered a huge portion of Asia and eventually was devastated by American bombs.

As the men engaged in battle, these women remained on the home front where they played very new roles for which they were not prepared. Before the American Occupation, their roles were so narrowly defined that they were entirely subservient to men. During the Wars, many became the head of the household even though they did not have a legal status commensurate with their responsibilities. However, upon Japan's defeat, these women gained an unsought and unanticipated personal victory when their legal status was made equal to that of men.

Observers and participants both have many questions about those women. How do they look upon the changes wrought in their lives during the War and the immediate tumultuous post-war period? How have they coped with and adapted to the modernization and rapid westernization of their country and to the new demands on them and their roles in the restructured society? Young Japanese women cannot answer these questions because they lack experience in the pre-war era. Because the elderly women lived through the radical changes in the social history of their country, they can not only give the answers but can also reveal the psychological strengths they had to discover within themselves in order to adapt to their suddenly altered society.

To secure an insight in the older Japanese women's lives and their perceptions of their changing worlds, the author, an American social work clinician and educator, interviewed a number of elderly Japanese women using the life review technique. I asked these women about their life histories, their pre-war (Sino-Japanese War and World War II) experiences, their ordeals during the two wars, their attitudes about the present society in contrast to the old, and the clues they distilled from the tumultuous events in their lives. The interviews were as fruitful as they were free ranging and open ended.

Being an outsider, my task would have been impossible without the invaluable consultation and assistance of Mrs. Yukiko Kurokawa, a gerontological psychologist, who also performed the role of interpreter.

The Tokyo Metropolitan Institute of Gerontology, through its Sociology Department under the leadership of Daisaku Maeda, sponsored this research. They gave invaluable assistance from the inception of this project to the final interview. Without the able assistance of Yutaka Shimizu, assistant director, and Toyomichi Sato of the research unit, this effort would not have been possible. They gave advice on sample selection to assure that the interviews would include women who were from rural and urban backgrounds; who had the desired variety of marital status, such as single, married, divorced, and widowed; who came from various socio-economic groups; who had differing educational experiences; and who ranged in age from 65 through the mid-90s. They helped locate the subjects through senior centers, welfare offices, nursing homes, and a class in the Elder University conducted by a university professor in the senior center of Setagaya-ku in Tokyo. They drew generously on their research knowledge and skills to assist in the task I set. I am most grateful for their time, effort, graciousness, and professional interest. Through them, I met social work, sociology, and health professional staffs in the community who were interested in the aged. I learned not only about individual aged and their families but also about community programs and institutions that serve the elderly.

A word about the use of an interpreter is in order in such a project. (Freed, 1988). Mrs. Yukiko Kurokawa taught me the proper role of such an interpreter. When, on a few occasions, several others who lacked her professional background acted in that capacity, unfortunately, the interviews were much less smooth and detailed. Mrs. Kurokawa was knowledgeable in psychology and gerontology. She understood thoroughly both the interviewing process in general and the specific purpose of the interviews. She interpreted with the approprite language nuances to help me, who could not master even the rudiments of the Japanese language, communicate effectively with the elderly women. She expressed herself affectively, duplicating my affect, to cause the women to truly understand and trust me. She and I were in effect a single person despite our basic language differences. As a result, the women shared a great deal about themselves. Finally, she helped me understand Japanese culture and its significance in the behavior and life histories of the

women.

Dr. Hiroshi Kawai, a famous child psychiatrist in Tokyo who is also interested in gerontological psychiatry, offered invaluable consultations and direction. His support was especially helpful as he encouraged me to conduct this project and gave me invaluable professional advice.

Without the assistance of my husband, Roy N. Freed, we could not have videotaped these interviews. He accompanied us on our visits to the women in their homes, senior centers, nursing homes, and hospitals, laboriously carrying the heavy camcorder. He rearranged furniture and backgrounds as unobtrusively as possible to get the best pictures, even moving sliding doors to enlarge the small living rooms temporarily. Many of the women were impressed with his participation and wondered if all men in the United States offered such assistance to their wives. Many saw him as a role model of how they wished a husband to act.

Thanks are also due to Viola Isaacs, Roy Freed, and Fuki Utumaru from the Boston area, who read the entire manuscript and offered both substantive and editing suggestions based on their extensive knowledge of Japanese culture and of editing.

The late Dr. Louis Lowy, Emeritus Professor and former Associate Dean of Boston University School of Social Work, a social worker, gerontologist, and scholar, was always available for discussion, advice, and inspiration. He deserves special mention and acknowledgement for his unique contributions to the field of international gerontology and for the insights he offered to me.

Finally, thanks are extended to the 27 women who were willing to share their life stories. I recognize, because of the dire warnings of many Japanese professionals, that that type of sharing of intimate thoughts and experiences was not thought to be possible in Japan. All the assistance we received enabled us to disprove this. Our greatest limitation was that we had only two hours for each interview.

The sample might be considered to be flawed by the fact that we interviewed only women who were willing to talk about themselves. However, that probably does not detract from the significance of the findings which apply only to the particular population under study. A few of the women stated that they were willing to participate even though they thought that there was nothing significant in their lives that would interest us. That might reflect self-effacement as much as a genuine belief. Most were clearly pleased that someone was interested in

learning about them because they rarely, if ever, had the opportunity to talk about themselves so freely. Many were happy to reflect on and evaluate their lives, and even philosophize a bit. Although our interviews lasted only two hours each, significant friendships were established that include the hope that we will see each other again. To these 27 women, "Thank you for sharing your changing worlds with us and for teaching us how you adapted and coped in your challenging environment."

Anne O. Freed, M.S.W.
Adjunct Professor, Boston College
Graduate School of Social Work

Chapter 1

ક&

Learning
From
Older
Japanese
Women

O lder women in Japan are particularly aware that a new era for women dawned when the American Occupation authorities insisted, in the mid-1940s immediately after World War II, that the new Japanese Constitution must guarantee equal rights to women. Spanning the pre-war and post-war years, Japanese women over 65 recall that, until the end of World War II, women were expected only to be "good wives and wise mothers," as prescribed in the Meiji era. However, during World War II, Japanese women learned through harsh experience that they had additional talents that were valued by their society in an emergency. They could be administrators, workers, and leaders in addition to their domestic attributes. Of course, poor women, farm women, women who worked with their husbands in family-owned small businesses, and young widows had been working outside the home for years, albeit mostly in lowly roles and at low wages, and they were aware of their other talents (Mishima, 1953).

Nevertheless, the resistance to women being highly educated and assuming responsibilities in the community was pervasive for centuries and is encountered even today. Very few women could become professionals before the War except in teaching and nursing, and then they retained their jobs usually until they married. Even though the War exigencies proved that women were as capable outside the home as within the family confines, after the War most men still resisted giving women the same legal rights as men, including the right to vote and hold public offices. Fortunately for women, the Occupation Authorities prevailed in getting their legal rights recognized in the Constitution (Robin-Mowry, 1983).

How do the women who lived through the War, during which they assumed unsought duties for which most were not educationally pre-pared and discovered hidden talents and abilities, look back at the dra-matic changes in their lives? What effects on their lives do they note? What do they think of the radical changes through which they have lived? How were their lives transformed by the Sino-Japanese War, World War II, and the westernization and urbanization they experienced? How did they cope with the stresses of war? How did they adapt to their

changed roles? What strengths and weaknesses did they discover within themselves? Have they remained wedded to the Japanese traditional demarcation of the role of women? Do they prefer the "old ways" compared to the new life they lead today?

We can learn about the perceptiveness of older Japanese women, those from 65 to 95, through their answers to the questions just posed. Asking them can be more fruitful than turning to younger women or to the experts for secondhand assessments. Having lived through two or three eras of Japanese history (those in their 80's and 90's lived through the Meiji, Taisho, and Showa eras), they bring an unique historical perspective. Furthermore, through their life reviews, they can describe their continuously altered life patterns. They also introduce the affective component so necessary in understanding the concepts of adaptation to and coping with change. Being just Japanese women rather than historians, psychologists or sociologists, they can share with us a non-intellectualized subjective approach that is sufficiently distant from the initial events to have validity when analyzed.

Interviewing older Japanese women is an ideal means for learning about individual adaptation to extreme societal upheavals and fluctuations because they experienced even greater changes than men did in the transition from an Eastern-oriented to a Western-oriented society. They had been taught to "endure" life within the home and family but were not educated to cope with the outside world. However, after 1946, "Modernization called for a redefinition and readaptation of women's ideal and actual roles in postwar Japan" (Lebra, et al, 1976, p. 268). It is important to know how women who lived through both pre-war and post-war Japan compare their new lives to their pre-war lives.

Although the life cycle itself inevitably brings many changes in the lives of women and men everywhere, that has been particularly apparent for Japanese women. Before the War, when a woman married, she moved in with her husband's family if he was the oldest son. She assumed the new roles of wife and daughter-in-law under the ie system and had to adapt to substantial changes, much more than her husband. She left her family and saw them only occasionally after that. In Japan, the female roles in the past were so strictly prescribed that women could predict quite well what was expected of them in general. Those roles were frequently very demanding, always constricting, and at times even tragic. Japanese literature is replete with tales of the trials of daughters-

in-law and unhappy wives (Aryoshi, 1984; Shimer, 1982).

The Sino-Japanese War and World War II changed the lives of women to such an extent that role predictability began to fade for at least three decades. During that period, they were confronted with circumstances which their culture had not anticipated. For centuries they were "taught to strive for modesty and selflessness and to spend their lives serving the needs of their parents, husbands, and children" (Tanaka and Hanson, 1982, p. xi). They could take an independent stance only in household administration when they became senior head. Beginning with the Sino-Japanese War and continuing through World War II, they were increasingly forced to become the breadwinners, the factory workers, the employees in responsible positions, the farmers, the local leaders, and the force that helped keep the home front operating. Thus, they discovered previously unrecognized talents.

After the War, many of the women had to continue working because their husbands were disabled or had died, and they had to earn a living to support their children and frequently their mothers-in-law. Even those whose husbands returned to assume their former roles and whose family life was reestablished discovered that their world, their functions, and their expectations had changed (Mishima, 1953). Families moved to the cities from the countryside in huge numbers. Women had to continue to work to supplement their husbands' income not only to maintain their traditional life styles but also to pay for higher education for their children. They wanted them to achieve more than they had. Their horizons had changed along with their roles. Today, the young mothers are known as the "education mothers," as they take this role seriously.

The women we interviewed were old. Even the youngest among them, those in their late 60s, can look back and compare their lives before and after the two Wars. Given their contrasting experiences, they had a great deal to say about their lives generally and their adaptive capacities in particular. Their observations are important to people interested in the concepts of adaptation and coping in the life cycle of women. Their life reviews reveal how they changed and coped under new and often traumatic conditions and a new life style. Although basic adaptation is an innate human quality, a close examination of the lives of these elderly women can teach us a great deal about the nurturing and development of their adaptive and coping processes. It was with such

questions and points of inquiry that this study was undertaken through a series of interviews with 27 elderly women in Japan. This approach was also taken by Lebra who observed that, "It is my belief that an elderly woman's life review, however old-fashioned, can provide valuable insights into the optimal way of life for younger women" (1984, p. xi). The Tokyo Metropolitan Institute of Gerontology sponsored this research and arranged for most of the interviews.

All but three women interviewed lived in Tokyo although most were brought up in the countryside and migrated to Tokyo as young adults. The three in the countryside lived in the small mountain town of Obuse, fairly close to the city of Nagano in the northern part of Japan. Five of the women were in a hospital or nursing home, and one was being referred to a home for the aged. All the women had at least a fifth grade education before the War, but most had completed eight grades, and half of them completed high school or a jogakko (a special school for girls). Three went to college. One who had lived in the United States during her adolescent years completed a liberal arts woman's college before returning to Japan. Another completed a nutrition specialization in Ochanimizu College, and one left college precipitously to her life-long regret when she was told by her parents that she was to marry a man they found for her. Another was raised and educated in China and returned to Japan as a young adult during the War.

There were other variations. Several were reared in poverty while a number were from moderate and even comfortable homes, but the tragedies of war reduced their standard of living for many years. All but two of the women had worked outside the home either because of economic necessity or because they were drafted by the government into the labor force, generally in munitions plants during the War. Many continued working after the War. Although the best educated women in Japan were usually not employed before marriage, the War found them in the ranks of the employed. Of the two who never worked, one was handicapped from early childhood, and the other went from college to marriage to care for an ailing mother-in-law with whom she lived for 35 years. Finally, three were still married (one had a husband suffering from Alzheimer's Disease), two were single, two were divorced, and twenty-one were widowed, many when quite young.

The interviews were conducted whenever possible in the homes of these elderly women. The exceptions were the five living in a nursing

home or hospital and the nine who attended a senior center. Present in the interviews were an interpreter and the author's husband, who took video tapes of the interviews. None of the women refused to be taped. Despite the need to rearrange furniture and to secure proper lighting, within moments after the taping began, they disregarded the camera and were comfortable talking with us. They generally offered us tea and cookies, and several insisted upon serving lunch. Given that each interview was two hours, divided between the questions and comments of the interviewer and the answers in Japanese with accompanying translations into English, an amazing amount of information was gathered. The women appeared to enjoy talking about themselves. In fact, several commented that no one had ever asked them to recount their life history, and they valued the opportunity to think about it and to reflect upon the events and their meaning. A number became very philosophical, though humble, when asked if they had advice for younger people stemming from their life experiences.

Although the author had an agenda as reflected by the objectives for this study, a questionnaire was not used. Instead, the purpose of the interview was explained after the author and interpreter were introduced and their credentials were described as being an American professor of social work and a Japanese psychologist. The women never questioned this. The interviews were unstructured. It was first important to put the interviewee at ease. Some women started immediately by recounting their present life and circumstances. In those cases, they gradually worked from the present back to their early life. Others gave a chronological review from early childhood to the present, even assembling pertinent dates. Several had so much to say that they hopped from subject to subject and had to be directed in order to clarify when certain events occurred or about whom they were speaking. If the data was too sparse, we asked more questions. Because we tried to put them at ease by learning about their present interests before plunging into their life reviews, it was easy to move into the discussion without the structure and constraints of a questionnaire. Their feelings and attitudes were as important to us as their facts. This was especially meaningful for it made them feel highly individualized, and many were flattered that we wanted to know about their "modest lives" and their thoughts.

The interviews were clearly meaningful to the women. A follow-up note from a 68 year old woman testified to this. "Thank you so much for

coming (to my home). Thank you for asking me about my modest life history. I never imagined talking about my life history to an American professor. I haven't talked about it even to any Japanese researcher. My feeling was that when my life was put to the spotlight, it was a small life, not a rich life. My life history is only mine, and I realized that though it may be a very modest life, I should cherish it because I cannot return to my past and re-experience my life. Instead of regretting, I want to enjoy my freedom." Another 68 year old woman commented in a note, "You were so kind and nice to listen to my humble story of my life and to support my past during the interview. It was a pleasant, happy day that I will never forget throughout my life." A 69 year old woman wrote, "It was really hard to say good-bye to you. I was, and am, very proud of my 'labor life' through which I could gain my own happiness so I was ready to talk about my own life to anybody who would listen to me. I wondered if I could talk well." The fact is, they all "talked well," and one woman, an artist, drew a picture to show her satisfied reactions.

Chapter 2

❧

Looking
Back

Mrs. Takahara, 84, met us at the door of her garden, her face wrinkled with smiles. She was attractively clothed in a brown and white print dress that she had bought for this occasion. No one had ever asked her to talk about her past life, and she was flattered that we were interested in her. After two hours, she ended the interview saying, "Thank you so much for letting me experience a wonderful time. I wish I could have the videotape you took. It will be a memory for me, and I would like to see myself on tape."

Mrs. Kaga entered the room bursting to talk about herself. An active 89 year old woman, she enthusiastically plunged into her life story, and, in addition, to emphasize her particular interest in good health exercises, she demonstrated them to us a number of times. She expressed regret when the interview ended and wanted to make another appointment. Later, she wrote us, "I was delighted to talk with young people. Old people love to talk with youngsters. I get excited to be with young people and listen to what they have to say." We, in turn, were excited to hear what she had to recall. Her life had been eventful as she pursued a nursing career in the battlefields of China and in leading hospitals in Tokyo.

Mrs. Matsuo, 82, was frustrated that she could not speak longer with us. She asked, could she write to us? And could she have a copy of the videotape? She wanted to show it to her daughter and to review it again and again. She did write to us. She told us how pleased she was that the Emperor, at the end of the War, was declared to be human and not divine. She could think of him just the way she thinks of other people. She wrote, "I had so many more things that I should have said, but I was not smart enough. I was very relaxed and dependent on Mrs. Kurokawa's interpretations, so that I felt safe and free. It turned out to be a good chance for me to picture the 20th century. I wondered if I can see the world with my eyes."

Not every older person enjoys reviewing her life. Nevertheless, it is an almost universal occurrence among elderly people as they turn within. The process of reminiscence has been reported in literature as early as Aristotle in Rhetoric in 367-347 B.C. (Butler, 1968). Novelists, carriers

of folk tales, and human relations professionals have always emphasized the importance of the past when writing about the aged. Reminiscence is part of the adaptation to life in the process of resolving questions about the present in the light of the past and in looking toward the future.

Mrs. Tomita wrote, "It was great fun to talk. Thank you very much. I could recall things of my past days while talking. The day was the happiest day among the days last month in Obuse."

Mrs. Hara not only reminisced but asked, "Did you understand the difference between Japanese and American people by visiting us and Japanese homes? The aged people in Japan are those who have overcome hardships, and they know the importance of the joy of living."

Miss Katase, in response to our follow-up note, wrote that she not only enjoyed the interview but "I have a dream to take part in mutual understanding of the American and Japanese people, different from what is reported in the newspapers and television, something more people-based."

Elderly people frequently like to reminisce about their past because it gives them a sense of continuity, an opportunity to obtain a perspective on their past life, and a chance to philosophize about their accomplishments, the world, and the future. While for some it is a preparation for death, for most it is an affirmation of life, their achievements, and their ability to have survived its many vicissitudes (Lewis, Butler, 1974; Carlson, 1984; Liton, Olstein, 1969; Kaminsky, 1978; Lewis, 1971; Austin, 1976; Coleman, 1974 and 1986).

Some people have looked upon life review by old people as their way of clinging to the past, as an example of their garrulousness, and as a reflection of their being unable to look toward the future that involves death. Some even insist that reminiscence is dysfunctional because it may lead to despair rather than ego integrity as described by Erik Erikson (1963). He claims that, in the last stage of life, people resolve their conflicts and feelings either by achieving a sense of integrity and wisdom or by succumbing to depression and dejection. But innumerable studies have shown that reminiscence is a normative process. (For an extensive review of such studies see Coleman, 1987; Lieberman and Tobin, 1983.) "Life review [is] a naturally occurring, universal mental process characterized by the progressive return to consciousness of past experiences and, particularly, the resurgence of unresolved conflict; simultaneously

and normally, these revived experiences and conflicts can be surveyed and reintegrated" (Butler, 1968, p. 487). Frankl (1963) insists that people should reflect upon their life as a necessary task before death.

At all ages, life review is connected with thoughts of death. However, it usually takes place at old age. It is a reflective, looking-back process, and may be part of a possible personality reorganization. The more intense unresolved life conflicts are, the more therapeutic it is to reintegrate the many strands and events in life. "As the past marches in review, it is surveyed, observed, and reflected upon" (Butler, 1968, p. 489).

Life review can be a creative and constructive process, an opportunity to integrate the past with the present, an opportunity to view oneself as one wishes to be seen by others, and an effort to express wisdom that only the passage of time allows. For many aged, it permits serenity to be established and a greater self-awareness to be achieved.

Nevertheless, life review can have negative consequences. Depression, guilt, rigidity, unresolved anger, conflict, and obsessive ruminations may occur. For those elderly who always lived for the future, who avoided current consequences, and who saved money for the pleasures of tomorrow, a life review might suddenly confront them with the fact that there are not many tomorrows, and they may not achieve their goals. This leaves some sad and frustrated, and others reflect with greater wisdom.

There is no doubt that a formal life review as described in this book and demonstrated by the 27 women we interviewed is not a process every elder would like. For a person who has experienced a series of failures in the past, who feels guilty about some past actions and behavior, and who still is ruminating about them, a life review might be harmful by precipitating depression, suicide, withdrawal, and anger. Nevertheless, it is "a potent force toward self-awareness" (Butler, 1968) most people welcome.

Reminiscence and life review may be therapeutic tools in work with older people. Psychotherapists see it as an effective method to help older people recognize the value of life as it has actually been lived. It also contributes to a sense of self-worth and enhanced self-esteem, engages the elderly person as she recounts the story of her life, and preserves her memories (Coleman, 1986). It permits the elderly person to take possession of the past, treasure it, and, at the same time, struggle with the regrets and sorrows by putting them into perspective. Ideally, it leads to serenity and greater wisdom. Inevitably, some past events are sanitized,

viewed with a rosy tint, rationalized to handle negative aspects, and glorified beyond reality. It is a subjective rather than an objective process and deeply personal.

Lieberman and Tobin (1983) conducted a series of life reviews with elderly based on the premise that large numbers of older people like to review their lives and particularly enjoy the interpersonal attention they receive. They discovered that those who are capable of introspection develop additional thoughts and conclusions about their lives as they review and reconstruct the past. It becomes a source of gratification and challenge and may lead to greater maturity. However, they did not find that life review automatically leads to acceptance of the finiteness of life or to better adaptation. Lieberman and Tobin learned instead that because of physical, mental, and personal losses, elderly looked to the past for comfort and a sense of control and mastery. Some even commented in amazement that they were the same person they have always been and had not become a different person because of old age. Those people maintained a stable, persistent, unique self-image in defining themselves in the present, thus reinforcing the "current me" (p. 264), the person of today. The process allowed some to create a self-portrait that reflected not only the actual person but, more importantly, the myth of how that person wished to be seen. In fact, some presented themselves as if in a drama with heroes and heroines. Life review in that way became a reaffirmation of their lives. This was therapeutic.

Life review by the elderly, whether individually or in groups, Coleman (1986) and Lieberman and Tobin (1983) found, has considerable emotional significance as they invest themselves in the past. For elderly whose present life is barren, it becomes an effective substitute, and the past takes on greater significance. There are individual differences. Some elderly prefer to think only of the present, even those who had a good life. Those engaged in meaningful current activities may not have a strong need to dwell too long on the past although they do not object to reminiscing. Others do not want to look back. They generally are people with low emotional reactions who have trouble articulating their feelings, feel neutral about their lives, or want to avoid the future with its connotation of death. These investigators also found that people in crisis (possibly when preparing to go into a nursing home) could, if articulate, use life review as a therapeutic method to counteract their sense of loss and abandonment. Similarly, they learned that in group

therapy life review is an especially helpful means for introducing the participants and creating a sense of both individuality and belonging. Hearing about other people in the group is gratifying and becomes a comfort and support. It may even break some elders' isolation. Likewise, for introspective people with good cognitive functioning and perceptual capacities, life review may lead to improved self-image and integration of the past with the anticipated future. It is interesting that they found that the old-old (age 85 and over) had already reviewed their lives to themselves or others and showed signs of resolution. Those people were not enthusiastic about repeating such a venture. Finally, all three investigators agreed that one could not generalize about life review. For example, those who preferred not to reminisce might be as well adjusted as those who did reminisce. They found that those who reminisce are not necessarily psychologically the best adjusted.

Peter Coleman (1986), in his extensive longitudinal study of reminiscence of elderly living in a housing project in England, observed that, "It is worth reflecting on just how many social changes this group of people had witnessed in their lifetime" (p. 20). These people grew up in a world where they had to be "disciplined, frugal, stoical, self-denying, poor." He found that what was taught to them was of little use to their children and grandchildren "who had been shaped by different purposes and by changed circumstances" (p. 26). Thus, they could see little in their life reviews that they could communicate to the younger generations. These people blamed World War II for social upheavals and condemned modern society and materialism, as if "accepting the values of modern society is tantamount to denying meaning to their own lives as they have led them" (p. 26). Nevertheless, they wanted to talk about their lives, present and past. When we summarize in Chapter 18 how Japanese elderly women responded to the changes in their lives that were even more radical than those in England, it will be interesting to compare the two groups. Both live on islands and were once proud empires, and both suffered severely as a result of World War II.

In life reviews, elderly frequently clarify their sense of self and continuity and, at times, are astonished to note their strengths and ability to survive. Surely, many of the Japanese women we interviewed were prime examples of survivors. A number were stranded in China and Manchuria at the end of World War II, others survived the bombings of Tokyo, and many were widowed at a young age because of the Wars.

They had to financially support their children and mother-in-law with little preparation for such arduous tasks. One woman was a battered wife, beaten by an alcoholic husband; others suffered in silence while caring for demanding, tyrannical mothers-in-law. Two women were considered physically weak or defective in early childhood and had to adapt to a rejecting environment. In these two cases, one succeeded in overcoming her handicap and at 89 is still working on it; the other is in a nursing home, still seeking an empathic family. Currently, many of the women have health problems, but, in all instances, they are finding ways of coping with their declining health. The saddest probably is Mrs. Hayakawa who wonders why her husband, who was so brilliant and learned, developed Alzheimer's Disease while she, who is unintellectual, is the healthy partner.

Religion, Coleman found, played an important part in the lives of those in old age who were able to philosophize. They sought existentially for a way to comprehend the meaning of life in general and not just of their own. In that regard, Miss Katase, engrossed in thought, observed, "If people everywhere would look deep into their own religion and look at what all religions have in common, how much better it would be. They would see the core of all religions is similar. Perhaps, in this way, they could find the possibilities for peace. People concentrate too much on their differences."

In summary, life review, while not suitable for all aged people, presents elderly with an opportunity to look back on their lives, to connect their families-of-origin with themselves as adult individuals and with the families they created, and to see themselves from a historical perspective within their families, within the society in which they were raised, and within the present-day society in which they have survived. Listeners to these elderly may discover how their adjustment today relates to their past lives, and they may "learn the riches that lie so often unnoticed behind our fellow citizens' front doors" (Coleman, 1986, p. 5). Most importantly, we learn how people cope with major life events. Further, we observe how today's elderly status and aspirations changed. This is particularly the case with Japanese women whose country and culture underwent profound changes as a result of the thirteen years of war and destruction of their large cities, their industries, and their economy. The life reviews of these women also tell us how they view their present life in contrast to the pre-war order, as well as their thinking about past

militarism, social constraints, and authoritarianism as compared to their present, more democratic situation. We can learn how they tap into their memories in the face of the difficulties and struggles many endured. We can learn whether they find it therapeutic to recount their life histories.

In a study such as this, we may draw conclusions only from the women who were willing to review their lives with us. We do not know from those who refused to be interviewed what rich or barren lives were being hidden. We do know, however, that after six of the women we interviewed told their friends in their Elder University class about their experience, their classmates volunteered to be interviewed. Unfortunately, time had run out, and we were unable to see them. With the exception of one woman, who could not concentrate on the interview because she was frantically trying to resolve a serious crisis, the others spoke freely and frankly and shared their thoughts willingly and happily.

When the plan to study Japanese older women's life histories using reminiscence methodology was discussed with Japanese human relations professionals, they doubted that older women would be willing to share their personal lives with a foreigner, albeit that the interpreter was Japanese. Some doubted that they would want to talk about their lives with anyone because this is not part of their culture. Yet, when senior centers, nursing homes, the Elder University, a hospital, several welfare offices, and individuals were asked for volunteers, there was no problem in finding as many elderly Japanese women as we could handle in our limited time. When we sent a follow-up note to each of the women asking their thoughts about the interviews, the answers were uniformly positive. They liked looking back and looking forward. Mrs. Hosoi summarized it well for all of the women. She wondered initially why we would want to interview her. "After all, my life has not been interesting or exciting," she insisted. Nevertheless, in her letter several months later, she stated, "I appreciate your giving me a chance to recall my own life. I thank you for picking me at the Senior Center. I had many more things to talk about, but I was happy that you listened to a modest woman's simple story. Singing songs together was a real joy." (She had commented that an uncle had taught her American folk songs as a child. When we asked if she could remember them, she did, even though she had not sung them in 55 years. We sang them together). She ended her note with, "God bless you. Hoping you will have a fruitful future."

Chapter 3

&

History of
Japanese Women
From the
Meiji Restoration
to Present

The women who shared their life reviews ranged from 67 to 94 years. The oldest were born in the latter part of the Meiji era (1858-1912), and the young-old, in the early part of the Taisho era (1912-1926).

If we are to understand these women, their experiences, thoughts, values, expectations in life, philosophies, and concerns, we must know a bit about the history of women in pre-World War II Japan. This includes their status and role, their culture, and their self-image as projected onto them by the Japanese society. Only in an historical and cultural context can one appraise them and measure their psychological and cognitive capacities as they have adapted to the many major changes in their society and in their lives (Austin, 1976; Pharr, 1976; Long, 1989; Lebra, 1976; Plath, 1980; Lebra et al., 1976; Robins-Mowry, 1983; Lebra, 1984; Cressy, 1955; Plath, 1974 and 1980; Kiefer, 1990; Mishima, 1953; Sugimoto, 1966).

By the 1890s, Japan had been open to westernization for thirty years and was in the process of rapidly industrializing and modernizing. The Meiji government was determined to transform Japan into a modern, industrial society from an agricultural nation that had been isolated for several hundred years. It sent its statesmen to Europe and America to study their governments, industries, and education systems and bring back ideas to be adopted in Japan.

Japan emulated the imperialism of the West as well, which was compatible with its feudalistic past. In the 1890s and early 1900s, it conducted successful military adventures against China, Korea, and Russia.

By the end of the 19th century, Japan ceased to be isolated economically, politically, and geographically; the culture and the status of its women had a different history. Historically, Japan experienced extremes in the status of its women. Its myth of the origins of the country describes the Sun Goddess, Amaterasu, sending her grandson from Heaven to govern the Japanese Islands. She is supposed to have established the present day imperial line with its divine origin. The first seven centuries were a golden age for women because many held powerful political positions. Those two hundred years were known as the Epoch of the Queens

who set standards for culture, religion, politics, and intellectualism (Robin-Mowry, 1983, Chapter 1; Lebra et al., 1976, Chapter 1).

However, during the same period, the Chinese philosophies of Buddhism and Confucianism gradually permeated Japanese society to the detriment of women. They were relegated to a position inferior to men. Those philosophies prescribed the family relationships and removed women from direct political life, except when they were influential figures behind their husbands. From that time, Japan became primarily a country emphasizing the aggrandizement of men.

Confucianism dictated the family hierarchy in which women were placed in subordinate roles. Buddhism did not allow women ever to achieve Nirvana. Both saw women as threatening, sexual creatures. To this day, these concepts persist in similar or modified language (Robin-Mowry, 1983, p. 21-22).

During the Heian years (the 8th through the 12th centuries), although women were hidden in their homes, the high-born among them were educated but not in the Chinese language as were the men. As a result, the women produced Japanese-language literature that laid the ground for indigenous Japanese literary works, for example, *The Tales of Genji* by Shikibu Morasaki in the late 10th century. They also served as social critics, "dissecting the events and morals of the time" (Robin-Mowry, 1983, p. 19). But in the ensuing period until the middle of the 20th century, "The woman had no way of independence through life. When she is young, she obeys her father; when she is married, she obeys her husband; when she is widowed, she obeys her son," as directed by the Doctrine of the Three Obediences (Robin-Mowry, p. 20). Those were the feudalism years when loyalty, obedience, and subservience were the values and standards demanded of women whether they were ladies of the rich and powerful families or those who toiled in the fields.

During the long feudal period preceding the Meiji era, Buddhism became especially strong. It degraded women increasingly as the priests preached that women were sinful, covetous, and instruments of defilement—a remarkable set of projections! Only its Nicheren and Zen Sects did not proclaim these ideas. Until the 1946 Constitution, women had no family rights except those allowed by their father or husband. With Buddhism as a dominant national religion, all families had to be registered in the community by the father or father-in-law during the period from the 17th century until 1946. Endurance, self-repression,

restraint, subservience, non-expression of emotions, and denial of individual thoughts and feelings were stressed as feminine virtues.

Confucianism, with its emphasis on passivity and negative feminine qualities (yin), combined with Buddhism and feudalism to reduce the wife's role to that of "a belly borrowed to bear sons" (Robin-Mowry, p. 25). Women referred to their husbands as their lord, and, interestingly, today their language is still sprinkled with such subservient terms. In essence, women were considered stupid, and, given their lack of education, this characterization was accepted as correct. Men had to guard against their "indocility, discontent, slander, jealousy, and silliness" (Robin-Mowry, p. 26). In fact, women were admonished not to form close relationships but merely to obey father, mother-in-law, husband, and oldest son.

During the feudalistic period that continued until the middle of the 19th century, women had minimum legal rights. Marriage was strictly controlled; only men could demand a divorce; only women committing adultery were punished, and, at that, by death. Inheritance and land ownership were not a woman's prerogative. The countryside was even more rigid than the cities in enforcing these legal customs. However, women in the merchant class were somewhat freer. They generally helped their husbands in their businesses. The most serious problem was organized prostitution into which poor farmers sold their daughters, sometimes even their wives. The geishas, who saw themselves as professional entertainers of men, really were in bondage, too. Women's status was frozen in this mold during the entire two hundred years of the Tokugawa era preceding the Meiji Restoration (Lebra, et al. 1973; Robin-Mowry, 1983).

Today, 150 years after the Tokugawa era, women are still struggling to extricate themselves from a rigid, formalist society with its hierarchies and formalism of relationships, speech, and actions. Many constraints are still ingrained from centuries of indoctrination. Although most people are probably not conscious of the teachings of the inferiority of women, they comply with it. Those women who resent their lowly status are still fighting to overthrow centuries of traditional teaching.

Although Japan had had earlier contact with the Western World, when the American Commodore Perry entered Tokyo Harbor and the American and European cultures increasingly began to influence Japan, the downfall of feudalism and the Tokugawa Shogunate was final. The

Meiji era was born. The first two decades of the Meiji era were exciting years for women of all social classes. Education for girls was encouraged, even to the extent of sending five Japanese young girls to the U.S.A. to be educated in an experimental project. By 1890, universal education was initiated. But, concurrently, Confucian ethics and filial devotion were strongly reasserted alongside nationalism and devotion to the Emperor.

The world into which the oldest of the women we interviewed were born was one in which women were stirring from their feudalistic constraints. Girls were being educated at least through the sixth or eighth grades, and there was a dramatic awareness of how limited the Japanese women's opportunities were in contrast to the West. A number of the aristocratic women became interested in the new, outside world. As they traveled with their husbands, they brought back ideas from the West that set Japanese society stirring. Unfortunately, in the 1890s and 1900s, Japan embarked on numerous wars with China (1894), Russia (1904), and Korea (1910). Patriotism brought large numbers of women out of their homes to rally and establish social welfare, charities, relief work, hospital work, and educational projects. One woman even established a branch of the Salvation Army. But legal and political rights continued to be denied them (Robin-Mowry, 1983).

Although women's status changed as a result of universal education in the Meiji era, nevertheless, the persistence of traditional relationships and expectations gave rise to a number of rebellions among women. They became the Meiji feminists, better known as the "Meiji women," a unique group concerned with women's inferior status, their lack of the right to vote or own property, their lack of higher education, their serious exploitation in factories, their parents' and husbands' right to sell them into prostitution, the use of child labor, and their desperate need for birth control (Robin-Mowry, 1983).

The latter part of the Meiji period, especially from 1890 to 1912, was particularly severe for women. Peasant women throughout the ages always worked hard, but industrialization gathered young women primarily from the farms and fishing villages into textile factories that housed them in dormitories and exposed them to such horrendous conditions that large numbers died. In the following Taisho era (1912-1925), relief came to women through factory laws that regulated working conditions. But life still was harsh in the Taisho years despite the beginnings of

democracy and enlightenment. Rural women staged a revolt against rice speculation, and soon it spread to the cities (Lebra et al., 1976, pp. 25-75).

Women's education, too, had its trials, and women leaders rose to demand more than the six mandatory grades. Furthermore, farm girls and those from poor families had never been encouraged to seek an education. In the Meiji and Taisho eras, women's education was meant primarily to prepare them for the domestic roles of "good wives and wise mothers." Christian missionary schools were an exception in that they emphasized academic subjects, but they were under constant criticism. Only as Japan engaged in its numerous wars did the government see the need for more comprehensive education for women because they needed them then to replace the men in the battle fields. Higher education was especially slow to develop until after World War II with the exception of teacher training, nursing, dentistry, pharmacy, domestic science, and medicine (a women's medical school was established in 1900). In 1938, a leading private university accepted women, but not until the American Occupation was the government prodded to allow girls to compete to enter the prestigious government universities (Robin-Mowry, 1983).

In essence, the ambivalence toward higher education for women reflected the fear that women would reject the traditional mores as they developed a broader outlook. However, the Meiji women were restive, and, in the latter part of the Meiji era, they pressed for higher education and a university for women. One of the earliest was the Women's Normal School established in 1874 that later became Ochanimizu Women's University. Two women we interviewed attended Ochanimizu. Tsuda College was another early women's college whose founder was one of the five little girls sent to the U.S.A. to study. In 1901, the Japan Women's University was founded, followed in 1918 by the Tokyo Women's Christian College. Unfortunately, the wars Japan embarked upon led the government to take a more conservative approach to education for women. It preferred to educate women to be "obedient wives and militant mothers" (Robin-Mowry, p. 43).

The family in the pre-Occupation years had been strongly patriarchal and patrilineal. The traditional ie system persisted. The oldest son inherited the family property and assumed the obligation to support his aging parents. When he married, he brought his bride into his family home, and for years she was expected to be obedient to his mother.

Japanese literature is rife with tales of domineering mothers-in-law and daughters-in-law waiting patiently to rule over their future daughter-in-law (Shimer, 1983). The Buddhist family registries became a way of controlling women. The elder of the family registered all new members, and, when the oldest son married, frequently the bride was not registered until she produced a son. Yet in numerous instances, she might not be registered even after a son was born if her father-in-law chose not to do so. Women were served last; men were given preference within the home. The daughter-in-law was the servant in the household unless she had an enlightened mother-in-law. A daughter who divorced was not welcomed back by her own family because she was considered to have disgraced them. (See also Christopher, 1983, Chapter 5.) An 84 year old woman we interviewed described how her family would not permit her to return to their home after she divorced her philandering husband. Families selected the husbands for their daughters without reference to their desires. This was the case for all but a handful of our interviewees. If a family had no sons, the husband of the oldest daughter was adopted and became the oldest son. If a widow wished to remarry, she needed the consent of her in-laws. (For a detailed description of the ie system see Lebra, et al., 1976.) As the reader studies the life histories of the women we interviewed, these cursory descriptions of the ie system relationships will come alive. A woman's life was one of burdens, responsibilities, duties, demands, obligations, and subservience. Those who could achieve a less demeaning role were the fortunate ones. A few even opted not to marry although this was rare except during World War II when most eligible men were away fighting.

With the emphasis on wars and nationalism in the late Meiji era and the pre-World War II Showa period (1925-1939), women were prohibited by law from joining political associations, as reflected in the infamous Article Five of the Peace Preservation Law of 1887. Women could only join literary and philanthropic organizations along with the Women' Christian Temperance Union, the Young Women's Christian Association, the Women's Patriotic Society, and similar organizations (Robin-Mowry, 1983).

The Blue Stocking Society (Seitosha), established in 1911, was the first feminist organization to encourage women writers. But when it became political, the government censored it, and, therefore, in 1919, it converted into the Association of New Women with the objective to

fight for equal rights for both sexes, to establish women's trade unions, and to safeguard women's rights. It did succeed in getting laws changed to allow women to attend and hold political meetings, but not until the American Occupation could women join or organize political parties.

Most dramatic were the efforts of women, especially during the Taisho era, to bring birth control to Japan. Families were huge, and women suffered severely. During the 1920s, the birth control movement started. However, with the onset of the Sino-Japanese War, the government wanted more babies for eventual soldiers and workers, and the movement was forced to cease. It was reestablished after World War II without government objections. The need in the post-war period for population control to eliminate Japan's overpopulation made it possible for women to limit their families. Today, the nuclear families generally have 1.7 children (Lebra, et al., p. 18). The older women we interviewed came from very large families; they had two, or, at most, three children. Their daughters have one or, at most, two children.

It is interesting to note that Japan's two greatest catastrophes, the 1923 Earthquake and World War II, provided conclusive evidence that women had significant capabilities when permitted to exercise them. Without being requested, after the Earthquake, they plunged in to organize relief and rescue teams and to assist with the reconstruction. They founded the Federation of Women's Associations of Tokyo to help the hungry, homeless, and destitute. During World War II, they flocked to factories to assume men's jobs. They also spent enormous amounts of time seeking food even though it meant selling their precious kimonos and other belongings. In their neighborhoods, they became leaders. They were constantly seeking new housing as their homes were destroyed by bombs. Some evacuated to the countryside (Mishima, 1953). One of our interviewees took her elementary school pupils to a mountain village for over two years. As is true for women all over the world, in national emergencies, Japanese women carried the burdens of the home front with remarkable ability.

In the '20s and early '30s, there were occasional movements demanding the right of women to vote. However, after the Manchurian Incident and the growing totalitarianism and militarism, the suffragettes were forced to shift to issues concerning women's daily lives. The suffrage movement was in eclipse until the end of World War II when the vote again became an issue. Women were told by government leaders that "it

would retard the progress of Japanese politics" (Lebra, et al., p. 19). They organized, lobbied, and, with the assistance of the American Occupation forces in December 1945, they were granted the vote. Nevertheless, the Imperial House Law still does not permit a female on the throne.

The post-war days have seen massive changes in women's rights, many initiated by the Occupation Forces. Licensed prostitution was abolished. Women were allowed to become leaders of local governments and assemblies. Mandatory school years were extended to nine years. An equal-pay-for-equal-work law was passed (but is not necessarily enforced). Limitations were placed on overtime, night, and underground work. Twelve weeks of maternity leave is now law. A Women's and Minors' Bureau was established in 1948 to protect working women. A Eugenics Protection Act provides for counseling concerning marriage, birth control, and legal abortions. In 1947, women were granted equal property rights, freedom of marriage, and equal grounds for divorce. The eldest son's inheritance rights were extended to all siblings in the family, thus eliminating the ie system. Widows were granted the right to be guardians. Husbands lost their right to manage their wife's property or choose their domicile. Wives could transact business without their husband's consent. Women were given equal opportunities to be admitted into tax-supported universities, including the imperial ones.

What is the world of women like in Japan today compared to the world the women we interviewed were born into? Women vote in larger numbers than men, but very few get elected to the Diet or local offices. Women are attending college in large numbers, but a 1956 law made home economics studies compulsory for girls, thus it is harder for them to compete with boys for university entrance. Equal numbers of girls and boys are admitted into higher educational institutions, but 90% of the girls enroll in two-year junior colleges, and only 20% of the students in the four-year universities are women. About one-half of the junior college students major in home economics. Most of the women's universities still stress the importance of being a good mother. The hard sciences, social sciences, and economics are not considered suitable for women. Most women major in the humanities. The government does not invest much in women's education on the assumption that "all women must sooner or later marry and become dependent" (Lebra, et al., p. 21).

Forty percent of the labor force are women, and one-half of all women over fifteen years of age work. Seventy-three percent are in clerical,

service, and factory jobs. The division of labor by gender is pronounced even in the professions, with women being primarily nurses, nursery school and elementary school teachers, and with men being judges, scientists, and managers. Women earn about one-half the amount of income men receive. The average working age of women is younger than of men, and their working lives are considerably shorter. Most women are still less well educated, less skilled, and receive fewer job promotions than men. Women are still opting for marriage first, but they marry at a later age than before the War. The birthrate has gone down; the divorce rate at first increased, but now has stabilized; there are more nuclear families; more married women work, many part-time, to supplement the family income and pay for children's education, especially if they go to jukus (cram schools) (Lebra, et al., 1976; Robin-Mowry, 1983).

Present day observers conclude that while more women are educated, working, voting, exercising legal rights, holding public offices, owning property, and getting divorced, nevertheless, "There is much of the fabric of the feminine tradition in Japan which has resisted change... For most women, the traditional domestic role identity remains a comfortable one" (Lebra, et al., p. 297). At the same time, women are seeking a dual role in work and at home, many because they get job satisfaction. They have choices that they did not have in the past, and that satisfies them. However, a group of present-day feminists want a more open and less rigid society, and this small group is trying to reach women as well as men with their demands. Whether their targets are achievable remains to be seen. The affluence of Japan presents a different climate from the immediate past, one that is not conducive to further change for the time being.

The younger women of present day Japan live in a society in which the relationships are described as vertical (Nakane, 1970), i.e., the mother relates primarily to her children and her family-of-origin, and her relationship to her husband is secondary. When this role becomes too unbearable for the woman, divorce or suicide result. Today, Japan is essentially an urban society and the "salary man" culture has evolved with most employment being in government and in huge corporations (Vogel, 1971). The feudalistic loyalties of the past to the daimyo or shogun are now transferred to the employers. The family does not get the man's primary allegiance. They rarely take vacations, and they spend their evenings with their colleagues dining, drinking, and "talking

shop" (Vogel, 1971; Christopher, 1983). The husbands turn over their pay checks to their wives who then control the family finances. Some women have become expert at investing on the stock market. Volunteer work is becoming more attractive to the women although still not as widely practiced as in the U.S.A. A growing number of housewives feel socially isolated and bored because they have little to do in their minute apartments. "Kitchen-drinking" is reported more prevalent, a certain and serious sign of boredom.

The farm women are feeling the effects of change, too. Older women have an especially low status as the younger farm women demand more independence. Our interview with Mrs. Minato, a farmer's widow, illustrated this when she complained about her daughter-in-law's determination to work (but not on their farm) in order to accumulate more money and be more independent. She was not about to take care of her mother-in-law as her counterpart fifty years ago would have done without a murmur. Farm women complain because they are still working long and exhausting hours. Young women do not want to marry farmers who, as a result, are importing picture brides from the Philippines.

Women continue to work in the factories, but the past inhuman conditions have changed. They have more legal protections. Married women even seek factory jobs without questioning the lower pay and traditional roles (Lebra, et al., p. 298). Today they are not as assertive as they were immediately after World War II when they were part of the trade union movement or the socialist movement (Robin-Mowry, 1983).

The present trend is for young women to work until they are 24 or 25 years of age, then marry, have two children, and return to work in their 40s at low paying, part-time jobs. They get no fringe benefits, pensions, insurance, medical care, vacations, or bonuses and generally are shut out of management jobs. Mrs. Mase was a rare Japanese woman having had two successive management positions. However, she stated that when her small company was purchased by a large corporation, she resigned, knowing that she would be assigned a lower position. If a woman becomes widowed before retirement age, she has a very difficult time economically because of lack of benefits. Divorcees have the same problems.

For centuries, women in urban areas frequently worked in small family businesses in which they had important roles. This continues today. Mrs. Sugita described how much she enjoyed helping build the family businesses consisting of several supermarkets and restaurants in which

she controlled the personnel practices and the finances. Now retired, she is depressed and misses the excitement and power. Mrs. Hosoi, too, played an active role in the business she and her husband inherited from her parents. Mrs. Ishii was left a widow while still a young woman with five children and a mother-in-law. She continued to conduct her husband's cattle business until World War II when she was forced to evacuate to the countryside. And Mrs. Nakai, when she returned from fourteen years in China, decided to establish her own business which she conducted successfully for eighteen years.

Women who work as bar-maid hostesses (two million), factory workers, stewardesses, and office ladies are generally expected to be subservient and to accept male superiority. Usually, they are not success-oriented and view the world from a very traditional point of view. Nevertheless, change is evident in the more elite occupations. It is interesting that this began when some of the women were able to achieve success in their endeavors because of early family support. The case histories reported in studies of women document dramatically how husbands and fathers and even mothers may have encouraged and supported these achieving women who generally became leaders (Lebra, 1984; Lebra, et al., 1976; Robin-Mowry, 1983). Women with Ph.D.s have been especially discouraged, however, because of the conservative attitudes at universities. Thus, especially on the higher levels, women are still struggling to assert themselves.

After their interviews with Japanese women from all professions and socioeconomic groups in contemporary society, Joyce Lebra and her colleagues concluded, "What shows through in the profiles of many individual women...is tremendous strength." Beyond the passive endurance women were socialized to anticipate, they found that the women they interviewed displayed courage and chose their own path. In a country like Japan, they observe, this is no small feat. These women who "despite a rigidly submissive, self-sacrificing feminine tradition describe themselves as stubborn, independent, and choosing their own ways. They are a moving testament to the human spirit" (Lebra, et al., p. 304). There still remain many who struggle ambivalently between the new roles to which they aspire, the dependence and subservience expected of women, and the overt resistances to a more liberal spirit. It does not appear to differ from many other countries. In Japan, women's status is considered a major social issue, one yet to be confronted because

the myths about women perpetuated by Buddhism and Confucianism and the long period of feudalism persist. Thus, Takie Sugiyama Lebra was correct in stating that the problems of women in Japan today are the polarization between constraint and fulfillment (1984).

Chapter 4

੨ð

An Overview
of the
Interviewees

S tatistics are boring. That is why we did not start this book with statistics. But we owe you, the readers, an overview of the interviewees, who they are, where they came from, their level of education, their marriage and other vital statistics, their interests, their attitudes and experiences with respect to major events (such as the 1923 Earthquake, the Sino-Japanese War, and World War II), and other such information that illuminates their backgrounds.

In the following chapters, you will hear seventeen women speak about their lives, experiences, and philosophies. The other ten we interviewed are referred to throughout the book and in this chapter, in which they are presented collectively or in brief vignettes.

If you relate these statistics to the preceding historical chapter, you will have a base line for comparing this particular group of women with Japanese women in general, both before and after World War II.

You should bear in mind that we made a decided effort to seek women over 65 who represented a variety of backgrounds (rural and urban; rich and poor; old and young-old; married, single, widowed, and divorced; healthy and unhealthy; well educated and minimally educated; and their variety of interests). We found them with the help of the Tokyo Metropolitan Institute on Gerontology primarily in nursing homes, a hospital, senior centers, the Elder University, and we found several through personal introductions. The only things the women in the sample had in common was their age and willingness to talk with us. The majority of the interviews were conducted in the women's own homes and the rest in institutions. The directors of the senior centers and medical institutions were most gracious in arranging for interviewing space large enough to permit us to videotape the interviews.

Age, Era, and Education.

Fifteen of the women were born during the Meiji Restoration (1858-1912), and most received their higher education in the more liberal and more democratic, but brief, Taisho period (1912-1926). The younger among them were born in the Taisho period but received their higher education in the pre-World War II Showa era, characterized by rising

nationalism, militarism, expansionism, and wars.

More specifically, fifteen women were in the oldest group, ages 75 to 94, and twelve were under 75. Eight women were in their 80s and one was 94. Of the entire group, two completed college, two left college before completion, four went to normal school for teachers' training, one graduated from junior college, and one attended nursing school. Only one born in the Taisho period went to college, but eleven others attended jogakko (a high-level high school). Thus, the older women were better educated than the young-old (under 75). Eight women completed six or eight grades, and one was taught by the family at home because she was handicapped.

As in most advanced countries, the children of these elderly women were, on the whole, better educated than their parents, especially their mothers. Among their sons, one had a Ph.D., one was a medical doctor, seventeen were university graduates, and five graduated from high school. Their daughters presented a strikingly different picture. Two graduated from a college, three went to junior college, three attended art school, one graduated from a technical school, three went to jogakko, eleven finished high school, one completed sewing school, and one graduated from elementary school. However, most reported that their grandchildren are going to universities, junior colleges, or technical schools.

Origin and Socio-Economic Status.

These women reflect well the trend toward urbanization. Thirteen were born in urban areas from as far north as Hokkaido to as far south as Fukuoka in Kyushu, and fourteen came from small towns and villages. However, only three remained in rural areas as adults, and even these women had worked in a city during their late teens and early twenties. Nineteen considered themselves middle class, three were lower middle class, three were upper middle class, and only two were really low income. In many ways, they demonstrated the typical upward mobility found in present day Japanese society. Six were originally from low income families, and two were from the lower middle class. At the same time, because of the slow demise of feudalism, seven identified themselves as coming from upper class families because they were the daughters of daimyos (feudal lords) or their fathers worked directly for the daimyo. One woman was from a banker's family, and, when her father died, her mother continued to operate the bank. It was our impression that most

who viewed themselves as upper class were not particularly wealthy. In fact, Mrs. Kobayashi stated that her father, a daimyo, had to sell land to send his children to college or normal school.

Family Size.

Even among this small group of women, we see dramatically the contrast between the pre-birth control era and post-war acceptance of the need for smaller families. Seven were born into families of two to four children, but twenty came from families of five to ten children (thirteen of the twenty had six to nine siblings). Several complained that their mothers' health was ruined by so many births. Fifteen women were among the older siblings in the family and were forced to assume considerable parental responsibilities. In contrast, six of our interviewees had no children (two being single and four, childless), seven had one child, six had two children, two had three children, and two had four children. Only three women had five children, and one had six. The latter were in their late seventies, and one was ninety-four. The younger among these elderly women had smaller families. One of the reasons may have been that the husbands were in the wars, and several were killed in war-related events.

Marriage and Widowhood.

The marriage age before World War II was reported to be earlier than in the post-war period (age twenty-five is now considered the time to be introduced to a potential husband); eleven married before the age of twenty-four, and fourteen wed between twenty-four and thirty-one (because of the War). Two never married, one because of her severe physical handicap and the other because she did not care for the few men left on the home front. Most of the women were introduced to their future husbands in the traditional way, i.e., by exchange of bio-data papers and by go-betweens handling the arrangements. But a surprising number of women had rejected such customs. For example, Mrs. Takahari was persuaded at age 31 by her cousin that they marry, and she accepted on the condition that she could continue her career as a teacher. She had never planned to marry. Mrs. Kaga, a nurse, only decided to wed when she realized that she would possibly outlive her relatives and, therefore, would not have anyone to bury her in old age. Mrs. Iwaki met her husband when they were studying Esperanto, and they announced to

their families that they planned to marry. However, they waited several years until his family approved. Mrs. Ishii married her employer (a cattle raiser), and Mrs. Minato's husband, a farmer, purposely sought a wife among the girls in the war factory in which she worked. Mrs. Sugita married the boy whose father owned the fruit and vegetable stand next door to her family's stand.

Several of the women painfully described their grief about being pressed into marriage by their families. Mrs. Matsuo, at age 18, was told by relatives with whom she was living that she was to take a train to Tokyo, and the man who would meet her and her twelve year old brother at the station was to become her husband. Mrs. Wakiro, when told by her parents that they had found her a husband, begged not to wed. She wanted to be a professional librarian. They refused to listen to her. Mrs. Sakurada recounted the saddest tale. Her family insisted that she marry a man known to be a philanderer, and later they rejected her for divorcing him after seven unhappy years. This was followed a year later by another marriage arranged by her family to a man who was an alcoholic, twice divorced, and who beat his wife when drunk. Several women complained that the War prevented them from marrying a more desirable husband. Their choices were severely limited. Thus, perhaps the older women in Japan who wed in the 1930s and early 1940s were more assertive than their culture demanded, and a number who succumbed to the cultural dictates had unhappy lives.

Our sample shows that women generally outlived their husbands by many years. Twenty-one were widows. Six of the husbands died during or immediately after the War; eleven were widowed well before they were 60 (six lost their husbands when they were in their 20s and 30s). One widow was also a divorcee, having left her first husband after seven years of marriage. After 20 years of marriage, another woman divorced her husband because he abandoned her many years before in favor of another woman. She decided to divorce only when her daughter was denied the job she had applied for because of her mother's "vague" marital (separation) status. The two divorcees described serious struggles in making their decision to divorce in the face of the negative and resistant attitudes in Japan. In one instance, the woman had to leave her child with the husband because the law mandated it. She remained guilt-stricken as a result and did not see her son again until her first husband died years later.

Their Husband's and Father's Occupations.

Among the twenty-five women who had been married, twelve husbands had professions, four were company men, three were merchants,
two were farmers, three were in government services (civil, army, diplo-
macy), and one was a manufacturer. The occupations of their fathers
were not very different. Seven fathers were merchants, five were professionals, three were in government service, four were farmers, three were
landowners, one was a Buddhist priest, one was a scholar, one was a
company man, and two were an impoverished laborer and a poor vegetable
stand owner. There were more farmers and more poor people in Japan
when these women were young than there are today.

Present Living Arrangements.

In Japan today, about 60% of the elderly live within multigeneration
families, but among the women we interviewed only twelve, or less than
half, lived with their children or in an apartment next door. Three lived
with their husbands apart from their children, eight lived alone (a high
percentage by Japanese standards), and three lived in nursing homes.
One was applying to an old age home because her daughter-in-law evicted
her from her home.

Religion.

Religion appears to have played a more important part in the lives of
the women who were Christian than those who were Buddhist. In one
case, the mother of the interviewee was a Salvation Army convert, and
her ten children were raised to be very active members of her religious
group. Another woman was very active in her Protestant Church. Mrs.
Wakiro became a Catholic late in life and was preparing for her death by
reading philosophical theology books on the subject. Mrs. Matsuo spoke
of her conversion to Christianity in her search for solace in adjusting to
her unhappy marriage. She was attracted to Christianity because it
spoke of love. Most of the Buddhist women did not discuss religion
except for Mrs. Iwaki who sought for the universal in all religions in her
quest for peace. Miss Katase revealed the same thinking. These two
women were well read and had very well defined personal philosophies
of life.

Work After Marriage.

We had too small a sample to compare our group with the employ-ment of present day women, but it is significant that nineteen of the women worked for many years after marriage and until retirement. For some, the Government had insisted, during the War, that they work; for others, their widowed status forced this upon them; and there were still others who were forced into the labor market by economic necessity. Only five did not work after marriage. One was handicapped very young. In contrast, one woman had three careers, first teaching English in college (she is the only woman educated in the U.S.A.), next as an executive in several small businesses, and, finally, as an administrator of several inter-national organizations. Three women were in their family business working closely with their husbands, and four owned their own small businesses. It is the latter who were unusual. Three were teachers, four had clerical jobs, three were in farming, one was a nurse, one was a nutritionist, one ran a boarding house for students, and one was a waitress. One of the women complained, as she described her dilemma when her husband was killed during the Sino-Japanese War, that she had wanted to have her own business to support her three children and mother-in-law, but having no skills she was unsuccessful in her business ventures. Finally, after a number of years farming, she established a boarding house for students. She was capable of more intellectual work but never could find the right business.

It is interesting that the mothers of twelve of these women had worked outside the home, most out of economic necessity. Several assisted their husbands, and one was a banker. This last woman was considered by her daughter as more competent than the father.

Health.

Considering the ages of these women, it is astonishing that only ten discussed health problems. Gall bladder, bladder, cancer, blood problems, rehabilitation, paralysis (three), and depression (two) were among the current health complaints. Miss Yabe contracted tuberculosis from her mother at birth, and later developed other illnesses that led to a paralysis. Mrs. Wakiro, in her 80s, found she could no longer walk and went into a nursing home. Mrs. Akimoto, at 70, suffered a paralysis of the lower body and had to move to a nursing home. Mrs. Konishi had the most serious health problems because of a blood disease that made the several

operations she had for cancer very dangerous. She always had a suitcase packed ready to enter the hospital in an emergency. And Mrs. Sugita was depressed since retiring from her very successful family businesses. She also feared that her daughter would not return from abroad with her family to live in the home they shared. In addition, she expressed concern that, if she ever became infirm, she would be a burden to her children. Our visit was meaningful because she could voice aloud her fears and anxieties for the future. No one else would listen to her.

Childhood Days.

All but four of the women spoke with nostalgia about their childhood. Mrs. Hosoi was able to recall and sing with me "Twinkle, Twinkle Little Star," an American song her favorite uncle taught her as a young child. However, nine women had lost a parent as a child, four, a mother, three, a father, and two, both parents. The four with especially unhappy childhoods described such situations as rejection by siblings or relatives after the parents died. Several recalled lives of poverty and hard labor. Even as a very young child, Mrs. Sakurada described an unreasonable number of duties and no time for play. When asked about the most significant events in their childhood, it was deaths, health problems, poverty, and very hard work that were discussed. Mrs. Konishi told of her blind sister to whom the entire family devoted their lives and made innumerable sacrifices. Mrs. Mase was particularly affected by the discrimination shown to Oriental children in the California schools. Finally, Mrs. Saka had to give up college to stay home to care for her bed-ridden mother and younger siblings. Despite their assertion that childhood was wonderful, many admitted to these unhappy recollections. Mrs. Kaga had the most amusing tale. Because the family did not expect her to live (she said she was a "fragile child"), she was given the freedom to play with, and act like, her brothers and their friends. When she teased them too much, she would ask to be spared from their anger because she was a "fragile child." At 89, she still thinks of herself as fragile in spite of a full career as a healthy nurse, mother, and wife, and having outlived her husband and daughter.

Family-of-Origin Attitudes.

While the number of subjects we could discuss in our two-hour inter-

views was limited, it was still possible to learn something of the attitudes and values of their families which were reflective of pre-war Japan. Twelve talked of the family's strong interest in and emphasis on education, and only two stated emphatically that their parents did not stress education. The twelve families were the forerunners of the obsession present day Japanese mothers have about their children's education. Mrs. Mase's mother toured the United States to find the right city in which to educate her children. Six families were strongly traditional about their daughters' upbringing, education, and marriage while seven families were considered by their daughters to be very modern and ahead of their time. In fact, four of the women stressed the stimulating environment in which they grew up. The Christian religion played a major role in the lives of several families influenced by missionaries. Fourteen women described their fathers' role in very positive terms. Only one complained about his dictatorial nature. Two even boasted of his modern ideas. One woman described her wealthy family who pampered her because she was the only girl, but six stressed the family philosophy of hard work and self-sacrifice. Six spoke explicitly of close family ties, but many others appeared to feel the same way. Mrs. Sugita developed such feelings of devotion to her family after leaving school in sixth grade that she spent many years diligently helping them in their fruit and vegetable stand. The community gave her a plaque of recognition for filial loyalty. She showed this to us proudly.

On the negative side, Miss Yabe saw her family as rejecting and insensitive, hiding her from the public, refusing to send her to school, and ultimately abandoning her because she had contracted her mother's tuberculosis in addition to several other handicaps. Mrs. Matsuo contrasted her parents' warmth and caring the first twelve years of her life with the insensitivity of the numerous relatives who took responsibility for her and her young brother after both parents died. They felt unwanted, rejected, and superfluous. The relatives could not wait to marry her off, particularly when the money inherited from her parents was used up.

The Earthquake of 1923 in Tokyo, the Sino-Japanese War, and World War II.

Because the education of girls in Japan did not prepare them for leadership, employment, administration, and management, we asked them to describe their experiences and tasks during those crucial catastrophic

periods when the entire community had to mobilize to assume major responsibilities. It is one thing to adapt to situations for which one is prepared or has skills but another thing to undertake tasks that are overwhelming, complex, and for which one has no training.

History tells us that the Japanese women, particularly, rose to the occasion in the 1923 Earthquake in a way which their masculine-dominated society had not anticipated (Robins-Mowry, 1983). Only eight women actually experienced the Earthquake, three as children and five as adults. One thought it fun, but several were frightened. One was sent to an orphanage with her sister until their parents could find new quarters. Five, who were adults, vividly described evacuation, death, fires, and destruction of homes. Mrs. Ishii and her family of five children and mother-in-law had to sleep outdoors and later rebuild their home. None of the women participated in the organizations that were established by women for the relief of families except for Mrs. Kaga whose nursing skills were in great demand.

The Sino-Japanese War presented a vastly different picture. Six of the women went to live in Manchuria and China. One spent her childhood there because of her father's business. The others went with husbands who were either in the Japanese Army or in business. They all reported enjoying the status of conqueror and living well until the Wars turned against them. Mrs. Matsuo admitted leaving her daughter in Japan with relatives because she feared Chinese children would be unkind to Japanese children in their schools. Mrs. Konishi's husband worked so hard in China that he dropped dead, leaving her pregnant and with a toddler. Mrs. Kaga described the true horrors of war when describing nursing soldiers from both sides as they were dying. She was a Red Cross nurse and lost her hearing in one ear from a bomb explosion. During the Sino-Japanese War, two women worked in factories, and two had husbands who died in battle.

All of the women described World War II as the most traumatic period in their lives. Three lost their husbands, one just three days before the War ended. Several had fiances or husbands in the army and worried about them. While nine were evacuated from Tokyo during the height of the bombings, the rest remained, moving whenever their homes or businesses were bombed or burned. Mrs. Takahari moved her entire classroom to the countryside for two and a half years and continued her teaching, a common practice during the War. Four described working in

a munitions factory, and several sewed uniforms. One continued her much needed nursing career. The twelve who never evacuated dramatically described the bombings and their fears. Two had husbands detained in Indonesia, one of them as a prisoner. All mentioned the food shortages and their need to scrounge about to find food, frequently selling their precious belongings. Four womens' husbands stayed in Tokyo because of business or work in the Civil Defense Corps. In one case, when her husband returned from China wounded, she and her husband rented a plot of land and grew vegetables that they sold on the black market. They made enough money to start a successful business eventually. The three who described the greatest hardships were Mrs. Saka, Mrs. Nakai, and Mrs. Konishi. Mrs. Saka's husband, a doctor, was killed in China, leaving her with three children and a mother-in-law. Suddenly, she had to support them without any preparation or skills. Mrs. Nakai was captured by the Chinese Red Army after she fled Manchuria. Her husband died just before she returned to Japan eight years after her captivity. He had been a prisoner-of-war in Siberia. In the Chinese Red Army Medical Corps, she held good positions but was constantly on the move helping set up field hospitals. Mrs. Konishi was captured by the Chinese and sent to an island off the southern coast of China where she endured many hardships with her two infants. She, like Mrs. Saka and Mrs. Nakai, learned to make her way alone and to speak up vigorously to have her needs met. Only two spoke of being well protected by their families when they evacuated to safe places. They did not present tales of serious stress and trauma.

Marriage.

Very few of the women described their husband's personalities to any extent though fourteen stated they had happy marriages. Only Mrs. Mase described her husband as handsome. Mrs. Iwaki admired her husband's intellect and adventurous spirit. Mrs. Koda considered that her husband was much cleverer than she. Mrs. Sakurada painted a vivid picture of a hardworking, hard drinking husband who beat her when he was drunk and worked her very hard when he was sober. Mrs. Kanai and Mrs. Sakurada admitted unhappily that they were angry that their husbands were not faithful. And Mrs. Matsuo sadly confessed that her husband was a very decent man, but she could never love him. Those with happy marriages enjoyed compatible relationships, worked with

their husbands in business, had activities together, appreciated their economic security, liked the traveling they did, and a few confessed they learned to love each other. The unhappy ones divorced or wished that they could. Several had never wanted to marry and accepted life fatalistically. One woman was overwhelmed by caring for her very sick husband, and only well after his death could she allow herself to become more social and outgoing. Several unhappily had to care for their mothers-in-law; one in particular was so dominated by her that only after her death did she begin to enjoy life and some freedom. Mrs. Akino was embarrassed by her husband's extremely short stature but appreciated that he had a steady income in contrast to her poverty-stricken family. Twelve women described a good marriage, but, unfortunately, a number among them were widowed before age 40.

Interests.

While many of the women had some interest in the tea ceremony, flower arranging, and haiku (a Japanese form of poetry), each had considerably more interests. Six were very serious about taking courses; twelve studied painting, dancing, and singing; six spent much time reading; and six concentrated on gardening. Two studied various arts and crafts to a point of perfection, and seven were particularly interested in politics, socializing with others, teaching English, and providing leadership in the community. Seven did volunteer work in the community as a librarian, a church leader, outreach workers for the aged, a social group work leader, and an artist. The artist won several prizes. All but Mrs. Minato, who was frantically reacting to her feelings of abandonment, were engaged in some interesting activities that they appeared to enjoy.

Perception of Changes in Her Lifetime.

We were particularly interested to learn how these women, 67 to 94 years of age, born in a different era and with a very different set of expectations, viewed the current world in which they lived. Spontaneously, fourteen enthusiastically spoke about the freedom and independence women now enjoy in Japan. They especially appreciate the educational opportunities for young women and are envious of them. However, they stressed that the freedom of today must be tempered with responsibility and respect for others, and they fear that many young people are not developing these traits and do not appreciate the meaning of free-

dom. One recommended that "old minds should be thrown out," and people should accept the new. Two particularly like the economic security of the present. In fact, none expressed a wish that there should be a return to the past. Two did feel that women should not compete with men, but, in both instances, they were very strong women who, indeed, had competed quite successfully.

Six women, while accepting the post-war modern life, preferred the traditions of the past. Only three spoke up strongly in favor of peace and a concern that wars should cease. Most of the women concentrated their thinking and efforts on personal affairs and relationships and were not as concerned with world affairs or politics. However, one, Mrs. Saka, liked to talk politics with her grandsons and expressed regrets for being too old to run for the Diet. She considered herself more conservative than her grandchildren but was pleased that they were interested in political issues. Three women spoke strongly about the importance of education. Another stressed the importance of equality but now realized that "happiness does not come from equality alone."

Several women had very definite concerns about children's attitudes today. They thought that children were too impatient, too wasteful of food, too dependent on parents, and did not work hard enough. In all instances, this reflected their own childhood when food was not plentiful and when they had to work strenuously with household tasks or on their family farm or store. Two women especially felt burdened and constricted caring for their mothers-in-law. Two, on the other hand, found that their mothers-in-law were particularly helpful with the children after their husbands' death. One woman, however, spoke bitterly about the ie system in which the oldest son and his wife assumed the care of the elder parent, saying that when her husband, the oldest son, died, his younger brothers and their wives did not offer to take their mother but left her with the burdens of caring for both a very young child and her mother-in-law.

The oldest woman, age 94, liked her present life better than any other time because now she was free, did not have to work, enjoyed socializing in the senior center, and knew that if anything went wrong, her sons would care for her. She was still healthy and walked a considerable distance to the senior center every day.

In summary, the women were not so nostalgic for the old way of life that they wished to return to it. The more conservative preferred old

values, but a surprising number, more than half, preferred the present and their current status. Many expressed envy that the youth have so much available to them and verbalized the irony that the youth do not appreciate their freedom and the more flexible society. Yet, they appeared unaware of the fact that Japan still retains a very traditional and rigid system with the emphasis on society and not on the individual. As women, they are still very family oriented, even those with considerable worldly experiences.

Only a few have ever traveled abroad, except for those who lived in China and Manchuria years ago. Three women had been to the North American continent, one having lived there and two having traveled to visit their children. Only one was confronting old age with economic insecurity, and most did not express fear of abandonment by their children. Seventeen knew that their children would care for them if necessary. But five had concerns and misgivings, fearing being a burden. Mrs. Kaga's only living child is in Canada; Mrs. Watari's son lives next door, but his wife is unfriendly and ungiving; Mrs. Sugita thinks that her son and daughter-in-law will not want to care for her if she is sickly; and Mrs. Kanai is upset by her daughter's marriage because she will now have to live alone. Six, who have no children, are either in institutions or are caring for themselves while living alone.

In my sample I found that in their old age, they were doing remarkably well, even those in nursing homes. Thus, one may conclude both from their explicit and implicit comments that these women have coped well with changes and appreciate some of women's new freedoms. Only a few really look back at the past with regrets for what might have been.

And now, in the following chapters, seventeen of the twenty-seven women will tell their own stories in their own way, mostly with their own dialogue. We found it a pleasure to speak with them, and, in all but one instance, they reacted with excitement at this new experience to have someone concentrate only upon them and accept every minutiae of data they offered. They liked being the center of attention for this brief time because they rarely have this type of opportunity. Such a positive experience can be very satisfying considering how rare it is for people to speak about themselves uninterrupted for several hours, without concern about the other person's reactions. This was their time, and they were the center of their universe.

Chapter 5

ક્ર

Miss Yabe:
Handicapped
for Life

M iss Yabe, at 67 years of age, is the youngest resident in the nursing home and the youngest woman we interviewed. She arrived seven years ago, four days after the home opened. Finally, she observed, she had a home in which she hopes to stay until she dies. She very much likes this place, particularly after having spent years living in a hospital because there was no place for her in the community. She is bound to her wheel chair having lost the use of her legs 27 years ago.

From very early childhood, she was "the sick child, the handicapped child" of the family. The secret she carefully did not wish to share with us was her family's rejection of their sickly, handicapped member. She was the "family secret" because of her handicap. At last she lives in a home where handicaps are accepted and friendships are extended. Her closest friend is an 85 year old woman with whom she can joke, share small talk, and participate in activities. At last, she has a real home where she is accepted!

Before coming to the nursing home, Miss Yabe spent 20 years in a hospital because of a spinal problem that left her paralyzed from the hips down. "My parents were dead. I had no other place to go." She did not add that her siblings did not offer to care for her. In fact, they had literally abandoned her until, when she moved into the nursing home, the social worker at the welfare department contacted them and insisted that they visit her.

Miss Yabe is a heavy-set, stocky. young looking woman, with wavy, short, dark, grey-streaked hair. She sits straight in her wheel chair and makes a pleasant appearance. She wears a constant smile and appears affable and sharing until questioned about her family. Then, her answers become brief and her face becomes sad. She was not an easy person to interview.

Born in Nagano prefecture, Miss Yabe is the youngest of eleven children. She lived in a small country town where her father owned a furniture shop. She has six sisters and four brothers. She describes herself as having been a weak child from birth and claims from her mother she contracted tuberculosis which eventually affected her spine. When she was three years old, her mother died of tuberculosis, having

been bedridden for the last six months of her life. She recalls spending considerable time at her mother's bedside, eating candy and cake. Her older sisters had to bring her up although it was her father who kept the family together. But her father died when she was age 10 of an infected tooth that poisoned him. It was a shock! "I had many troubles after that. I endured many sad experiences."

Miss Yabe does recall some happy moments as a child. In particular, she described, with a wistful smile on her face and many gestures with her hands, going with other children to hunt crabs at the river's edge. "We pushed a big rock and under it were many crabs. We collected buckets full as souvenirs. It was fun."

Because she was weak and paid frequent visits to the doctor and the hospital, the family never sent her to school. "I have no education except for what my sisters taught me. I never did much reading but spent many years watching television." In talking to Miss Yabe, it is evident that she is quite intelligent and missed not going to school. However, she does not express openly any feelings about it and appears to take for granted that her physical condition made this impossible. Actually, she was ambulatory until age 40 and, therefore, could have been offered a formal education.

The death of her father came as a shock, and many changes took place. "I had many troubles from that time, endured many sad experiences. Several of my sisters moved to Tokyo, and I went with them. We lived together until the sister with whom I lived married and told me that I would have to leave. My sisters supported me economically for a while although I had to live alone. I could walk then, but, because I was weak, the activities I could engage in were very limited. I was in the hospital frequently. Finally, during the War, my sisters evacuated from Tokyo and ceased supporting me although I did continue communicating with them for some years. This, too, slowly tapered off, and for many years I did not hear from any of them until the social worker in the welfare department insisted they reestablish relationships. Now, three of my sisters and a nephew visit me occasionally. Our relationship has been very complex. After all these years, it was like meeting strangers when they came to see me. Nevertheless, when I met my sisters and nephew, I was happy because one cannot forget one's blood relations."

All during the War, Miss Yabe remained in Tokyo, first in a hospital in the Itabashi section of Tokyo, and, when it burned, she was sent to a

tuberculosis sanitorium. Upon discharge, she lived in her own apartment supported by government disability insurance. At age 40, she again entered a hospital and told the doctor, "It is no good to continue having a weak body. He suggested an operation might help me. It didn't! It was a failure! The nerves at my spine were cut, and I could not walk again." We empathized with her, observing, "You were alone, your family had disappeared, going their own way, now you were completely dependent and could not live independently as you had in the past. It was very upsetting." Miss Yabe sadly nodded in agreement but did not share more of her thoughts and feelings.

The next 20 years, from ages 40 to 60, Miss Yabe remained in the hospital. She was paralyzed from the hips down. For five years, she was bedridden, then allowed to get around in a wheel chair. She learned to do this remarkably well and could go shopping whenever she wished. But she could not return to an apartment. In the hospital, she made many friends who, after they left, would return to visit her. However, there were very few recreation activities in the hospital unlike the nursing home. She spent hours watching television and had to wash her own diapers. Here, in this nursing home, she does not have this disagreeable task, she said with a smile.

We asked Miss Yabe about her conversion to Christianity. This occurred when she was 18 years of age. "I was in the hospital during my teens when some nuns came to visit patients. I was moved by their friendliness and their interest in people. Before I met them, I had tried to study about other religions, but none seemed to fit what I was seeking. I liked what they had to say; I liked the Catholic religion and its concept of God. So I became a Catholic. I felt very positive about how God in Catholicism relates to people. I am happy about my choice, and now I am in a Catholic nursing home; I find the people are good to me; I feel at home here; the nuns are warm and friendly. I am cared for and have many friends." She is clearly settled in for the rest of her life.

In the light of all the struggles with her health during her entire life, we commented that she showed tremendous strength to be able to face so many health crises alone and to endure so many losses. Yet, she is able to reach out to people, make friends, and find satisfactions from her relationships. In response, she commented, "I feel much better now because the aged people are so nice; I'm popular among them. Everyone teaches me something. They don't just take my hand, but they talk to

me about their lives and their experiences. I have so much to learn from them. Some are 90 years old. My closest friend is 85." Apparently, Miss Yabe is living through the lives of the many women who have befriended her in the nursing home. In addition, she participates in many activities such as flower arranging, choir singing, clay work, and outings. Once a year, she goes to Atami (a hot spring resort) over night with the nursing home group. "I keep busy here."

In spite of her cheerful exterior and positive attitude, Miss Yabe revealed her self-image when we asked what she would tell young people about life. "I'm not good enough to give advice to the young. I have tried my best throughout my life. My feelings now are gratitude toward this nursing home, optimism, and a wish to establish good relationships here. Friends I have known for 20 and 30 years come to visit me, especially on special occasions and cultural events. My sisters visit from time to time, and now I have friends in this home." She feels she can ask for nothing more at this time of her life. Nor does she see herself as offering much to young people. Her entire life has been a physical and emotional struggle to survive.

After the interview, the nursing home social worker commented that the nurses consider Miss Yabe a difficult patient. She presents an attitude of entitlement, makes demands of them rather than requests, and is crisp, pressuring, and insistent. However, with the very old women patients she gets along fine and eagerly seeks their friendships.

Miss Yabe is a sad and angry woman who never had a normal life. The loss of both her parents, her poor health, the frequent medical intrusions, her isolation, her sisters' rejection, and the denial of a normal childhood including attendance at school with other children, left her emotionally deprived. While her sisters took responsibility for her upbringing, obviously she was a burden they found troublesome. They likely did not want the world to know they had a tubercular sister. She was completely dependent upon them and their good will, and, because of her illnesses, remained dependent well beyond the time most children begin asserting some independent thinking and action. Although ambulatory until age 40, emotionally she clung to them until one sibling after the other abandoned her. Given her demanding attitude in the nursing home, one wonders if she made the same demands upon her sisters when she lived with and was economically supported by them..

In Japan, handicaps are viewed with alarm. Conformism being a

dominant cultural expectation, a handicapped child presents serious problems and reflects negatively on the family. Tuberculosis, in the past in Japan, was a disease to hide from the public, as was mental illness. It was common practice to reject and hide such relatives. Thus, from early childhood, Miss Yabe was different from other children, weak, sickly, and a burden. Although she described crab hunting with friends, she did not give the impression she played very much with other children. While she does not dwell at length about her sensitivity about being different and enduring a life of rejection, isolation, physical ailments, frequent hospitalizations, and abandonment by her family, she is now asserting and displacing previously repressed hostility by making demands on the staff of the nursing home. The home is her family. Fortunately, she knows that they will not abandon her and, therefore, finally feels free to express herself.

Miss Yabe may be considered a remarkably strong woman who has suffered physically and emotionally all her life. She still has a deep need to seek out friendships, and, in particular, parent figures. In the nursing home, she has finally found what she has wanted all her life, stability, predictability, and caring. The very old women who befriend her represent the mother she lost at age three. They will die, as her mother did, but, in the nursing home, there will be others to take their place. Now that she knows she may stay here until she dies, she feels free to assert her needs and wishes, and, through the elderly friends, she can have these met. Nor can the staff abandon her. She is more in control than she has ever felt in the past.

Life was not good to Miss Yabe. Behind her smile, there is anger and frustration. So much energy, in the past, went into repressing and denying her negative, hostile, and depressed feelings in order to protect her self-esteem and sensitivity about being rejected that now, in a safe place, she feels free to direct her hostility toward authority figures, namely the staff of the nursing home. But with it all, she has survived remarkably well. Reaching out to make friends, and adopting a religion which could help her accept her physical condition and her life reveal that beneath her dependent, demanding exterior, is an assertive spirit, determination, and strength.

Chapter 6

ᨀ

Mrs. Konishi:
Confrontations
With
Life and
Death

S lender, well-dressed, 67 year-old Mrs. Konishi met us at the station and guided us through the maze of streets, past large attractive apartment houses, and up a long, unpaved path to her small, two-room, old-style Japanese house, hidden by trees and bushes. Mrs. Konishi has rented this house for the last twenty years and now lives in it alone. But there was a time when her parents, two sons, and she shared the tiny quarters consisting of a kitchen, living room, and toilet. Adjacent to one wall of the living room was a small greenhouse full of plants. Several bookcases and a sliding-door cabinet filled another wall.

Mrs. Konishi was so eager to talk about herself that she could hardly wait for us to arrange the video equipment. Unlike many of the other women, Mrs. Konishi did not tell her tales of hardship and endurance with a smile. She did not need this defense. She was straightforward, very verbal, and had so much to share that we had to help her maintain some chronology to her life review if we were to understand it. She would have ignored her childhood in the process of reciting one tragic event after another during her adult life. She bore a worried expression and spoke with great intensity. As is true for so many of the other women, she had never been asked about her life story. Now, she had two hours just to talk about herself. One could sense her need and her relief.

Twenty years ago, Mrs. Konishi explained as we entered her house, she was searching for an apartment. Her house in Shiguyama had burned, and she moved from one apartment to another, dissatisfied with her accommodations. Her friends finally told her about this house in an excellent neighborhood, and she called her parents who were living in Kushima north of Tokyo to come live with her. She is pleased with her accommodations.

Mrs. Konishi was born in Hokkaido, north of Honshu, and lived in two small company mining towns until, when she was age 10, the family moved to Tokyo. She enjoyed Hokkaido. Her father, a mining engineer, worked for Mitsubishi Company, having studied mine engineering in a technical high school. She has many pleasant memories of the company town that consisted of twelve houses. They went skiing, picked grapes

in the vineyards, and had many enjoyable outdoor activities. Laughing, she described how cold it was in the winter. Because there were no baths in the houses, everyone used the communal bath, and, as they dashed home after a bath, icicles would form on their eyebrows.

"But those happy days ended when I was in the third grade. My youngest sister was born with defective eyes, and my father decided that we should move to Tokyo where she could get proper treatment and help for her eventual blindness.

"We had many other physical problems in my family. My oldest sister is not well; I was the second child and was never strong. I'll tell you more about that later. Another sister died in infancy of a brain disease, and my last sister is blind.

"My father gave up his job, and we moved to Tokyo. There, he went to school for a year to learn clock making and opened a clock repair shop in Shibuya with money borrowed from his brother-in-law. Those were hard times for the family. My father eventually did well in business and repaid his debts.

"My parents devoted themselves to my blind sister, sending her to special schools to be trained to earn a living. She studied massage and acupuncture and did very well. But she could not go places alone. I accompanied her when she went to her customers.

"I was always considered a weak child. I could not go to the school outings and had to rest frequently. It was not a happy feeling being apart from my friends and their activities. Because of my health, the teacher recommended to my parents that I not go beyond the 8th grade to a jogakko. It was dull living at home without work. I could not bear it, so I took a job in the Tokyu Department Store where I worked for four years until marriage. Those were enjoyable years. I went swimming, skating, learned Japanese music, and sang in choruses at concerts. I was thrilled to meet the Japanese Olympic swimmers who practiced in the pool that Tokyu Department Store rented for us. In fact, I was very happy not only during those four years but for four years after marriage. Then, my many troubles began.

"First, let me tell you about my physical problems. Actually, it was not until 1951 that I learned what was causing my weakness. It seems that I have a serious blood disease; my blood does not clot adequately. Therefore, when I bleed, it is hard to stop. This discovery came about when my blood appeared to have burst." (She probably has idiopathic

thrombocytopenic purpura according to a hematologist we consulted.)

"When I returned from China seven months after the War ended, I worked day and night to support my two young children and my old parents. I would finish my office work in the insurance company at 4 p.m. and then took a job washing towels for hairdressers and restaurants. I also learned to be a masseuse. I was exhausted and finally collapsed. I had to stay in the hospital for six months while my parents cared for my sons. My father returned to repairing clocks to earn extra money. At that time, he was retired. My insurance also helped. But it was a rough time for all of us.

"I've had a number of jobs. After my long hospitalization and several brief jobs, I quit work until a friend recommended me for a secretarial and clerical job where I worked for eight years. Then, I met the president of an architecture company who persuaded me to work for him as a secretary. In all, I worked for forty years until retirement.

"Ten years before retirement, my mother died, and later my father broke a bone. I would awaken at 5 a.m., prepare food for my father and sons, and then go to work. I worked and worked and worked. I did not know what it was like not to work. The welfare people tried to persuade me to put my father in a nursing home, but it was 300 kilometers from here, and it would have been too difficult to visit him. I resisted and tried to manage. If I came home late from the office, my sons cared for my father and prepared the meal. They were very helpful, and I appreciate the support they gave me. It is not because they are my sons that I value them, but they are good human beings, and, when I worked so hard, they pitched in to help me and my father. Eventually, I did have to send my father to a nursing home, and, then, I traveled every weekend to see him until he died.

"During all those years, I had to go to the hospital frequently for blood transfusions. At one point, I had hepatitis and that necessitated transfusions, also. I have lived from one health crisis to another. And, not long ago, I discovered that I had breast cancer. I knew that I had a lump but decided to ignore it. Operations are risky for me because of my blood problem. I was afraid of an operation and was prepared to die. Finally, I did consult a doctor who assured me that with proper care and treatment, I would survive. It was a fifty-fifty chance. Three doctors and eight nurses were in the operating room. When I opened my eyes, I was surprised to be alive. The nurses told me how worried the doctors

had been, as well as how helpful they were. I cried to think that they thought so much about me that they would worry. I made every effort to cooperate in my recovery, went to rehabilitation, did the prescribed exercises, and followed instructions faithfully. I'm sure that the sports I used to engage in when young helped me a great deal, as did my mental strengths.

"Now let me tell you about my husband. You asked me about him. That is an interesting story. He came from Nagasaki and was in the trading business. My father met him and his family in Kyushu when he was on a business trip. When he came to Tokyo to go to Meiji University, he stayed at our home. I was 14 years old at the time. I liked him like a brother. However, when he proposed six years later, I hesitated, but my mother convinced me that he would make a good husband. I was in love with another man; my mother did not object to him, she just thought that I should take a second look, and I did. I decided that he was a good choice and we married. I was 21 years old.

"We moved to Hong Kong; the Japanese occupied Hong Kong at the time where my husband had his business, and, later, we transferred to Canton, China. At one point, an army officer sought him out because he had a big warehouse and ordered him to use the storage space for the munitions industry. He did not like this but was told he must be an interpreter and a supervisor in a factory making bombs and munitions. He worked all hours intensively and exhaustingly.

"One night, my husband came home late, as usual. As I opened the door, he fell at my feet. I rushed him to the doctor, but he was already dead. He died of a brain hemorrhage. I had a two-year old son at the time, and two weeks later my second son was born. I was in such shock that I fainted at my husband's funeral. Several days later, the War ended, and I was confronted with many more trials. It was an exceedingly difficult period for me and my two children. The nurse felt sorry for me when she saw me leave the hospital with my infant and two-year old son holding my hand. Knowing that I was a new widow, she ripped apart her kimono, and made me a coat that would cover both my new baby and me when I carried him on my back. I cried and cried because she was so kind to me. I was touched.

"We were sent by the Chinese Army to an island off the coast of South China. Because I was carrying my infant son and toddler, I could not take many belongings with me. I lived in one of the destroyed

houses that was still liveable. Fortunately, it was in a warm climate so that I did not have to worry about heating my home. But I could not keep the rain out, and I had no cooking facilities. I would gather wood which I placed between two bricks and built a fire to prepare boiled rice porridge for my children. The Chinese issued us some food rations, but these were not enough. Eventually, the Japanese captives negotiated for permission to go to the market to buy food and other necessities. Because those who had big families were able to take a large number of belongings with them, they had goods to barter for the food they needed. But I was not able to do this because I was a widow carrying two small children. I bartered my watch, then my rings, and, finally, other small items to obtain food. Soon, I had nothing to exchange. That is when I thought of making rice porridge to stretch the food.

"When living on the island, I didn't have enough diapers. In winter, when it rained, I could not dry the diapers. First, I would wash them in the river, then string them in my house, and when I had used the last dry one, I would place the wet diaper on my body in order to use my body heat to dry it. I recall how I would cry when the baby wet his diaper just as I was putting a dry one on him. I felt desperate.

"Our captivity lasted seven months. That is not a long time considering the chaos and disorganization. I had prepared myself psychologically for a long stay. One day, it was suddenly announced that a ship was being readied to take us back to Japan. That boat ride turned out to be a nightmare. My baby could not retain his food and was getting weaker and weaker and sicker and sicker. When we finally arrived at Kurihama where we were to disembark, the doctor refused to let anyone off the boat because he discovered cholera on board. I was frantic because I had to get my baby to a hospital. I pleaded with the doctor until finally he wrote a note giving me permission to leave the ship. After hospitalizing my baby, I telegraphed my father to tell him where I was. He came to help us return home.

"My second son, the baby who survived as a result of my pleading, is still very close to me. When I had my mastectomy, he came to the hospital to see me daily. He visits me frequently and even massages my neck to help me relax."

We asked her to tell us more about her two sons, now grown. "My older son works as manager of a branch of the Tokyu Department Store. When I was severely ill a number of years ago, both boys were in junior

high school. I could not afford to send them to a university. Instead, they went to a technical and commercial high school. My second son lives alone, having been divorced. He recently gave up his job and is looking for another. But he refuses to let me help him. I have so many good contacts from my working days. I can introduce him to my former boss, and I am sure that he would help him. But my son insists upon being independent. He is afraid that if he is not successful as a result of my helping him find a job, he will feel that he has let me down. He does not want to be pressured to do well and wants to make it on his own. I wish I could help him.

"In my retirement, I am very busy. I go to the Elder University to take courses for women and on the subject of aging. I've taken several other interesting courses. Once I start, I don't like to quit. I also read a great deal." She pointed to the books on her shelves. Some she has designated to take to the hospital in the event of an emergency. "I always have a bag packed for an emergency hospitalization. I'm always prepared. I am not afraid to die. I have friends who are helpful and can be called upon to assist me quickly.

"People have been very kind to me. Tears come to my eyes readily when I experience kindness. It is because of such friends that I have survived. People tell me I am considerate and warm. But I can't help feeling that I should be warm and helpful to others. I have many good friends in all the companies in which I worked. I go back to visit them, including the president of the last company. I could not have made it without their support. In that sense, I have had a happy life.

"I have been given so much help that, when I hear others say that there are evil people in the world, I say that there are no evil people, only generous people. It depends on how you relate to others. If you feel free, you can make good friends. I am glad to help people who are having troubles. I can relate to them because I have experienced joy, sadness, and tragedy, — every kind of human emotion." We wondered if children today can understand what she is saying. "I'm pessimistic about present-day children. I experienced a different life and have different values. Children would say that I had a terrible life. Yet, I regret nothing, and am prepared to die at any time."

Finally, we observed that some of her hardships related to the fact that she was a woman, especially her heroic efforts at making a living in order to earn enough money to live more comfortably. "I don't know

about that. I liked working and worked as hard and as much as any man."

"But did you get paid the equivalent of a man's salary for the same work?" we asked.

"No, that is why I had to work day and night, carrying two jobs." And implicit in her assertion was the comment, "I survived and am still alive."

What enabled Mrs. Konishi to survive, retain her optimism, and fight for life instead of succumbing to depression and helplessness? Her many strengths are apparent, both internal and external. Her family relations and personal supports were always available and loving. Her father presented a model as he sacrificed his engineering career in Hokkaido, one he enjoyed, in order to seek medical and educational assistance for his blind daughter in Tokyo. Family cohesiveness characterized their approach to the illnesses and deaths they experienced.

Family and collegial cohesiveness are the secret of the successful adaptation of many of the women when facing crises. Perhaps they could have managed alone. But family relatedness, reinforced by a series of culturally mandated obligations and responsibilities, contributed to making it possible to confront tragedies and crises without a serious breakdown.

Mrs. Konishi's life history presents one crisis after another involving the death of one sibling and blindness of another, her husband's death and her captivity, her struggle with a serious, death-threatening blood problem, and finally a cancerous condition. From the time her husband died when she was still in her 20s to the present, she has encountered a series of devastating personal crises. War, captivity, deaths, sick infants, insufficient income, care of frail elderly parents, blood disease and cancer, and innumerable hospitalizations plagued her. Her defenses against these events were work and more work and relying upon friends, family, bosses, and colleagues. She did not see herself as a victim. She did not feel sorry for herself. She used relationships for emotional support when she could not care for herself. She has been living on the brink of death at least since 1951 when she learned the nature of her ailment. But, by keeping involved, busy, working, and caring for her sons and parents, she never permitted the threat of death to interfere with her life. She is still prepared for death, and, even in retirement, she is not brooding or obsessing about it. Instead, she is using her intellectual interests to make it possible to cope. She takes courses, she reads, and she maintains her

many relationships accumulated through the years. She does not allow her unhappiness about her son's divorce and unemployment (we guess that he is depressed) to interfere with her relationship with him. She respects his wish for independence. It is interesting that she does not cling to her sons, as many Japanese women do, and insist that they take care of her. Her sons presumably identify with her independent and assertive spirit. But she does see them as helpful and loyal. Although she says that she is prepared for death, she has her bags packed to dash to the hospital at any moment in order to continue and save her life. She is not ready to give up. She is a survivor and a determined one at that!!

Chapter 7

ᔥ

Mrs. Sugiura:
Successful
But
Apprehensive

Youthful-looking, sixty-eight year old Mrs. Sugita was eager to talk about herself and to share her life experiences and apprehensions. She is a very attractive, slender woman with delicate features and black wavy hair but looks anxious and sad. She was hospitable and leaned forward as she spoke, determined to understand our questions and to share accurately whatever information and feelings she could. It was very clear that she looked forward enthusiastically to our visit and that she wanted not only to talk with us but to show us her very attractive home in an excellent neighborhood. She is proud of her home; she and her husband occupy the first floor; the second floor is for her daughter's family when they are in Japan. At this moment, they are living near New York City, and the apartment is empty.

Mrs. Sugita was smartly dressed in an attractive yellow sweater and black skirt. Her appearance was matched by her ability to articulate her thoughts. She spoke with much feeling, eager to be cooperative and accurate.

She began our session by announcing, "I want someone to listen to my story! I was born in Shibuya in 1919, the middle child of seven brothers and sisters. My father had a fruit and vegetable stand, and we were a very poor family. We worked very hard. I couldn't have the things I wanted; I couldn't wear the type of clothes I wished for. I could only complete high primary school (eight years). Then, I stopped to go to work to help my family economically. We were a happy family in spite of our poverty. Our parents were loving and cherished us.

"I had two brothers and four sisters. All but my oldest sister finished high primary school. She went to joggako. I did not want to continue my schooling when I saw how much my parents were suffering from lack of money. I wanted to help them and, therefore, accepted a job as an office lady in a bank. It was not a particularly good job. Because my education was limited, I had to serve tea, do some clerical work, and generally be helpful.

"I worked in the bank until my brother was called to the military service. My brother's departure was a hardship for my parents who relied upon him in their business. At that point, I decided that I ought to be of further assistance to my parents. Therefore, I offered to work in the

family business, taking my brother's place. I did heavy work, not the kind women generally do. My eldest sister was not available because, by 1933, she was already married, and my younger sister was very weak. I was the next in line. My mother worked with us, too. Yet, in spite of all our efforts, it was difficult to earn an adequate living. We had to work hard if we were to have enough to eat. Our problem was that we did not have enough customers or sell enough fruits and vegetables to accumulate sufficient money to buy produce in advance. Every morning, we had to go to the market to buy food to sell on that day. For thirteen years, I worked with my parents until my brother returned from the army in 1942, and, then, I could leave my parents to get married."

Mrs. Sugita insisted that she did not mind the hard labor because she had such a nice family and lived in a pleasant atmosphere. The people in the community were aware of her devotion and efforts on behalf of her family. With pride, she told us, "I was given an award by the community for being a good daughter and helpful to my parents. This is a Confucian idea that persisted at that time." With this, Mrs. Sugita left the room and returned with an official appearing award inscribed on parchment. She treasures this certificate because it asserts that she is a model daughter who was devoted to her parents while her brother fought in the War.

We asked about her siblings. When her brother returned from the War, he was ill with tuberculosis and needed care, but, eventually, he took over her tasks. Another brother died in North China. The husband of one of her sisters had a furniture business but was not taken into the army because his heart was in the wrong side of his body. After the War, when Mr. and Mrs. Sugita's business expanded, that brother-in-law worked for them. More recently he became a fortune teller. Apparently, that is a lucrative occupation, and he is doing very well. "Maybe he gives good fortunes," she smiled. Another sister was born with a handicap; several of her fingers were missing. For that reason, she did not go out much because it was so conspicuous. (In Japan defects are hidden, if possible, because the defective person, as well as other members of the family, might find it hard to acquire a spouse.) The sister eventually did marry, but now is a widow.

"I met my husband through my father. Our fathers were good friends and had fruit and vegetable shops next to each other. Each of us was helping our father. However, my husband's father opposed the marriage

because my sister had a defective hand. But we were in love and decided to marry in spite of his objections. Unfortunately, the year we wed, my husband was called into the army. I was married in January, my son was born in October, and, in December, my husband received the call. He stayed away for three years. I was 24 years of age when I married.

"While my husband was in the army, since I was now a member of his family, I worked in their business. It was easy to get along well with my in-laws. We had to cooperate with one another to share and earn a living.

"The War years were awful. Bombings and food shortages made life very tense. We had to work doubly hard. When a neighbor's house burned to the ground, my parents-in-law rented the land and we raised vegetables. Thus, we had food. Also, we had to move during the War. The house we rented was located along a railroad track where many bombings occurred. We were struggling in the businesses of farming and selling vegetables and were not doing well in either.

"My husband was fortunate to survive the War. He was sent to Vietnam, in French territory. Many soldiers lost their lives there. He broke his hip bone in such a way that the bone pierced his body and made a hole in his back. He was lucky that he could walk eventually. He spent considerable time in the hospital, and, by good fortune, was able to walk when he returned home.

"When the War ended, there was no rice. We were in trouble. My husband helped the family obtain rice, and we ate only the food we raised. Everybody in Tokyo had similar problems. In our case, we obtained seeds from a relative living in Setagaya-ku. At that time, Setagaya-ku was a rural area, and people living there did not have food shortages. It is strange to think that we now live in Setagaya-ku and that it is part of Tokyo. Then, it was the countryside. With my husband's help, we raised enough food to sell on the black market in Shibuya. That was a good market, and we amassed a considerable amount of money. We had many customers, and business thrived.

"During the 1950s and into the '60s, we worked very hard selling fruits and vegetables. Then, my husband opened a supermarket, and now we have six of them and several restaurants. I worked with him all this time. I did very little work at home, and my children had to learn to be independent. We let them choose their own studies and careers. My son went to Tokyo University, and my daughter selected an art

school. Now, my son works with his father in the supermarket and restaurant businesses. Eventually, he will inherit them.

"My daughter married a man who works for a large company, and they have two children. After completing her art training in Tokyo, she went to France where she studied both French and Japanese painting. My son is 43 years old, and he, too, is married and has two children. My daughter is age 40. My son lives nearby and has a nice wife. I see them frequently. But my daughter has been away with the children for some time. I am not happy about that. First, they went to London for two years, and now they live in Connecticut, outside New York City. I am planning on their return but don't know when. I keep their apartment clean and ready for them. However, even when she returns, I don't know what her plans will be. I won't hold on to her. I know that I must let her be independent. That is how I raised both my children. I worked and had a housemaid. I allowed my children to make decisions that other parents would force on their children.

"Yes, I did a great deal in the business. I did not feel like a wife merely helping her husband. I had my own special responsibilities. I was in charge of the accounting department and the supervision of the employees. That was a big job! However, it was my husband and son who decided on the new business ventures, the restaurants. They wished to do more than sell food and to expand into new areas. I watched over the business to be sure it was running well. My husband is the kind of person who cannot say `no' to people. If anyone asks him for a job, he employs him without knowing where he will place him. I had to be the practical one in the family. Too many people asked for jobs. I was the person who placed them and saw to it that they did a full day's work. I enjoyed my work and the responsibilities. I miss it now that I am retired.

"Twelve years ago, I retired when we moved to this house. Since then, there are too many employees. It cuts into the profits. But I no longer get involved. Now, my husband and son make all the decisions. Since retiring, I work in the garden, care for my house, baby-sit for my grandchildren, and take courses at the Elder University. In the past, I had no time for hobbies and still do not have any. I worry about that because, in the future, I may find myself without enough to do. I should have a hobby. I have tried, but my memory is bad, and I get confused by directions. If I were young, it would be easier to remember things.

"I particularly like the family sociology course at the Elder University. I have made nice friends there, and Dr. Takahari, the instructor, is a fine teacher. I find that I am reviewing my life as we study about families."

We asked if she had come to any conclusions as a result of her studies. "Yes. The conclusions involve the future. I am anxious about many things about my future. I am anxious about my life after my husband dies and my body gets weak or ill. What will happen then? My children may support me and care for me. But I fear to be a burden. I'm satisfied with my life at this moment but cannot forecast the future.

"I have seen many changes in my lifetime. When I was young, I thought primarily about my husband, what would he want and what he was thinking? Only after that, did I think about myself. I observe that my daughter-in-law is different. She thinks first about herself and second about her husband. I think that is good. It is better to speak up. I devoted myself to others and either ignored or sacrificed my desires. In that way, everything went smoothly. There were no problems. Everyone was happy.

"I wouldn't want to relive my life. I have done quite enough. I had a happy life although I had troubles and hard times. My efforts were fruitful. I have a sense of completion and achievement. I lived at a time when, if I loved a person, I could let it be known, and I would be loved in return. Now, it is different. People are not responsive. They do not show their true feelings. I don't like living that way. I want feedback. I want to know how others think and feel. Even though I did not get an advanced education, I observe that people today don't respect each other. They have a sense of loss.

"Society today is too affluent. We are surrounded by too much materialism. I don't know how to handle this. I worry about the future, about my grandchildren, and about the type of society in which they will live. What will happen? I note, for example, that when I was young, I would invite my nieces and nephews to join us when I would take my children on an outing. Now, when my daughter or son go anywhere, they take only their own children. Relationships have tapered off, and people concentrate only on the nuclear family. Relationships have shrunken. My children have excellent educations. My son-in-law went to Hitotsubashi University and my son to Tokyo University. Yet, there is more selfishness and self-centeredness than in the past."

We commented upon Mrs. Sugita's pessimism and wondered how she

visualized her children would help her if the occasion demanded it. "I don't want help until the last moment, until I really need it. I've been independent for so long that it is hard to picture being dependent. That is exactly the problem. I look back on a hardworking but happy life. But I'm not sure about the future for myself and for others."

While no one woman we interviewed can be said to be representative of all Japanese elderly women, each in her own way presented fragments of general significance. Mrs. Sugita is no exception. Through her, we learned of the importance of Confucian filial duties and pride in such accomplishments; the lowly position of the "office girl" in Japan; the poverty of many families before and during World War II; the results of the black market after the War; the latent skills of many undereducated women who, when challenged, rose to the occasion; the fears of aging Japanese women; the typical family constellation of two children; the contrast in education between children and their parents; retirement activities and dilemmas; and the influence of Western culture on the Japanese family. We learned a great deal from Mrs. Sugita because what she said can be generalized. Many other older women had the same experiences and expressed the same concerns and doubts. Fear of being a burden in old age yet longing for the security of knowing she will be cared for is a common international concern.

We were struck by Mrs. Sugita's eagerness to talk with us and to express her concerns. She obviously did not have anyone with whom to talk and share her worries and anxieties. It was immediately apparent that, in spite of her economic security and affluence, she was anxious and worried about the future and about her aging. She saw that family life has changed appreciably in Japan, and the anticipation that the eldest son and his wife will care for his aged parents was no longer a certainty. Actually, like many Japanese women, she feels closer to her daughter, but her daughter's life abroad renders her unavailable. As Japan becomes more internationally oriented, more families will experience what Mrs. Sugita is feeling and dreads. Will her daughter and family decide to stay abroad? Or, upon return, will they find living with parents no longer attractive? Will there be more traveling and more distancing? Mrs. Sugita sees herself as a modern woman, but she is conflicted because no longer can she anticipate that her children will be available when she really needs them. On the other hand, she is independent, and she established such a model for them. Perhaps she regrets

her past emphasis on independence. She also modelled devotion to parents, but her children never observed this; they merely heard her speak of it, and that was not enough.

Mrs. Sugita's concern about what will happen to her if she is widowed or too fragile to care for herself is understandable. As we listened to her, we heard aging women in every society ask the same question. In traditional Japanese society, the answer was dictated by Confucian philosophy and societal practices. Today, it is different. While most people accept and even prefer the nuclear family, they look forward to their future with anxiety because they are uncertain that the multigenerational family automatically will evolve to care for them. The East and West are shedding their differences and are becoming more similar in development. However, in Japan, the process is slow because 60% of the aged are still living with or next door to their adult children (Maeda, 1983).

Mrs. Sugita is an excellent example of the hardworking older Japanese women, probably more hardworking than present day young women. This was the case of most of the women we interviewed. Some had been supported by their husbands, but a large number worked during their early years, most at low paying jobs, because of either family poverty or early widowhood responsibilities. The educated women who achieved professional status could more readily attain self-sufficiency and greater self-esteem. However, for most Japanese women reared in pre-war society, life was difficult if, either during or after the War, they had to support themselves and their families. They revealed remarkable strength and resilience. As we listened to Mrs. Sugita, it was evident that she felt more comfortable, competent, superior, important, and needed when working in the family businesses. She found her identity in work and not exclusively in motherhood. She rationalized that her children should learn to be independent and, therefore, she need not feel guilty for having left them in the care of a maid. But, at this time of her life, she is conflicted because her children are so independent that she fears they will abandon her if she becomes dependent. She does not share with them her hidden thoughts that perhaps, when very young, they had felt abandoned by her psychologically. As a result, she fears that they will not be responsive when she ages. Also, she cannot imagine her daughter-in-law sacrificing or extending herself to care for her, nor her daughter being available.

Retirement has left a vacuum in her life, and, like many older people,

she has not been able to fill it. She no longer feels depended upon in business by either her husband or son, or by her children at home. Perhaps she may not feel close to her husband anymore. We could not ascertain this. Gardening, baby-sitting, and taking courses at Elder University apparently are insufficient to occupy or interest her. She was so busy in the family businesses for many years that she did not develop other interests. However, at this time, she is depressed because she misses her daughter and worries about widowhood and ill health. While she ostensibly appears to approve of her daughter-in-law thinking of herself first, ironically, she is aware that if she needs help, her son and daughter-in-law may not come forward.

Although she did not verbalize it, Mrs. Sugita is aware that when she was poor, she had the security of a cohesive family. Also, she was the giver and felt strong and superior in that position. Whatever resentment she had because of her poverty, she repressed. Now, ironically, when she is affluent, she fears there will be a lack of emotional support for her in the future if her husband dies before she does. The cohesive family upon which Confucian thinking was premised is no longer a certainty. When she was needed, she felt in control. Now, she no longer feels needed, as she perceives it, and she experiences a psychological vacuum.

It is unfortunate that she does not seek psychological counseling to resolve her fears and conflicts. Many older Japanese women suffer from precisely these feelings and need help in acknowledging and confronting them. But, in Japan, this is not available. In the United States, while it is not common for older people to seek counseling services, more are seeking psychological assistance in confronting the conflicts about their family relations and the future when their family will become even more important to them as their physical status changes. Mrs. Sugita has the company of many women who are afraid to verbalize their fears. They need to be helped to do so in the hope that the depression that engulfs them can be dissipated, and they can continue to enjoy the healthy years ahead of them.

Chapter 8

&

Mrs. Kanai:
Her Father's
Daughter

We visited with Mrs. Kanai in her small Japanese home, hemmed in by similar little cedar houses, in an attractive, old section of Tokyo. Her diminutive garden was meticulously planted, reflecting careful planning. Mrs. Kanai is a slight, nice-looking, bespectacled 68-year-old woman with dark wavy hair. She is highly intelligent, very serious, thoughtful, peaked, and tense. Her reserved manner led us to anticipate that she would find it difficult to talk about her life although she had volunteered to do so at the Elder University. While it did take her some time to speak freely, eventually, she became more relaxed and sharing of her life history, thoughts, and concerns. We sat around her low dining table. Although her younger daughter was present during the entire interview, she offered no comments at any time. Instead, she sat looking glum and expressionless, listening carefully to her mother. Rarely did either the mother or daughter smile. The atmosphere was one of sadness, and both appeared anxious and worried.

Mrs. Kanai plunged in by asking what she should talk about. Were we interested in her independent life after she obtained her divorce? "I married at 29 and divorced at age 44 and brought up my two daughters alone." We encouraged her to start at any point in her life that she wished. Significantly, she began by telling about her outstanding father.

"I lost my mother at age 12. My mother was 42 when she died of kidney and heart failure, leaving seven children for my father to raise. He never remarried and reared all but the newborn baby himself. The baby was adopted and raised by my father's cousin. My father was a remarkable man, unusual for a man born in 1880. He had very modern ideas. For example, he declared to his children that he did not expect to be cared for by his eldest son when he grew old as was common in his generation. He proclaimed his independent stance very early in his life and stayed with it until he died. He was a wonderful teacher, and I learned a great deal from him, including how to be independent."

Independence and her unique, wonderful father became the two themes of her life review. Interestingly, she set this stage at the beginning of her life review in order to describe her life conflicts and struggles and the many events related to these two issues. This is what she said.

"I was 12 years old when my mother died, the second child in a family of five girls and two boys. But I did not grieve the loss of my mother; I did not feel lonesome for her; I had no strong feelings about her death. I had enjoyed life up to that time and continued to do so. You must remember that when a mother has so many children, she cannot pay much attention to any one child. She was always busy caring for a new baby. Mother was seen by the children as the person who cooked, cleaned the house, and had babies. I was sad when my father died. He was the significant person in my life.

"My father was mother and father to us after my mother died. He was a scholar and, therefore, stayed at home doing his research and writing. That is why he could manage so well. He was always available to us. He believed that children should be free, another innovative idea for a Japanese man, and let us run around the farm freely. Today, he would not be able to do this. The family of today is different from the family structure in my youth. We were bonded to each other and had good relationships. We had respect for each other and, most important, we respected our father. My daughters never respected their father. I divorced their father because he went out with other women. I felt comfortable being a woman, but I surmise my daughters likely don't feel the same because they do not respect their father.

"My father was an expert on Chinese subjects and published textbooks for junior high schools. Today, these would be used by high schools. He was a brilliant man.

"I don't recall any sad events during my childhood. I always had a positive view of life. We were carefree and enjoyed ourselves. I remember playing games with my brother and sisters. I preferred climbing trees and playing baseball with boys. Mostly, I was in the field picking up the balls. Even in school, I preferred physical education to academic subjects.

"My sisters and I went to Tokyo Metropolitan High School. We did not go to a university, except for one sister. Our school was considered a superior high school for girls. There were eight metropolitan high schools, and this was the best. I didn't study to prepare myself for any particular job or career. However, I learned Japanese typing, and that was very helpful when I sought a job after I separated from my husband. I worked as a typist for some years to send my daughters to junior college to study English literature because I believed in education. After the War, girls started going to college in large numbers. Times did change, and women

are better educated now. My brother went to Waseda University, but I don't know if the brother adopted by relatives was sent to a university.

"After finishing high school, I worked as a typist in several companies. I met my husband in the steel company in which I worked. I was not introduced to him formally. He was an administrator in one of the divisions. We dated and did not have a go-between arrange the wedding. None of my sisters or brother had a go-between. My father did not believe in such traditions. He was open-minded."

We asked if Mrs. Kanai recalled the Earthquake of 1923. "I was only 4 years old at the time. I remember people were in a confused state, but I thought it was fun. We escaped to our neighbor's house that was well constructed and considered safe. It was a playful experience for me; I was excited being together with all my friends. We lived in Chiba then."

The other experience elderly women in Japan have in common is the Sino-Japanese War and World War II. Mrs. Kanai remembers the bombings very well. "I was living in Tokyo at the time, working in a defense factory. No one in my family was evacuated. Our house was never bombed, but a house 100 meters from us had a serious fire. Generally speaking, we were in a safe area. Other neighborhoods were completely destroyed. For example, Setagaya-ku was not harmed much, whereas the Akasaka section of Tokyo suffered severe destruction.

"The most unhappy time for me because of the War was my father's death, resulting from the War. I was 28 years old at the time, and my father was 67, in 1947. He died of malnutrition because he did not take adequate care of himself. Immediately after the War, food was especially scarce, and he did not have enough to eat. He had been in good shape and had no diseases during the War. Father kept saying that he was not hungry when we urged him to eat. He insisted that he did not feel like eating, and he gave his food to his children saying, `You children have a longer life to live, so you take this food.' He would go to the black market to get it. Without that, we would not have survived. Everyone who could, did this.

"I recall his fingers became puffed, and he said that when the swelling reached his wrists he would die. He died on a Saturday. I remember it vividly. He prepared everything for his death and said everything he wished to say to his children. He urged us to live together in harmony and not quarrel. He was in total control of himself to the last moment.

Even when very weak, he went to the toilet himself. To this day, when I recall his death, I am moved to tears.

"The year after my father died, I married. We had our own apartment, and I quit my job because my husband did not want me to work. I had two children, both girls, and, when not caring for them or doing the usual household chores, I read a great deal. I had been brought up surrounded by books so this was a natural thing to do. As I am a Christian, I also volunteered to work in the church library.

"My marriage did not last. My husband ran after women so I told him to leave. I feel that if there is no love left, it is best to get a divorce. For a long while, however, I did not go through the legal procedure; I considered that we were permanently separated. I didn't actually get a divorce until my oldest daughter sought a job at K.D.D. (International Telecommunication Company) and was told that they did not object to hiring the child of a divorcee but would not employ the child of separated parents. I contacted my husband to ask him for a divorce. I did not care about my status, but I did not wish to make things hard for my daughter. It was the right time for my husband to divorce, too, because he already had a child by the woman with whom he was living. Therefore, he was very agreeable. The reason I say that it was the right time for a divorce is that not only was my older daughter seeking a job but my younger daughter was entering college. I had to anticipate her future, too.

"A question arose concerning what name I should assume upon my divorce. I was not forced to change my name, but I decided to resume my father's name. I loved my father." During this part of the conversation, Mrs. Kanai's daughter, the younger of the two, sat looking particularly sad but remained silent.

When they separated, Mrs. Kanai retained the house in which she is presently living. We commented that it was a comfortable one, but she laughed, saying it is a traditional Japanese house, cold in winter. The humid Japanese summers make it necessary that houses be open to allow the wind to blow through and prevent rotting. "That is why these wooden houses last 50 or more years." Mrs. Kanai's older married daughter, in contrast, lives in a modern house that has many good features, especially good cupboard space and much insulation.

Four years ago, Mrs. Kanai retired. "My last job was with the Association of Metropolitan Governments, handling social welfare questions. I was in charge of accounting for the home helpers of handicapped aged. I

was 64 at the time of retirement but had not planned to leave until 70. Unfortunately, because I like gardening, I fell while working in my garden and struck my head. That created a circulation problem in my brain, and I had difficulties understanding small things. So, I quit my job, retired, and went to work for the church. I'm fine now, am on a pension, and I also get paid by the church for my once-a-week job organizing the library, ordering books, and the like.

"All the years during my separation and divorce, I was the sole support of my daughters and myself, except when my daughters worked. My older daughter is married, and now my younger daughter will very soon be wed. She is receiving unemployment compensation now because she gave up her job. She will be living in Saitama Prefecture after marriage. It is not close to my home. When she settles in her apartment, she will seek a job in Saitama. My daughter was recently confronted with the question of whether she should live with her in-laws or opt for her own apartment. She and her fiance finally decided to live apart from his family. I thought that was the right decision.

"There have been many changes over the years, but the most important problem I am confronted with is how I will manage living alone in the future. In the past, I lived by the saying in the Bible, 'The tiny flowers in the field are precious, and not just the big, gorgeous ones.' I must accept the present, but I don't know about the future. It will be different. When my daughter marries, I will live independently. I have two daughters and don't want to be dependent upon either of them. I have told my older daughter that if I cannot manage, she should send me to a nursing home."

We observed that she is apparently quoting her father whom she described as being very independent. "Yes, that is true. But it was different then. He was born in 1880, and he could not imagine the development of the nuclear family as we have it today in Japan. It was the absolute duty of children in the past, especially the oldest son, to care for their aged parents. Today, children feel that they must be rich, or the parents must be rich, if they are to be provided care. I would like to use public services for the elderly if I need help. But, if public services are not sufficient for my needs, then I will ask my children to help me. Three of my neighbors are old, and their children live separately. After the War, this new way of life began, and it is not unusual in Japan today. In the studies of family sociology that I am taking at the Elder Univer-

sity, people say that at first living with children works fine, but after a few years problems arise, and there are difficulties. It is not good for parents to ask to live with their children; it is best that children should do the inviting.

"I'm not sure just what I will do after my daughter marries and moves to her new apartment. I'm not one to stay at home and do nothing. I'll have to decide on some activity. I like volunteer work. In Japan, that is not as common as in the United States. My neighbor's wife participates in volunteer activities and sometimes comes home as late as nine or ten o'clock at night. I plan to ask her what she does."

We remarked that in many ways she is not like the average older Japanese woman in that she does plan to live alone, however much she dreads it, and that she does plan to do volunteer work to keep herself alert and busy. We wondered how she viewed the present as compared to the past in terms of family relations and child rearing.

"That is a difficult question. If I talk too much about the past, people will say I'm too conservative. The world has changed. I have many complaints about modern child rearing. As I look around my neighborhood at the children and the kind of upbringing they have, I think that they should be freer, should not have to go to juku (cram school) after regular school hours, and should not have to compete in the examinations. It would be better if children could go to the mountains. I was raised to be free to run about in a large cattle field. If we tried to get out of the fence, my parents would pull us back. But we had lots of room to run around. We were encouraged to be productive, creative, and imaginative. For children today, society is too mechanized, too computerized, and is not free and creative. Nevertheless, I do agree with the nuclear family structure in preference to the ie system of the past."

Thus, Mrs. Kanai is caught in the conflict between the security that the past traditional family system offered and her loyalty to her father who raised her to be a modern woman in the late twentieth century. It appears clear that she really would prefer to live with her daughter but does not feel comfortable requesting it. How she wishes one of her daughters would invite her!

Mrs. Kanai's daughter's pending marriage is a real crisis, a crisis that coincides with her retirement and the onset of old age. Although she professes independence and self-reliance, up to this time, there has always been someone upon whom she could rely for emotional support. For 28

years, it was her father; for some years, it was her husband. Her daughters, although economically dependent upon her, were emotionally supportive. Like many women around the world, in old age, when widowhood occurs and the children are no longer living at home, she is confronting the event that she had dreaded, namely, the price of independence and living alone at this time of life is loneliness. Psychologically, many women are not prepared for this eventuality even though on a intellectual level they anticipated these developments. Mrs. Kanai is worried, anxious, and depressed as she confronts the departure of her second daughter. Judging from her daughter's reactions, I think that she feels the same way. She is aware of her mother's mixed feelings about her approaching marriage and is conflicted, sad, and very likely guilty. Not once, as her mother recounted her life experiences and feelings, did she show any reaction while listening carefully.

Mrs. Kanai is struggling with ambivalent feelings toward both daughters leaving home. She is true to her father and verbalizes his teaching of independence, but in reality she is not ready for it. She strongly supports her daughter's decision not to live with her in-laws but wishes that one of her daughter's would invite her to live with her. As a result she feels depressed and helpless, conflicted and frustrated, anxious and unhappy.

Throughout the recitation of her life history, her father plays a dominant role. As her father's oldest daughter, she probably thought of herself as taking her mother's place after her mother's death. With six children to raise, he probably assigned the older children numerous household tasks. She, the oldest girl, would have had many. Any annoyance about these responsibilities, she successfully repressed. Instead, she presents herself as important to him and worshipping of him. His sacrifice of food so that his children could have enough added to her need to put him on a pedestal and view him as a saint or martyr. It also left her, and possibly her siblings, feeling guilty about his death from malnutrition. Most of them were adults or teenagers during the War, and he was an elderly man. Unless he was an extraordinarily stubborn person, they could have pressed him to share more of their food. Mrs. Kanai is still mourning his death. She has not separated from him psychologically, and she remains emotionally over-attached to him although he has been dead for many years. When divorced, she resumed his name and obliterated her marriage name.

She cannot even permit herself to mourn the death of her mother who died just as she was entering puberty. Her denial of any feelings toward her mother's death is extreme; perhaps it is her way of denying her negative and angry thoughts toward her. She may have resented the numerous babies her mother was preoccupied with since she had to help care for the younger children. Instead, she repressed both the good and bad feelings about her mother. She sees women as feeling womanly only if they are accepted by their fathers. She does not comprehend femininity as related to identification with the maternal figure, but, instead, sees it only if the father values women.

Mrs. Kanai is a resourceful woman with considerable strengths. She was able to support herself and her daughters; she was able to separate herself from an unfaithful husband; she is able to volunteer her services to others and take courses rather than restrict her life and activities during retirement. She has an active mind, seeks creative outlets, and, although still tied emotionally to her father, has not been immobilized. She quotes him to help herself rationalize why she must adapt to the new situation she now confronts. She has the capacity to adapt and master life crises, and it is likely that, after a period of grief reaction to the loss of her daughter, she will create a new and meaningful life for herself. Eventually, one of her daughters will probably invite her to live with her and her husband.

Throughout the world, as family systems alter in modern urban societies, elderly women face the same dilemma as Mrs. Kanai. Families are available to the elderly; they are not deserting them. But they are not necessarily all offering invitations to live with them in their homes. Communities are developing home care and nursing home services previously rendered only by families because families cannot continue, in many instances, to offer these services themselves. It is the daughter or daughter-in-law who has shouldered the burden of caring for her frail elderly parent. With women in many parts of the world now working out of necessity, some pursuing careers, there is a limit to how much of this burden they can be expected to shoulder. Mrs. Kanai, as an individual, is encountering what Japanese society as a whole is confronting. The Japanese Government is at present engaging in long-term planning for the care of the aged who have no families or whose families cannot or do not wish to care for their elders. Increasing numbers of Japanese aged, like their American cohort, are concerned that they will be a

burden to their families, especially when ill or disabled, and are even accepting institutional care if necessary. Gerontologists and private and governmental agencies are struggling to create solutions. Mrs. Kanai's father prepared her for a more Western societal outlook, but at this crisis point, the conflict between the past Japanese cultural expectations with regard to the care of the aged and the present day realities dramatizes the fact that intellectual preparedness and emotional preparedness rarely coincide. Nevertheless, the ego strength she demonstrated all these years stems from her identification with her father, and we hope that this will permit her to adapt to her new status as a divorced aging woman living independently.

Chapter 9

ও

Mrs. Watari:
Rejected
But
Philosophical

Mrs. Watari lives in a tiny, two-room house, consisting of one six tatami-mat room, a small kitchen, a bathroom and a toilet. It is separated by a high metal fence from a large modern, attractive home in a residential area of Setagaya-ku. It is located on what was once the garden of the big house. Flowers and shrubs no longer grow there.

Mrs. Watari's living room is distinguished by the bookcase filled with books and western classical music records. Because she lives alone, she spends much time listening to music and reading in her snug, minuscule home.

Mrs. Watari is a 69 year old, short, heavy-set, plain-looking woman who dresses casually in slacks and sweaters. Her curly black hair is pulled back off her full, round face, and she peers through wire-rimmed glasses. From all appearances, she is a smiling, optimistic person. However, when she begins to speak, it becomes clear that she is also very serious and thoughtful. She spoke with ease in a relaxed, engaging manner, presenting herself as an unassuming, modest person, astonished that anyone would be interested in her life story. As was the case with the other women interviewed, she grasped this opportunity to review her life, seeing it as a welcome, exciting task. She had given much thought to it before we arrived. But first we had a cup of tea in the usual Japanese hospitable manner, sitting on the floor around the table.

Mrs. Watari has been living in this humble house for two years. Before that, she lived in the big house next door with her son, daughter-in-law, and grandson. She was shocked when her son announced that his wife requested that she move from the home that she and her son had occupied for many years before his marriage six years ago. He built this small house for her in the garden. How lonesome it was at first, she declared, but now, she enjoys her privacy and has found much to keep herself busy. Among other things, she is taking numerous courses at the Elder University, including a course in family sociology. When her professor asked for volunteers for life reviews, she responded readily and with great interest.

"I will start from the beginning. I was born in Gumma Prefecture, northwest of Tokyo, an essentially rural area although it has some small

cities and towns. I am the third of five children, three boys and two girls. My father was a successful businessman, the president of a movie theatre and branch owner of a company selling stocks and bonds. Life was pleasant, and there were no financial problems until the Earthquake of 1923 when his business slowly starting failing.

"I was six years old when the Earthquake occurred. We felt only slight tremors in Gumma, but Tokyo was in terrible shape. My father's headquarters were in Tokyo, and that business was seriously affected, thus hurting my father financially. However, the financial impact crept upon us slowly before we realized how serious it was." By 1937, when he died, there was very little money left to inherit. She was 19 years old at the time. After that, life changed radically for her.

"I had a very happy childhood. My father was a generous and kind man and spent a great deal of time with his children. I recall the many family picnics and outings we had together. My mother was always with us, too. With five children, she did not work outside the home. She was always available. Except for my father's fights with my oldest brother, life was very peaceful. Outsiders criticized my father for not being strict with my brother. But he was not that kind of person. He spoke up, but he did not act forcefully. My brother ignored him, in any case."

The only other unhappy event she could remember involved her school marks. "My sister was a very good student and had good marks. My memory wasn't as good, and my marks were poor. I never liked to study." We observed that she was what in the United States is called a "late bloomer," that is, a person who develops her intellectual capacities later than the average child, and then goes on to do well. She assured me that all of her clerical jobs in accounting and bookkeeping were modest, but now she does like reading and studying.

All of the children in the family went to high school, but none went to a university. She and her sisters went to a joggako. Her father wanted his eldest son to continue his education but, she explained, "He was not a good son; he was a ne'er-do-well and wandered away from the family." She is convinced that this hastened her father's death. He was heart-sick and depressed by his son's behavior. People used to tell him that he pampered this son too much. They had many disagreements and it was evident to him for a long time that his son had no loyalty to him and the family. He worried about him for many years, and she partially attributes his failing business to this, also. Her brother never fought

with his father overtly. He merely ignored him, and this infuriated her father, leaving him frustrated and angry. Unfortunately, her younger brother could not take his older brother's place. He was much too young, and, furthermore, the Sino-Japanese War in 1937, the year her father died, "took him away to the army and to China." There was no one to inherit the business. No one even knew where in Tokyo her older brother was living.

" As my sister was married and living in Tokyo, after my father died, my mother decided to move there, too. So my brother and I went with her. But, because my brother went into the army and my oldest brother took no responsibility for the family, I had no choice but to go to work to support my mother and myself. At that time, women were not educated to work outside the home. I worked all during the two wars, and in 1945, when World War II ended, I found myself having to continue to care for my mother. My younger brother died in New Guinea, and my older brother had completely disappeared. I do not know where he is to this day. I understand that he is married and has a family, but he has never maintained a relationship with us. He is totally alienated.

"During the War, my mother and I lived together. I supported her by doing clerical work. My younger brother helped a little financially, but, being in the army, he could not do much. I had to face the reality of our situation and assume the major burden of caring for my mother. My first job was with the Tokyo Metropolitan Government calculating the census, and then I moved to a simple job maintaining record books. That was easy. It was before World War II. When that War came, I had to work in a munitions factory for the Air Force, again in a clerical position. It paid more, but life was very hard. We did not have enough money. Food was difficult to obtain. Bombings were frequent. I worked long hours. I worked there until 1947. In fact, I met my husband while working there."

At our request, she elaborated upon the War years. "We suffered from food shortages. I went to markets to stand in line just to get potatoes, I recall. And I built a shelter to protect us from the bombs. It was a hole in the ground, and, as I look back, it really wasn't very good. It probably would not have saved us if a bomb fell near it. The bombings were aimed at the airport in Mitaka. I recall hearing and seeing a huge airplane flying very low. I was frightened. Eventually, we saw many B-29 planes. There were bombings day and night. We became so used

to it that we would stand outdoors watching the planes fly overhead. We realized that they were aiming at factories and airports and not at our houses. But all the homes were close to such facilities. I recall March 10 when, close to my home in the Ogikubo section, blocks of houses burned, and the entire area had a red glow. It was scary. The railroad station was destroyed. Our rented house was not hurt fortunately. We were lucky. The family from whom we rented had evacuated to the countryside. Unfortunately, we had sold our house in Gumma Prefecture and had no place to flee. We had relatives in Maigoshi and left our furniture with them. Ironically, their house was bombed, and we lost everything."

When the war ended, Mrs. Watari was 28 years old and unwed. In 1947, her friend's father introduced her to Mr. Watari who was working in the accounting department of a train manufacturing company.

"He had never been in the army because he had a frail body and was ranked in the third category. I had wanted to marry earlier, but there were so few men. Most were in the army; many had died. At age 29, my choices were limited. He was 37 years old, and his wife had died. They had no children. We learned to love one another, but unfortunately he lived only three more years and died of tuberculosis. He did not have the disease when we married.

"My husband's father was a professional calligrapher who did formal writing for people and made a modest living. About five or six years before his death, my husband and his brother had to support their father. My husband made a reasonable income, and we could manage. We lived in a big house that he owned. The present modern house is on that property. Years later, I had the old house torn down and built the house you see next door.

"After my husband died, I had to care for my son, age two, and my mother-in-law. To support them and myself, I rented two rooms in our house to boarders, and I took a job in the neighborhood in the accounting department of a small business. I worked in several such places until I retired on a pension. My mother lived with my youngest brother after I married, and my mother-in-law remained with me. Although my brother-in-law should have supported his mother because he and his wife worked and could afford it, they did not offer to do so. My mother-in-law said that she preferred to live with me. I could not refuse. So I had to work to care for the three of us even though I was not bright and capable. My

mother-in-law lived with me for 23 years, until she died.

"I have a stereotypical answer when you ask me about the War. I want no more war! We suffered! Our bodies suffered! I want to stress the importance of peace! In particular, I object to the restrictions of information at the time of war. The Japanese people were being told in the newspapers that we were winning, that we had to be patient, and that we had to be loyal to the nation and to our leaders. Even when the atomic bomb fell, we were told only that it was a new type of bomb, and we did not get the real information about it until much later. People were asking, 'Are we really winning?' We knew nothing. I hate control of information. We were educated before the War to be loyal to the Emperor in an absolute way; no questions were to be asked. I cannot imagine this belief today. We had to believe that the Emperor was always right, that he was so powerful he could cause the wind to blow, win the War, and he did this for the kamikaze (suicide airplane pilots). We had to believe everything the people in power said. It is no good to live under such conditions when people do not get correct information. I was working in the factory on August 15 when we heard the Emperor announce over the radio that we had lost the War, that it was unconditional surrender. We were stunned. Everyone was weeping. In my day, we had to apologize to our ancestors for losing a war. Now, this was happening, and there were no apologies.

"I think that things are different now. We educate people to think differently. There is more skepticism today. When I was in school, teachers taught us unquestioning loyalty and acceptance of Japanese imperialism. I think that it is important to tell people the truth and to create a public opinion based on truth. Information control is not extreme now, and people are not forced to follow orders. Nations that control information, as Japan did in the past, will never really prosper. I believe that Japan is a better nation now than when I was young."

After these observations, which Mrs. Watari asserted with deep conviction and emphasis, she returned to talking about her life.

"I lived with my son and mother-in-law while working in an accounting company. After my mother-in-law died, my son and I continued to live in the big house. Now he is 39 years old, a graduate of Hosei University where he studied economics. Currently he works in a bank. When my son was 33 years old, he married. He met his wife through a friend's father; there was no formal go-between. I did not object to his

marriage. Only sons have a hard time finding a wife because young women do not want to take care of their mother-in-law. I thought that we got along fine. I had my own room and tried to keep out of their way. Nevertheless, his wife decided that she did not want to have her mother-in-law live with them. Now, my son comes to visit once a week in my house. He says 'hello', but not much more.

"Actually, I am worried about my grandson. He is a sick child and coughs a good deal. I don't know the name of his illness. Every two days, my daughter-in-law takes him to the National Children's Hospital. They can walk there. The beds are full so he has out-patient treatment. There appears to be something wrong with his blood. He needs frequent transfusions. It has something to do with his immune system. He has about one-quarter of the amount of antibodies that he needs. His parents worry, and so do I. He is only three years old. His parents are so concerned about his condition that they are afraid to have another child.

"You asked why my daughter-in-law wished to live separately from me. Today's young people have different ideas from those of the past. She told my son that she felt constricted by my presence. Actually, I did not interfere with her because I left early for work, and did not return until late. But these days many daughters-in-law do not want old parents, especially a mother-in-law, around. I can understand that. Things are different today. I felt that there was a tense atmosphere when I was with my daughter-in-law. However, it was a surprise when my son talked to me about the need to live separately. But I am accustomed to it now, and I am no longer lonesome. With my pension I can support myself in this small house.

"The greatest change in my lifetime is the abolition of the ie system (the family system in which the oldest son inherited the family property and assumed care of the aging parents). It was based on the premise that parents and children could live in harmony together. That is the ideal situation. But when parents and children have different ideas, it is very hard to force them to live in harmony. I suffered from the ie family system. I had to take care of my mother because my oldest brother refused to conform; and I had to care for my mother-in-law because my brother-in-law did not conform. Both my brother and brother-in-law did not accept their responsibilities and forced these on me even though I had no money, no skills, and no obligations. I could not abandon

these two women. I liked them, but it was a terrible financial and physical burden. The present system is not ideal, but it is better than the past system of absolute obligations. It is essential that families live in harmony, and it is not good for old parents to be too dependent on their children. Recently, I saw an article in the newspaper that stressed that old people should not be too dependent on their children. I agree.

"Today, I keep busy. I am independent. I have my own income, and I go out daily to take courses. I enjoy the Elder University, and, in addition to the family sociology course, I am studying comparative governments with the professor from Tokyo University. I don't totally understand him, but the course is interesting. In that course, there are people from age 30 through retirement age."

We asked if she had more thoughts to share with us in comparing the past with the present. "Yes. Women became freer and began working more outside the home. This is good for women because it makes them more independent, especially financially. But not everything is good. I look at television and see some bad things. Nevertheless, the young people are healthy and doing much better than my generation did at their age. I don't expect the present to be perfect, but it is better than when I was growing up." With these thoughts she ended, and we had another cup of tea.

Mrs. Watari's perception of herself as an ordinary Japanese woman who accepts events in her life with fatalism is found among many women in Japan. She was born at a time of many changes during the Taisho era that brought democratic thinking into the political and social system, but it did not last long enough to be integrated into the fabric of Japanese society and culture. It ended while Mrs. Watari was still a child. The conservative and feudal ideas of the previous period had not been erased. And the new Japanese imperialism was accompanied by education and information that were directed by the leaders to promote nationalism and war. Mrs. Watari, no different from other citizens, believed what she was told. But she is unique! Once she knew that she had been given propaganda, she was repelled. She has the capacity and vision to recognize the importance of free speech, free press, and freedom of information. She can conceptualize the political and social implications of the experiences through which she lived. Interestingly, in old age and retirement, she is even pursuing this subject at the Elder University. She does not present herself initially as a deep thinker or an intellectual.

Her strength lies in the fact that, even while assuming a passive, seemingly resigned stance and apparently accepting whatever comes along in life, she does look back, analyzes what has occurred, and arrives at independent conclusions.

She had a difficult life for which she was unprepared. She felt inferior to her more intellectual sister and never could overcome that perception of herself. Furthermore, brought up in a comfortable, happy home life in which she expected to marry shortly after completing the jogakko, she unexpectedly had to assume responsibilities to support herself and her mother, to worry about the family after her father died and her older brother refused to assume his traditional role, and to move to a new city. She was realistically aware of her limitations and did the best she could.

Although she considers her life to have been difficult from age 19 to the present, she rationalizes her disappointments and hardships and does not feel sorry for herself. Only when she explained the ie family system, how she felt trapped by it, and how she was forced to assume roles she had not anticipated or sought because the various men in the family abdicated their obligations, did one detect her bitterness and sense of irony. None of the men in her family, except for her father, could be depended upon. In fact, given her limited resources and strong sense of responsibility, she managed very well. Even as she describes her son's and daughter-in-law's rejection, she is able to acknowledge the hurt and rationalize the situation by saying this is the reality of the new era when aged parents should be more independent and not routinely cared for by their children as in the past. Instead of succumbing to anger, martyrdom, or immobilization, she has found new interests and new activities. Their rejection has a familiar ring as she thinks back on her older brother's fights and flight and on how her father felt about it. However reluctantly, she has settled into her tiny house, grateful that it is next door to her son's; she has not become depressed and acrimonious.

It is only possible to speculate why Mrs. Watari's daughter-in-law and son asked her to move. She may have been critical of their handling of the sick grandchild; she may have interfered with their lives more than she was aware; she may have been too close to her son; or she may have unconsciously made her daughter-in-law feel unwanted. We do not know what her daughter-in-law and son are like. But we do know that they are under the strain of caring for a very sick child. Perhaps the

daughter-in-law does not feel guilty for rejecting her mother-in-law, but the son clearly does. In the meantime, Mrs. Watari is keenly aware of the irony that she cared for both her mother and mother-in-law in their middle and old age and for her son since age two, yet she is now made to feel unwelcome and uncared for. However, being next door to her son, it is likely that in the event of an illness, he will be responsive although it is improbable that she will reenter her former home again.

Mrs. Watari is a thinking, feeling woman with a good capacity to adapt to life's crises without disintegrating and fragmenting. She can rise to the occasion when pressed and function very well, accepting the situation and taking her strengths for granted. She can philosophize about the past and view it realistically. She is an unpretentious woman, highly verbal, and a modest but admirable thinker. She had considerable suffering and losses and now stoically accepts whatever comes along, not fighting but coping.

Chapter 10

૨ઢ

Miss Katase:
A Single
Woman Who
Enjoyed
Serving People

T his gracious 74 year old woman was meticulous in appearance and beautifully dressed. Her white hair was styled perfectly, and she carried herself with great dignity. She clearly pays much attention to her appearance and does not look her age when one notes her smooth, unwrinkled skin and very lively expression. Yet, she is a serious, thoughtful woman who weighs each word carefully and deliberately. She was poised and comfortable as she talked about her life. There was neither the laughter nor nervous smiles with which many women responded to hide their anxiety and eagerness to oblige. She had a paper in her hand that she consulted from time to time when we asked about dates having given considerable thought to this prior to our meeting. She wanted to be accurate and helpful, she explained.

Miss Katase was the oldest of six children, three boys and three girls. "I was born in the Taisho era in 1914. My father came from the countryside to Tokyo where he worked as a salaryman on the Ginza in the jewelry and machinery business. It was a big operation because the company traded with other countries. The company is still functioning but now has more varied operations. My mother, too, came from the countryside, and met my father in Tokyo. She was a very healthy woman who raised six children. However, suddenly in 1943, in the midst of the War, she fell ill with cholecystitis (gall bladder disease) and died. It came as a shock to the entire family.

"I had a happy childhood growing up in a big family. We lived in our own home, and, because the family was large and my father's income was limited, we were not rich. But we had no complaints. Education was important so my sisters and I went through high school, and my brothers went on to the university. I took special post-graduate training in nutrition. I enjoyed studying, especially reading, and I still do. In fact, I was frustrated during my working days because I could not find time to read as much as I would have liked. Now, I am making up for it. I recall no really unhappy events growing up except for my mother's untimely death when I was 29 years of age. Of course, my brothers and sisters were all younger so it had a greater impact on them.

"I graduated from Ochanomizu joggako, a famous girls' high school

that eventually became a university, and I continued studying there to receive a diploma in nutrition. From 1960 until I retired, I worked for the Tokyo Metropolitan Government Health Center as an advisor and counselor for the citizens of Tokyo on nutrition and food affairs.

"Of course, during the War, our family was engaged in war activities. My three brothers went to war, and my father and sister and I lived together after my mother died. Father's company shifted into armament production, and my sister and I worked in a factory sewing buttons on uniforms. Yes, the whole family participated in the war effort. Amazingly, all three of my brothers survived the War, but my middle brother was kept in Siberia by the Russians for five years and returned home suffering from serious malnutrition. Two of my brothers graduated from Waseda University, and the third went to a different university after the War. They all became salarymen. One sister married during the War, and one married a considerable number of years after. But I never married and remained with my father until he died. I am still living in the family house alone. It is a very old, wooden house built in 1923 after the Earthquake and now is so crowded by high rise apartments that I get no sunshine, wind, or light. It's really very unpleasant, like a "rabbit hutch," and it makes me feel very small, but I am not about to move." With this, Miss Katase laughed. Up to this time she had been very serious, hardly even smiling.

"I was always a student and decided that I wanted a career, a job for life. As a woman, I wanted to be helpful to people, and I thought that I could accomplish this by studying about food. In that way, I could care for myself and my family and be useful to society. It is a good career for women. Most of my friends at Ochanomizu studied literature and family management and did not continue their education after high school. If they did, it was to master flower arranging, the tea ceremony, and the like. They planned to marry and were not interested in a career. My family encouraged me when I announced that I wanted to pursue a career. I was fortunate that they were so supportive. It is traditional in Japan for women to prepare for marriage even while studying, but, as I looked around, I did find that many families encouraged their daughters to study beyond the required courses.

"I worked at the Health Center until I retired at age 60. Then, for seven more years I stayed on as a lecturer. I liked that. Finally, at 67, I retired entirely, and now I am doing what I always wanted to do but was

prevented from doing by the War and my career. I am studying, reading, and traveling. I write haiku (Japanese poetry), take painting lessons, go to the theatre, travel on short trips, and foster relationships with my friends. I enjoy everything that I am doing.

"You asked me earlier about the War. It brought many changes apart from our work in the war effort and the men going off to battles. What I recall especially are the bombings and lack of food. We even had to be evacuated for a while. Everyday life was severe, and we spent much of our time and thoughts on how to find food. We were hungry. We were fortunate that our house was never bombed. Every place around us was devastated, yet our house escaped. In light of the fact that it is wooden, we were astonished by its condition when the War ended. It did not need extensive repairs."

We asked her about marriage. Surely, given the institution of go-betweens, she could easily have found a husband. After considerable thought she answered, "I did not have a strong will to marry. My brothers and sisters did. We all lived with my father until each departed one by one, and I remained to care for him. He died in 1975 at age 89. I had many chances to marry, but most of the attractive men were away at war, and later no one really interested me. Also, I had a career and didn't have to be dependent on a man. I became intensely interested in my career and liked it so much that I kept working with pleasure and satisfaction. I did not avoid marriage because of any strong antipathy to it. It just worked out this way. Most of my friends married, and some became widows during the War. Furthermore, some of the husbands of my friends who did come home from the War were so run down that they died shortly after their return. So many of my friends lived alone or with their young children that I didn't feel unique.

"Why did I elect to specialize in nutrition? Food is important in everyday life. With the right food, you can have good health. I decided that health education is urgent and that a nutritionist has an important mission in life. During the War, we had to survive on limited food supplies. But, after the War, people needed to be educated about balanced diets. We had to reconstitute our health, and in what better way can that be done than through nutrition and food."

We observed that many young women today want to have both a family and a career. She had chosen just the career. Did she have any advice to the present generation of women?

"I think that it is hard to have a career and a good family life. If you want both, then you need a good partner who will help with domestic activities, and you also need good parents and parents-in-law. My sister's daughter is an ophthalmologist and has two children while continuing her career. If one of the children becomes ill, she has to ask her mother or mother-in-law to help her. It is difficult unless you have auxiliary help. She is strong and healthy, but it is hard to manage without backup assistance."

With increased animation, Miss Katase spoke of her retirement. "I enjoy my present activities and feel creative. So long as my health allows, I want to continue what I am doing. I want to avoid memory problems and the sicknesses of the aged. Keeping active does prevent some memory loss. And I also have other thoughts about this time of life. Every human being has to die in the end and, when dying, does review her life. I don't want to regret my life. I want to feel that I did my best. I want to cherish each day until I die. That was my thinking when I was young. I look around the world now and see so much riches and so much waste. It seems that there are more riches now than when I was growing up, but people do not really have a richer life. I don't like the wastefulness I see about me.

"I still want to be helpful and contribute to others. My career helped me do this, and I want to continue. But I have another thing I would like to say. I want to talk about religion. I was raised a Buddhist, but I like to think about religions in general and not about a particular religion. I seek the essence of all religions. As I view the globe, I see so much war, terrible international relations, and so much emphasis on religious differences and disagreements. If people everywhere would look deep into their own religion and look at what all religions have in common, how much better it would be. They would see that the core of all religions is similar. Perhaps in this way, they could find the possibilities for peace. People concentrate too much on their differences. I pray and want so much to have a peaceful world. I want to contribute to world peace through my own efforts." With these words Miss Katase ended her life review.

Miss Katase understood perfectly what is meant by a life review. Although she brought a chronology of her life events with her, she recognized that it is not the dates that are important but how you perceive your life and your accomplishments. Having a philosophy of life

and the wisdom to look back at her life, while at the same time looking forward, are the signs of maturity and intelligence of the highest order. Miss Katase arrived at the interview ready to go beyond her life story — the happy and sad moments, the tragedies of the War, and her contributions in war and peace. She had had her conclusions, her reflections, and her thoughts about life and death, war and peace, religion and philosophy for some time. A self-assured, confident woman, full of compassion for others and with an inner strength, she is satisfied with her life thus far and is facing the future with confidence. She demonstrated to us that she can act independently; she can take care of herself; she can make her own decisions and complete tasks with competence. Yet, she makes clear that this self-reliance does not come at the expense of withdrawing from or avoiding people. She depends on friends to fulfill an important part of her life. Now that she is retired, she acknowledges how much this means. She can give and take in relationships and enjoys both. Those whom she served very likely gained a great deal from her warmth and her wisdom. She is a woman who has experienced suffering but does not dwell on it. She focuses on the positive aspects of her life and draws conclusions from these, putting the negatives in perspective.

Interestingly, Miss Katase expresses the concern of many women of her generation, namely, the waste they see in modern Japan. Before the Sino-Japanese War and World War II, affluence was limited to a small group. Because families were very large compared to the present, even the salaryman's income was insufficient. Also, during the wars, particularly World War II, rich and poor alike in the large cities suffered extensive bombings and food scarcity. Many people sold treasured belongings in exchange for food. Miss Katase, as a nutritionist, learned from experience to have a great respect for food. Thus, the materialism and food waste of today's society is upsetting to her. It reflects a value that she rejects.

But Miss Katase goes beyond her concern about the attitudes she observes. She has the wisdom, creative thinking, and capacity to examine the world and not only her immediate environment. In this way, she is broader in her outlook than many people. She sees what divides people and mourns the fact that they are unable to probe below surface superficialities to see their common experiences, their common needs, and common values. She is able to arrive at the core. Although she has

never left Japan and has never traveled extensively, through her own thinking, analysis, and readings, she has achieved a cosmopolitan and universal understanding of human beings and a philosophy that makes her unique. She can talk with people of different religions, races, countries, and continents, and arrive at a common understanding. As a result, her life is richer and more meaningful than most people's lives.

Chapter 11

੨

Mrs. Akino:
A Woman
Marked by
Poverty

S eventy-three year old Mrs. Akino was wheeled into the room by the attendant in the Obe Nursing Home in the small mountain town of Obuse in northern Japan where she has been living for the past year and where she likely will stay until her death. This neat, fairly attractive, smiling, dark haired woman is paralyzed in both legs; apparently, the condition is irreversible. She was brought here by her only child, a daughter, who lives in a neighboring community. The interview was a difficult one for Mrs. Akino and the interviewer because several people alternated in translating our conversation. Despite the various interruptions, Mrs. Akino good-naturedly shared bits of her life. Because of time restraints, it was a brief interview, lasting only one hour.

Mrs. Akino explained that she is not a native of this rural area. She came from Tokyo and, before her marriage, lived in Yokohama. Over a year ago, she suddenly developed severe trembling in both legs. After a month in the hospital in Tokyo, her daughter brought her to the hospital in a nearby community. One year in the hospital produced a diagnosis of "affliction of the lobar vertebrae, a very serious disease," she stated. She will never walk again and now is bound to a wheelchair for the rest of her life. All this was recounted with a smile, a typical pattern we observed among Japanese women who wished to avoid expressing the pain of an unpleasant and disagreeable subject.

"This illness came to me as a shock. I had no previous symptoms and was thoroughly unprepared for it and for the changes that it brought in my life. I was working at the time. My daughter is married and has three children. She could not help me from a distance. So here I am. She visits me every week and brings the children with her. At this time, the children are too young for me to play with them. When they are older, I hope that we can play together. Nevertheless, I have many interests and try to keep busy. It isn't easy to keep occupied in a nursing home when you are confined to a wheelchair.

"I fill my time here reading books and newspapers, knitting, and sewing. I enjoy these activities. Also, I participate in the group activities. But I still don't have enough to fill my days. I cannot move about easily to clean my room or do any household-type tasks. I go to the shop next

door to this nursing home to buy small things, but that is the extent of my travels. At first, I felt very sad because it is so difficult to go anywhere in a wheelchair; I now accept the situation.

"Before I lost the use of my legs, I traveled a good deal with my friends. We went to Hong Kong, Okinawa, and many places in Japan. That is what I like doing.

"I was born in Yokohama and lived there until I married during World War II. My father worked on the boats and docks of Yokohama but did not make much money. In fact, we were very poor. He died when I was 25 years old. Because I was the oldest of six children, I had to help support the family. My mother could not go out to work because she had to care for the younger children. I had three brothers and two sisters. Life was very difficult. My father left us with no money, and my brother and I worked in Chinese restaurants to support the family. I was a waitress. My other brother and sisters also worked in Chinese restaurants when they grew up. I liked working in them, and, even after my husband died when I returned to waitressing, again I sought a Chinese restaurant.

"I only went to school for six years, completing the primary grades. At age 15, I started working and never studied after that. Even as a young child, I had to work at home to help my parents and, therefore, did not have time to make many friends. I had very little fun as a child. Life was harsh and demanding. We were so poor.

"I recall, when I was in school, that there was a huge Earthquake (1923) in Tokyo, and my family had a particularly hard time. My mother and sister were sent to the countryside to be with my grandmother. My sister, who was close to my age, and I stayed in Yokohama in an orphanage while my father and brother remained together. Because our house was destroyed, my father had to find another place for us to live. Actually, my sister and I were taken to the orphanage separately, and, by coincidence, we came to the same one. (One brother was born after the Earthquake.) One month later, we were sent to the country to be with my mother until my father was ready to have us return. I was nine years old when the Earthquake occurred, but I will never forget it."

Mrs. Akino could recall no happy events in her years of growing up. She merely reiterated that the family lived a life of poverty; food was scarce because they could not afford much, and life was austere and bleak.

"I was 30 years old when I married during the War. We were introduced to each other by my uncle. My husband was a construction engineer engaged in building large structures. The reason he was not in the army was that he was too short. (She showed embarrassment when she shared this information.) We went to live in the countryside with his family in Chiba Prefecture. It was safe there because, unlike the cities, there were no air raids. We were in Chiba until well after the War ended.

"During the War, we did have problems with food shortages. However, life after marriage was better than at home, but I was not particularly happy. We did not have enough to eat. I had to help my husband's family plant and raise food. I had never farmed. It is hard if you have never done it before. I didn't like it. I'm not a country girl and prefer the city. It did not make for a happy marriage at that time. After the War, the food shortages persisted for some time. As a result, we did not move back to Yokohama until 1953. By that time, I had a child. First, we moved in with my mother, brother, and sisters. It was crowded, but later we had our own apartment in Tokyo. My brothers worked in Chinese restaurants. I always stayed close to my family.

"My husband never received a good salary. He was a poor wage-earner. I did not work outside the home except for farming in which we were all engaged. I was occupied caring for my child. When she was 22 and I was 55, my husband died. At age 54, he had a successful operation for stomach ulcers, but 10 years later he again had a stomach operation and later died of cancer of the colon. Just before his death, the doctor diagnosed his cancer, but it was too late. The pension he left was inadequate, and I had return to work. I chose waitressing again because I liked it.

"Actually, after my husband's death, life was better for me. I had a job plus my husband's pension, and that added up to an adequate income. I had money so I could do whatever I wanted. Also, I was free after my daughter married. I no longer had any responsibilities. I could spend time with my friends. We went out to dinner together, shopped together, and traveled. For 15 years, life was good for me, until my illness. I am happy to have had those years."

We asked Mrs. Akino what advice she would give to her grandchildren about life in the light of her experiences growing up. She could think of nothing special and could not imagine she could give them

advice or that they would be interested in what she had to say. But, after a long silence, she made the following remarks that summarized her life experiences and reflected her personality.

"I think children today are not taught to be patient and are too wasteful, especially of food. They are not expected to help their parents. When I was a child, I did not have enough to eat because we could not afford to buy the food we needed. Children today do not appreciate how precious food is, that it should not be wasted. We were poor and hungry and valued whatever we were given. Now that it is plentiful, it should not be taken for granted. Also, as I look around me, I see that many children are not giving to others and expect only to be given to. They are impatient and demanding. I learned to accept life, to be patient, and not to get frustrated. Tolerance of hardships and difficult situations is important. I learned to stick to things and not give up. Children today are not learning these things." These were her final words to us about her observations concerning the present generation.

Mrs. Akino's life is typical of many older Japanese women brought up in poverty before the wars. Being the oldest daughter of a large family, she had no choice but to accept many responsibilities as a mother's helper as well as to work outside the home to help support the family. Being given to was not an expectation, it was a wish. Instead, mature obligations were imposed early in life, and the family needs took precedence over individual needs. Thus, when she was widowed in middle age and freed of familial demands, she eagerly indulged herself, finally satisfying her long suppressed desires. When she advises patience and tolerance, she speaks from the heart and from painful experiences. She had to wait 55 years before she could gratify her narcissistic requirements and had 15 happy years thereafter.

Several themes emerged as we review Mrs. Akino's brief description of her life: her impoverishment, the importance of food, her joy when freed and released from meeting other people's needs, and her pleasure in gratifying herself. Throughout her childhood and the War and post-war years, food was more than a symbol of being given to and of being nurtured. It was the realistic fear that without it she would not survive. She was hungry. Thus, for her, food represents life. It is no wonder then that she is upset to see the waste that affluence has brought to the Japanese family. And it is no wonder that she and her siblings sought employment in Chinese restaurants where they were surrounded by an

abundance of food and were assured of meals. To her and to her siblings, food represented the psychological security they sought for survival. What her parents could not provide, the restaurants could, and they were like an extended family.

It is of interest that a number of older women whom we interviewed commented about their enjoyment of late middle age or old age when the family's and husband's demands no longer ruled their lives. From early childhood, girls were taught, explicitly and implicitly, to nurture others, to serve others, and to be caretakers. Many, unlike Mrs. Akino, had a mother-in-law they had to care for, also, who frequently dominated them. Thus, when the elderly women talked of a new-found freedom upon widowhood, they made clear that this was the best stage of their life. Unlike in the American culture where old age is not welcomed by either society or the elderly, these Japanese women welcomed the freedom of widowhood and old age. Also, if they are incapacitated, they expect that they will be cared for by their children.

Mrs. Akino was typical of many of the elderly Japanese women in her passivity, her fatalistic acceptance of life, her tolerance of adversity, her patience, and her reluctance to admit anger and despair. Loyalty to family and promotion of family relations are very important aspects of women's lives and only when these are satisfied do they have time to nurture friendships. When family demands were no longer pressing, Mrs. Akino comfortably cultivated friends. Fortunately, she is the kind of person who could make friends easily.

Mrs. Akino is a very resilient woman. Much of her life was spent in poverty, hard work, and an unsatisfactory marriage, yet she coped well under the circumstances. She has worked through her depression around the loss of locomotion, accepts the dependence and inactivity resulting from this condition, and complains only that she cannot keep as busy as she would like. Instead of bemoaning her fate, she seeks creative outlets to make survival under present circumstances meaningful.

Chapter 12

❧

Mrs. Matsuo:
A Seeker Of Love
And Caring

At 74, Mrs. Matsuo is a busy lady with little time to waste on trivialities. Her days are consumed with volunteer services to others, with concern for the handicapped elderly, and with offering loving care and even hot meals to those who cannot manage for themselves. She is a leader in a senior center outreach program. She cares about people and is a woman who thinks. She has a philosophy of life; she knows why she engages in her present activities; she practices her religious beliefs; and she constantly compares the present with the past. Despite an unhappy life and an unwanted marriage, she still seeks the love and caring she lost years ago when her parents died.

This attractive, aging woman is alert, sophisticated, and youthful appearing. Yet, her enthusiasm and energy hide a frail body. Mrs. Matsuo approached our interview with great seriousness, giving deep thought and concentration to the content of our questions and her responses. From the first sentence, it was clear that she saw this as an opportunity to summarize her life experiences and express her thoughts and conclusions. Articulate and highly intelligent, she approached the task with ease and pleasure. We began the life review of Mrs. Matsuo at the senior center.

Currently, Mrs. Matsuo lives in an apartment next door to her widowed daughter and grandson. Her days are devoted primarily to volunteer work, which excites her.

"I help those who cannot walk. I push them in their wheelchairs, take them outside their homes, take them to a park where they may converse with other people, or to places where they have precious memories. When families can't do this, I do it for them."

When prodded to tell us more, she explained that she and three other women conduct an outreach program once a month to identify isolated elderly in order to bring them to the senior center, hoping to engage them in the regular program and to draw them out of their tiny living quarters where they sit isolated, lonely, and depressed. When encouraged, she added, "I help people go shopping for food. While it isn't a contract, people ask me freely now, and I'm glad to help. I have a dream of providing food for shut-ins. The senior center does not have a kitchen,

but I found one, and some elderly people come now to get my hot meals. In the future, I would like to deliver food to shut-ins." This was our introduction to Mrs. Matsuo's life history.

Mrs. Matsuo has been a widow for 23 years. Her 67 year old husband died of stomach cancer when she was 55 years of age. She has one daughter, now age 57, whose husband died several years ago. From the time her daughter married, Mrs. Matsuo lived in the same building as her daughter. Because she inherited enough money from her husband and she has a pension, she was not faced with the need to support herself.

"I can't give money to people in my volunteer work, but I can give of myself and my time. When I take them home, they shake my hand with tears in their eyes. I'm moved. I feel happy when I see such people happy."

Mrs. Matsuo was born in a large city in the northern part of Kyushu, Japan's southernmost island. Her father owned a clothing store, and they lived very comfortably until she was 12 years old and her brother was five. Then, her father died of tuberculosis; six months later her mother died of a brain hemorrhage. Suddenly, they were orphans being cared for by uncaring relatives. "It would have been easier if I had to face this alone, but I had to be supportive to my brother." We commented that she has been emotionally supporting people for a long time. "I feel keenly the warmth of other people because of my family history. It is important to me to communicate with people warmly. I tell this to my daughter."

Because neither of her parents had siblings, distant relatives took responsibility for her and her brother. So long as the money her parents left lasted, various relatives shared in caring for them however grudgingly. When one of the relatives tired of the responsibility, they would be sent to another. Mrs. Matsuo was permitted to go to a joggako and was encouraged to study sewing. She recalled one event especially during that time that still saddens her. She needed material for her sewing class. Although the relatives with whom she lived gave their daughter fabric, they would not provide Mrs. Matsuo with any. In fact, all the girls' parents gave them materials.

"One of my mother's friends learned about this and ripped apart her kimono, giving me the pieces for the sewing class. I come to tears thinking about it even now. People should be warm and more sensitive to others.

"When I was 18, my relatives suddenly announced that I was to go to Tokyo and that the man who would meet me at the train would marry me. I was thoroughly unprepared for this. I didn't want to marry. They said that he was a nice man, 12 years older than I, and he was willing to care for my 11 year old brother as well. My brother was still in primary school. I had no choice. I could not support myself and my brother. So off we went to Tokyo where I married a man I did not know and never learned to love. He was good to my brother, taught him to be a jeweler, which was his trade, and my brother lived with us until he married. My brother died five years ago of tuberculosis.

"If my parents had lived, I would have had a different life. I would have had anything I wanted. Before they died, I lived a happy life. I was the only daughter, and my brother the only son. They were very giving to us. I received good marks in school and never had any problems. If I didn't experience their death, I would not have my present attitudes and feelings. Experiences shape one's thoughts and actions. Because I was unhappy, I went to church. I was not a Christian, but I studied the Bible and learned the importance of the spiritual aspects of human beings. After I married, I did become a Christian. I still practice my religion. It is important to me.

"My husband lived next door to my relative's relative. That is how they found him. He was a warm, generous, and honest person. He gained people's respect. But I could never love him. Actually, this is not unusual in Japan, particularly in my generation. Women rarely knew the men they married. Even to use the word 'love' was shameful. I recall that when I was in school, if one student received a note from another, the teacher would insist that the note be read in front of the class. So, boys and girls avoided one another. If a girl traveled alone, she always sought a seat in the women's section of the train or sat near a woman. Merely talking to a man could get you into trouble."

Mrs. Matsuo admitted that she didn't realize what marriage was about then. Her husband, being so much older, did not feel like a companion to her. She repeated that he was a generous man, earned a good income, and took care of her and her brother, but she could never find real meaning in the marriage.

"When I grew older, I began to worry about it. I didn't feel that we were a real couple. I didn't experience any joy in my marriage. Nevertheless, I stayed in the marriage; I did not seek a divorce. It was unusual

to divorce in those days; I had no place to return to, and, in our culture at that time, it was mandated that a woman must be buried in the tomb of her husband. If a woman divorced, she had no way of supporting herself. She could either get a job living with a family as a housemaid or become a street girl. Children were considered to be the bond between husband and wife, and the marriage rested on that base. In a divorce, the husband was awarded custody of the children. Since the end of World War II, things are different. The relationship between men and women is freer now. They may talk with each other and do things together without criticism. Social welfare is available to help women, and this, too, is very important. Senior centers are open to men and women, and they socialize together.

"Other important changes have taken place. Before the War, there were areas in the city restricted to street girls. This is illegal now. No longer may families sell their children when they are poor. While children did not become slaves in the past, they were treated badly. Girls from poor families became geisha girls, street girls, or worked in textile industries without the freedom to quit their jobs. This is now prohibited by the law."

Mrs. Matsuo returned to talk about her husband. He had a good job working on the Ginza for a large jewelry company. She learned enough about the jewelry business from him to open a small shop herself. But, during the Sino-Japanese War, that became a dead industry. Hence, in 1937, they went to Shanghai, leaving her brother in Tokyo. Her husband worked for a new company there and later in Nanking. They did not return to Tokyo until the end of World War II.

"Life in China was good. We had food and all the goods we needed. It was less feudalistic than in Japan. Occasionally, there were bombings, and I was frightened, but our house was never hit. I saw wounded soldiers sent into Shanghai and Nanking by trains, and I met many attendants caring for them. I even helped them with the dead soldiers and took the wounded ones to the hospitals to be bandaged.

"The return home was a shock and a tragedy. In China, we never worried about food, shelter, and clothes, but, in Japan, I saw long lines of people waiting to get beans and other food. I saw people wearing rugs as kimonos because their kimonos were worn out, bartered, or destroyed. I saw houses that were bombed beyond repair. My brother had lived in three different homes that had been bombed. Our house was destroyed.

"Our daughter did not come to China with us. She stayed with my husband's relatives in the countryside and attended school there. Although Shanghai and Nanking had good schools, people were unfriendly to Japanese children; in fact, they were very impolite. Therefore, it was best for my daughter to stay behind. I did not see her for eight years and missed her very much.

"My daughter did not go to the university because of the War. When it ended, she took special courses in sewing and English. Everyone tried to study English then in order to get a job with the Army of Occupation. Later, she married and had two children. Five years ago her husband died. Her daughter is now married and lives in Hokkaido, and her son is studying photography while living with her."

Mrs. Matsuo changed the subject to tell us about her health. "I have had many operations. In 1970, I had a cancer in the womb and had a successful operation. I still go to a good cancer center near my home. A year and a half ago, I fell from the second floor down a flight of stairs. I was exhausted from running and fell while rushing down the stairway. I broke my breast bone and hip. I was in the hospital for two months and then took a long time recuperating at home until I could learn to walk well again. I still get pains as a result of that accident."

We asked Mrs. Matsuo her thoughts about life in the light of her experiences and her feelings about people. She is a person who analyzes events and is philosophical about her life, she stated.

"That is why I became a Christian. My family were Buddhist. I go to meetings in which we discuss books on religion. Initially, I was drawn to Christianity a year after I married because it stresses love and caring. Such subjects are not discussed in Buddhist writings. Actually, each religion reaches the summit in its own way, but the summit is the same. Many Buddhists quote from the Bible because their ideas agree. I don't attend church regularly because I am more interested in the feelings and attitudes it expresses than in the rituals. Because of my unhappy life, I find the writings of the church and its philosophy have helped and comforted me. Today, I feel that I help others and bring some warmth and happiness into their lives. That is what religion means to me. This gives me great satisfaction and contentment.

"I do compare the past and the present. At any age, older people complain about the younger generation. When I was young, they did. That's the way the world progresses. There is always change, and hope-

fully it is positive. After the War, the American influences were good. They brought many freedoms to us and made life easier in many ways. But I am sorry to see traditions in Japan being neglected as a result. Also, the democratic way of life introduced to Japan was good, but now I am concerned because some people think freedom means that they may act any way they wish. They do not pay attention to the fact that democracy requires a sense of responsibility if there is to be freedom. It is worrisome that there appears to be so much irresponsibility among many people.

"Finally, I'd like to say that women's status has changed. For this I am grateful. Before the War, men were considered superior, and women were neglected. While there is still much more that needs to be done about women's rights, I am grateful to see the changes that have already taken place." With these words the interview ended.

One week later we received a letter from Mrs. Matsuo stating that she had forgotten to mention another change in Japan, namely, that the status of the Emperor had been altered. She explained that, before the War, he was a god, and the people could not speak to him. Now, he is a person, the same as all others in the country, and she does not have to worship him.

Mrs. Matsuo, despite her outgoing personality and the warmth she expresses, is still grieving the loss of both parents at the beginning of her adolescence. Furthermore, her anger and hurt at her relatives have not been resolved. She still feels keenly their rejection and hostility because they made her feel unwanted and a burden. Also, she still is resentful that she was burdened with supporting her brother at a time when no one empathized with and understood her need to mourn the loss of her parents. She probably has never before been able to express these feelings. Beneath her exuberant exterior and her activity is still a depressed and unhappy child longing for the love and caring of her dead parents. Her husband could not fill that role, and, therefore, he was a disappointment. Nevertheless, by taking her brother into his home, to her he felt more like another relative than a husband.

Very likely she has never adequately acknowledged her ambivalence toward her brother. People probably felt more sorry for him losing his parents at such an early age and ignored her. She was made to feel responsible for his care as the big sister, and she was forced into a parenting role. His presence even determined whom she was to marry.

She did not feel she was accepted as an individual but was part of a "package deal." Mr. Matsuo was selected to be her husband because he was willing to take her brother, also.

Her marriage was both a shock and a disappointment. At 18, she was still very immature and unprepared to marry a man who appeared so old to her. She, also, possibly had the fantasy that in marriage she could recreate the idealized family she lost when her parents died. It did not work out that way.

Mrs. Matsuo is a highly intelligent woman who is introspective and gives much thought to her feelings. She tries to be philosophical about her experiences. She has considerable strengths, adapts well to the demands of the moment, and relates very warmly to people. Now, in the last stage of her life, she is hastening to compensate for her past losses and sense of incompletion by putting her managerial energies to work in helping others. She identifies strongly with the fragile people she helps, thus contributing to and enhancing her self-image. Some of this she attributes to her religion, and she uses religion to help her find a way to express the emotions she had bottled up within her for so many years. She is giving the handicapped older people the kind of caring relationship she longed for over these many years.

Finally, Mrs. Matsuo does not cling to tradition because she fears change. She is open-minded, thinks for herself, and is able to accept the new society and new ways of doing things. She relates to others with remarkable skill and ease. Intellectually, she is an interesting, thoughtful woman, but most important in her life is her search for love and caring. This is the theme of her life in its last stage. It is giving her the satisfaction she sought since she was 12 years old.

Chapter 13

❧

Mrs. Nakai:
She Lived
History

W omen in small businesses have long been a familiar sight in Japan, and we were pleased to find such a woman in Mrs. Nakai. Such women generally work with their husbands and maintain a low profile (Lebra, Paulson and Powers, 1976, pp. 89-107). However, in Mrs. Nakai's case, she started the business herself and ran it for 18 years before selling it upon retirement. From her, we were able to learn why a Japanese woman would start her own business, what motivated her, and how she managed. We were introduced to Mrs. Nakai by a faculty member of the Elder University in Setagaya-ku.

Mrs. Nakai, a short, slender, perky woman of 74 with dark black cropped hair, was clad in a heavy sweater over a long wool skirt and blouse when she met us at the bus stop to guide us to her apartment because directions are so difficult to give and follow in Japan. Her pleasant, almost prosaic, appearance gave us no clue to the story that she was about to share with us of her eight years of difficult, satisfying, involuntary service in Communist field army hospitals in China after she was captured following the Japanese defeat.

In retirement, she lives in a typical small Japanese city apartment of three tiny rooms in the attractive Setagaya ward in western Tokyo. Two rooms had six tatami mats, and, with the exception of a low table in one of the rooms and a chest in the other, they were devoid of furniture. The third room was a narrow entrance corridor that served as her kitchen. The walls were hung with her own paintings as well as a few contemporary works from China.

Mrs. Nakai is a self-assured woman with many interests in art, crafts, dance, and studies. She had no difficulty or hesitation in talking about her past or present. In fact, she clearly enjoyed sharing her life experiences as she plunged into her life review eagerly and readily.

Mrs. Nakai was the fourth of seven children, five boys and two girls. After her older sister died quite young, she was the only girl. As a result, she saw herself spoiled by her parents and brothers. "I was cherished by them." She could recall no unhappy events in her childhood other than her sister's death and talked of her family life in a small town in Kyushu as being an especially happy one.

Mrs. Nakai's father was a graduate of Keio University, a famous private university in Tokyo. In their home town, he was the only graduate from that university; this made him unique. He spoke English very well, and read English newspapers every day. He had a good job in Tokyo but, as the oldest son, when his mother became ill, he dutifully returned to Kyushu upon the family's demand. Because the family owned considerable land, he did not have to work. Being available, he was invited to take a position with the local government; however, his pride prevented him from working for local bureaucrats. If he took such a job, he would have to bow to those people, which he was unwilling to do. Therefore, he decided instead to open a bookstore that carried primarily high school textbooks. Actually, he was not a good businessman. It was her mother who helped him to make the business successful. He, instead, was busy as president of the Chamber of Commerce and in similar activities.

"My parents had to make a living by this time because World War I and, later, the Great Depression had forced them to sell much of their land. Two of my brothers could not even afford to go to a private university. So they applied and were admitted to Tokyo University."

Her older brother became a judge, and the second brother, who now lives near her, became an insurance company executive. Another brother teaches Japanese in a high school having graduated from a national university in Kyushu. One brother died as a child, and the last brother could not go to a university because of World War II. Upon graduation from high school, he was drafted into the army. Her only sister, older than she, was very clever and entered teacher's school but suddenly became ill and died. It was a shock to the entire family. In contrast, Mrs. Nakai did not think of herself as a scholar. She did not want to continue studying after graduating from a joggako. Instead, she did what most traditionally educated girls did in her day, she studied koto, a traditional musical instrument, ikebana or flower arranging, and sewing. Years later in Antung, China, when she had to earn money, she was to learn how useful it was to have learned to sew.

Mrs. Nakai's life changed when she decided to go to Manchuria during the 1930s to marry. She explained that she did so to marry a desirable husband. When she and her family decided that it was time to marry, Japan's involvement in the Sino-Japanese War and in the Manchurian occupation had drained Japan of the eligible men who might have interested her. Most of those who remained home were either too old, too

young, too sickly, or too disabled. This was a problem many young women faced in those days. Someone she knew, acting as a go-between, introduced her to her husband-to-be by way of the mails. He was from a town not far from her home, but she did not meet him before they agreed to be married because he was an officer in the Japanese Army of Occupation in Manchuria. After six months of exchanging pictures and correspondence, they agreed to marry. "And that is how I happened to come to Manchuria."

Until the end of the War in 1945, when the Soviet Union entered Manchuria, life was pleasant; as Army personnel, they had many special privileges and lived well. "We did not have to stand in line for food as in Japan." She never expected the Japanese military might to disintegrate and end as it did. Nor did she anticipate that she would experience the adventures that followed.

Mrs. Nakai left Manchuria with a group of civilians, mostly women, as they fled eastward to evade the Soviets. They stopped at Antung, a small city on the border of Korea, where they stayed for two years.

"It was impossible to leave. Those were two very hard years. I lived with a Japanese family, but I could not communicate with my family in Japan. I felt so alone. I had to earn a living, however I could."

When Soviet troops occupied Manchuria, her husband was captured and taken to the Soviet Union as a prisoner of war. He was assigned to hard labor in Siberia for five long years before he was repatriated to Japan, several years before she returned. But she never saw him after his capture. He died of physical exhaustion in Japan a few years before she returned. As Mrs. Nakai recited this sad story, she showed no outward emotions and expressed no regret that she did not return in time to see him. Whatever feelings she had appeared to be controlled or to have been resolved.

The Japanese government apparently did not know that a large group of Japanese women were "trapped" in Antung, although it probably could not have done anything about it.

"We had a bad life there. The Soviet soldiers took over for a while and were nasty to us; when they left, the Korean and Chinese soldiers were no better. I had left my belongings behind when I fled so I had nothing with me. For the first time in my life, I had to make a living. I had to earn money so I did sewing. It was the only skill I had. Japanese girls in my day were not taught to earn a living unless they came from

poor families. Unfortunately, I could not earn much with my sewing." She repeated, "Those were hard times."

She continued, "In Antung, I found myself among some people who had worked with the Japanese Red Cross, and that was the beginning of another chapter in my life in China. I remained with the group, as well as with a number of young Japanese women, for eight years, pressed into service traveling and working from north to south China with the Chinese Communist Army. We were not allowed to write home. No one heard from me during all that time. No one knew that I had escaped from Manchuria and was still alive."

It was interesting to watch Mrs. Nakai's expression as she recalled her China experience. While she appeared to speak in a matter-of-fact manner, there was an intensity about her demeanor that made us feel that she was pleased and eager to talk about her Chinese adventure. She expressed no regrets. With great concentration she continued to tell her story, leaving us with the impression that she thought about it frequently. Having listeners who were so receptive, she spoke rapidly and with ease, giving as many details as she could within our limited time.

"After we left Antung with the Chinese Communist Army (in 1947), I worked in a field hospital unit. The patients were Chinese soldiers. Because I was not a nurse, at the beginning I would sit with the patients to help care for them. I guess you could call me an attendant, but, because I was older than most of the Japanese girls in our group, I was elected their leader and was put in charge of assigning them their tasks in the hospital. They turned to me for help and advice. Eventually, because I spoke Chinese, I took life histories of the soldiers admitted to the hospital. I ended my hospital career with the Chinese Army having had many job assignments. In my last job, I was in charge of hospital records and statistics. I kept track of the number of Chinese soldiers in the hospital, to which hospitals they were sent, how many days it took to recover from specific physical problems and medications, and other such pertinent information.

"As new battles took place, new hospitals had to be set up hurriedly. Our group had that task. We were moved from field hospital to field hospital, following battle movements whenever there were large numbers of wounded soldiers. I recall one day walking 40 kilometers to set up a hospital. I started in the north of China, and, by the time I left China, I was in the south.

"We had free time in between these moves and battles when there were few soldiers to care for. That was when the girls and I studied medical care. There was much to learn because we had never done anything like that. There were Japanese doctors among us from the Manchurian railroad who also were caught by the Chinese Communists, and they taught us. The administrators were Chinese, but the rest of us were Japanese.

"After we returned to Japan, we kept in touch with one another." With this, Mrs. Nakai showed us several group pictures of now aging people. "Twice a year, we meet for a reunion, once in Kansai (the western part of Japan), and once near Tokyo. We became very close. And we became friendly with the Chinese, too. One of the Chinese men in our hospital is now vice president of a university in Beijing. Six years ago, I went to China to visit him. He gave me those paintings," pointing to two paintings on the wall. "And his children have visited me. I hope to go to China again soon."

All this was announced with considerable satisfaction and delight. We, in turn, observed to her that she had a remarkable capacity for making friends and enriching her life.

If we had had more time to talk with her, we would have heard many more tales of her Chinese adventures and relationships. We wonder how many people ask her about those years in China. Likely, the only time she talks about it is when she meets with the group during their reunions. Nevertheless, for her those years are vivid and full of meaning. She never once said that she wished that she had returned sooner from China to be reunited with her husband. She accepts the events of her life without expressing remorse.

"Eventually, the international community forced the Chinese to give us up. We had expected to return earlier, but the Korean War kept us in China longer." She admitted that if the Korean War had not occurred, she might have seen her husband.

Home to her was the town in Kyushu where, at the time of her return, her aging mother still lived with a maid, her father having died. People in the town read her name in the newspaper listing those being repatriated and the ports of arrival.

"Many people rushed excitedly to show my mother my name on the list. Now they knew that I was alive. My mother and several brothers came to the boat to greet me, but they did not recognize me. I was

wearing an army nurse's uniform, and I was fourteen years older than when they last saw me. The reunion was dramatic and even tearful," she laughed. "Yes, for years they had not known that I was still alive, and now I was back. But, when I visited China years later, I, too, had tears. In the hospital, I did not feel that there were differences between Japanese and Chinese. We were alike, and we had become friends."

After her return from China, Mrs. Nakai was confronted with having to support herself. She did not consider remarriage. Consequently, she came to Tokyo to study sewing, but soon gave up the idea because factory production of women's garments made hand-sewn clothes obsolete and expensive. She was not interested in studying dress designing. Therefore, after consulting her brother, she decided to set up a cleaning business in Chiba Prefecture, near Tokyo. With his financial help, she developed a good business which she ran for 18 years. She employed a number of people. Although it was successful, she admitted that she had expected it to be a simple operation, but instead she learned through hard experience that it had many complexities. She needed more machinery than anticipated, and some operations still had to be done by hand. As a childless widow, she devoted all her efforts toward running the business. She wanted to sell it several years before she finally did. It was the many friends among her customers who begged her to stay longer. But, finally, when she turned 70, she decided that she should not delay any longer.

Now, Mrs. Nakai is happy to be free from the pressures and responsibilities of business. "There were so many tasks, so many details, so many things to go wrong. And, in my retirement, I love living in Setagaya-ku. There are many things to do here. I'm on the board of trustees of my condominium, and that takes up much time. I have classes at the senior center, and every day I go to a different place to study art, dance, exercise, or crafts."

Mrs. Nakai enthusiastically showed us some of her craft and art work. She is a woman of many talents and will never be bored.

"I chose this neighborhood not only because it offers so many educational opportunities and good housing, but it is close to my brother, the one who helped me establish my business. He is sickly and needs my help. I go to see him every day to massage him."

In addition to the fact that she has made many friends in Setagaya-ku, Mrs. Nakai finds this is a fine area in which to live because it has

many services for the aged.

"I don't need the welfare services yet. I'm healthy and exercise, and I keep busy. But, if I should need the services, I know that they are here for me."

We commented that one of Mrs. Nakai's strengths is her ability to make friends. This she revealed in her China experiences as well as with her business customers. She is doing it again in retirement. She readily admitted that wherever she goes, she manages to make friends.

"Because I am alone, I try to form relationships. It is an important part of life. It is important and exciting to have many friends. Now, I go with them to hot springs. We stay at hotels and enjoy ourselves."

From Mrs. Nakai, as from the other women we interviewed, we sought to learn about her perspective on life as well as how she viewed the differences between life before and after World War II. Her answer revealed a great deal about her personality and adaptability.

"I do not cling to tradition. I accept the present as different from the past. It means more to me than the past. I love being here now; I enjoy good health and take advantage of the many activities available. Changes in society and the world cannot be helped. Yes, young people have more choices than I had. They have more education, and many of them marry whomever they wish. There are new kinds of marriage today, some with good results, and others with bad outcomes. New types of marriage can be good if young people respect each other, are careful, and understand each other. Respect is essential. But, what I don't like is free sex and marriages that result from instant heat. That can only lead to divorce.

"We cannot think of divorce as being only a present day solution. In the old days, Japanese women knew how to endure. They did not like divorce because husbands were generally awarded the children. Now mothers can ask to keep their children. I received a call recently from a friend with whom I worked in China, who is divorced. She has her children with her. Women's options and rights have expanded. We can inherit property, go to universities, and work if we wish."

She sees women in Japan today as being in a favorable position. Many young women have more choices, and let their families know that they want higher education, and some even want a career.

"Parents used to prepare their daughters only for marriage. But they need more than that; they need specialties. They need to learn to be

independent. This is important for them. It is something that needs to be. Young women in Tokyo are in an especially fortunate position because they can get higher education and learn more specialties. These young women are lucky."

We observed that her life history proves how urgent it is for women to be learned and prepared to work if they wish, or more important, if they must. "You successfully became independent and took care of yourself. You had to. But you had to learn skills when forced to by circumstances. Having them without the pressure of necessity would have been better," we commented. Mrs. Nakai agreed.

"Life is full of ups and downs. One lives through so many events. I have worked at many kinds of jobs. I have raised rice, sewn, nursed, and conducted a business. The only thing I did not do is play mah-jong."

Again, she returned to her favorite subject, China. "I had a hard time while in China. But now, as I look back, I think that I was lucky. I saw the changes as they were occurring in China. I saw the revolution. I saw with my own eyes what was going on. I enjoyed working and traveling in China. I was part of history. Not everybody has such experiences. In that sense, I was lucky. I made the most of things. I see my past in a positive way. I'm not sorry about my days in China. I was in the middle of the history that was being made."

Indeed, it is evident that in Mrs. Nakai's life review that her years in China were the most significant to her. Other facets of her life fade in importance; the Chinese experience remains vivid. She speaks of it with spontaneity and warmth. For her, reminiscing about it is joyful. She welcomed having someone interested in her adventures. If we had more time, very likely, she would have shared more incidents about China. Her Chinese odyssey overshadowed even the sadness of losing her husband. We are left with the impression that, well before she learned of his death, she was resigned to never seeing him again.

For Mrs. Nakai, life review became an affirmation that her life had been rich, that she had achieved the capacity for self-reliance and independent thinking and action, and that she could make her way wherever she went. She discovered attributes in herself that she had not known she had. She was a leader; she gained respect from her peers; she acquired new skills and was rewarded for them; and, most important, she made friends everywhere. Her ability to form relationships and her self-confidence have been her greatest strengths. These she acquired in child-

hood through close family relationships; they sustained her throughout her adult life. Her capacity to relate, combined with her obvious good intelligence, maturity, and leadership abilities, contributed to a strong ego, a capacity to confront serious crises, and an optimistic disposition. Losses were accepted without descending into depression. She coped with them through numerous creative activities and a social network of friends and family. She does not look back on her life with a list of things she wishes had been different. She expresses no serious regrets and resolves inner conflicts sufficiently to enable her to enjoy her retirement.

Even Mrs. Nakai's decision to start her own business, rather than seek a job, reflects her independent spirit and a growth that likely took place as a result of her experiences with the Chinese Communist Army. Before that time, she was dependent on her family, and, later, on her husband. She learned to make her way without family supports. Also, she identified strongly with her mother who had successfully run a business. To be an entrepreneur and make her own business decisions seemed natural to her. However, her brother supported her in these endeavors.

Today, in her old age, she is busier than ever with her art interests, dance, exercises, body care, intellectual studies, leadership role in the condominium, and assisting her beloved brother. These activities are not merely a way of filling time. She enjoys them and makes the most of the present while savoring the past. She has an impressive support system which she creates wherever she goes. Even in China, when it was she who had to comfort and bolster the younger women, she used that ability to establish a support network for herself, and it continues to this day. She voices no regrets about being childless. However, when one scrutinizes her efforts to form relationships, it appears that she compensated for the loss of her husband and her childlessness through the mothering and care she gave to the young Japanese women in China and to the wounded Chinese soldiers. This capacity was reflected even in her business; when she was on the verge of selling it to retire, her customers and friends persuaded her to continue because they enjoyed her friendship. In whatever she does, she goes beyond what she insists is the Japanese mandate to women, namely, to *endure* gracefully. She can turn a series of crises and stresses into positive experiences. It is no wonder that she can look back on her life without serious conflicts and without obsessing over her losses. She can see her place in history,

however modest, and savor the experiences, acceptance, and relationships she enjoyed. China opened her life; it challenged her to become an independent, assertive woman; it forced her to discover her strengths; and it enriched everything she accomplished since then. She is indeed a fortunate woman! These are the lessons people of Japan can learn from Mrs. Nakai.

Chapter 14

és

Mrs. Iwaki:
An Exponent
of Peace

Mrs. Iwaki is a pleasant, delicate woman with a beautiful smile. She wears her grey hair pulled back in a knot and presents herself as a gracious, serious, deep thinking person. She understands some English although she does not risk speaking it. At age 78, she has been a widow for one year having been married for 50 years to an intellectual and unusual man. She lives with her daughter and her family with whom she and her husband shared the attractive, traditional Japanese house in the Mitaka section of Tokyo for many years. While we were conversing, her grandson, a handsome young man who attends Tokyo Metropolitan University, joined us. Her daughter is a social worker in a neurological institute.

Mrs. Iwaki was born in 1909 to the wife and priest of a Buddhist Temple in Tokyo next door to the famous Red Gate of Tokyo University. She was the oldest of three children, having two younger brothers.

"I lived on the grounds of the Temple and worked very hard helping my parents care for the place. I was not a spoiled child and worked from early childhood. My brothers, being younger, did not do as much as I did. One of my brothers eventually became a Buddhist priest.

"Growing up next to Tokyo University was an interesting experience in those days. I had many friends my own age. In addition, I found the people from the University who came to my father's Temple very stimulating. They joined my father's study group on Buddhism. I always attended the classes and looked forward to Sundays. A well-known professor from Tokyo University was the first student in the class; the next year, he became an assistant teacher.

"I enjoyed my childhood. My parents were liberal, worldly people and encouraged me in my many interests. Although we were poor, they sent me to Ochanomizu joggako, and then I continued studying for three more years in junior college until I qualified to be a teacher. I wanted a career even though it was not common in that era for girls to pursue careers. But that was in the Taisho period when attitudes in Japan were liberal and democratic. I wanted a teaching career because, at that time, the distinctions between the rich and poor were great. I thought that it would be nice if society could become more equalized. The poor needed

more money, and the rich needed to be more understanding. I thought that education was the path that could accomplish this goal.

"Unfortunately, there were not many teaching jobs when I finished my studies. Therefore, I thought about my father's philosophy concerning the world and decided to learn Esperanto, the universal language, in order to participate in working for a peaceful world with no wars and good communications. I thought that it was essential for the countries of the world to move toward peace and unity regardless of their racial and religious differences.

"For several years, I worked in the foreign division of the Central Post Office. Because the world was heading toward World War II, we had to check every bit of mail coming from abroad. I checked foreign mail written in Esperanto. A woman I knew was doing the same in French.

"It was through my studies in Esperanto that I met my husband. He had the same interests I had. He, too, was studying Esperanto. However, we did not marry for some time. My husband was the oldest son in a family that owned a kimono shop in the center of Tokyo not far from the Ginza. He came from a family very different from my free thinking family. His parents expected their son to take over the kimono business and did not approve of his studying Esperanto. They particularly objected to his marrying a woman who was also studying that language, fearing that I would discourage him from assuming his proper role in their business. They were sure that the business would collapse if we married. As it turned out, although he was in charge of the business eventually, he spent so much time studying Esperanto and writing a text book for the language, in reality, he was not running the business. He let the banto (the employee apprentice) do all the work. His parents began to fear that if they waited too long to approve our marriage, they would be very old before he married. Finally, they consented. My parents had consented all along. I was 28 when we married."

Given both Mr. and Mrs. Iwaki's concern about peace in a time when war, not peace, was on everyone's mind, we wondered what happened to them during the War.

"We had two very young daughters when the War started. My husband was still in the kimono business. The government controlled the clothing industry and permitted only small deliveries of fabrics. Business became tight. Everything was controlled by the government. Also, employees were being drafted into the armed services, and, one by one, we lost

them. Older employees were being forced to work in munitions and other war factories. Finally, we had to work in the kimono shop. Then, a law was passed restricting businesses unrelated to the war effort, and we had to close our shop.

"My mother-in-law, two daughters, and I evacuated to a town 200 kilometers northwest of Tokyo when the bombings became serious and food shortages worsened. My husband stayed behind doing civilian work as a guard, protecting the neighborhoods from looting, and helping people whose homes were bombed. I did not work during the evacuation. I had many relatives, and, among us, we were able to find enough food. My relatives owned a book and stationary store and I, also, helped them get materials they needed."

We asked if her husband had any difficulties in the light of his aversion to war.

"Not really. He was very philosophical and tried to think constructively. He had been among the first students of Seikei University, a private institution built by Professor Haruji Nakamura. He had lived with other students, and they were all influenced by their teacher's thinking. Many famous professors and philosophers came there. The Itoan movement of the Nichiren religion had its roots in Kyoto and became so strong that my husband wanted to go to Kyoto after the War to work with them, converting people. It was not a Buddhist group but a mixture of different religions aiming to create one religion and to eliminate the multiplicity of religions. It was similar to Esperanto in that respect, advocating a single religion, just as Esperanto advocated one language.

"After the War, we lived in Kyoto for 18 months. We had no income while there. Our return to Tokyo was a nightmare! Our shop had not been bombed, and, therefore, we found many refugees camped in it. Strangers wandering about looking for a place to stay, lived there. Before leaving Tokyo, my husband, being open-minded and concerned, originally invited in some of the homeless. Many of them had shops in the past, and, therefore, sold their goods in our shop while living in our house."

We laughed together as we pictured this to be like a miniature department store.

"But, as time went on, these arrangements became troublesome. The people did not want to leave. My husband was finally forced to go through many court battles and, after a number of years, the Supreme

Court of Japan ordered them evicted. This was a victory as the courts, reluctant to evict people after the War, had tended to side with the squatters.

"In the meantime, we had to live with my parents because we could not use our house. Eventually, Seikei University asked my husband to be a counselor for troubled graduate students. When he took that job, we built our present home.

"I did not work outside my home when we returned from evacuation because I became ill with tuberculosis and had to rest for several years. My mother-in-law cared for my children. Fortunately, we had income from the rental of the house connected with the kimono shop, and, when my husband began to work at Seikei University, we had a steady income so things were better.

"My daughters were six and nine years old when the War ended. They went to public school in the primary grades, and, later, we enrolled them in the junior and senior high schools affiliated with Seikei University. From there, my oldest daughter continued her education in the nursing school of Tokyo University Hospital while my younger daughter went to Tokyo Metropolitan University to study geography. She received a master's degree and still teaches in a high school. Both daughters are married, and my oldest daughter is now a social worker instead of a nurse. When she married, she continued to live with us in this house. Her husband is an engineer, and she has two sons. Currently, she works in the Tokyo Neurological Hospital.

"My husband continued to counsel at Seikei University until he retired. Then, he did many things that he had always been interested in. He wrote a book on the history of Seikei University and its founders. When that was finished, he turned to writing the history of Mitaka City. Our city is very unusual and has many social services, especially for the aged and the handicapped, that are unique to Tokyo. It is a very progressive and interesting place. And, when that was finished, he did not stop. He became interested in waterwheels and started studying that subject intensively. This took him to Turkey, Afghanistan, and other places. When in Afghanistan, he was old, and it was a risky place to visit. Nevertheless, he went. Sure enough, while there, he found himself in the midst of a bomb scare, and it turned out to be the beginning of a rebellion. Getting out of the country was no easy matter. He was in a troubled area and needed help. My daughter had to appeal to the

authorities to get some action. Finally, she went to meet him in Afghanistan. Shortly thereafter, I received a call from them in India, saying that they were safe and on their way home. That was a frightening experience."

She recounted this adventure with a smile, indicating that he was an unusual person doing unusual things. Accordingly, she could expect anything to happen.

"Before my husband died, he was quite ill. He first slipped in the bathroom and broke some bones, could not walk, and had to use a wheelchair. We adapted this house, building ramps and widening doorways, so that he could move his wheelchair from room to room. Eventually, he had a brain hemorrhage and died. I had an interesting and exciting life keeping up with him and his interests. I enjoyed it. Life is different now."

We asked what big changes Mrs. Iwaki experienced during her life time that she considered significant.

"My husband and I worked very hard devoting ourselves to our projects and our beliefs. We had many strong convictions. Even in old age, we were very much involved in the world around us. My daughters are the same. They worked before and after marriage. I took care of the grandchildren. All of my family are hard workers and deep thinkers. In many ways, our lives did not change much because we were always busy and involved. We got the most out of everything we did. My grandchildren are the same. One is at Tokyo Metropolitan University as a freshman, and his brother is in the University of Washington in Seattle, U.S.A."

As a young woman before her marriage, Mrs. Iwaki expressed a strong interest in peace, one world, and one language. She married a man who had the same beliefs, and they added one religion to the list. We asked if she still feels the same about these social and political issues. She did not answer "yes" or "no." Instead, in her response, she focused on people.

"When I was a young girl, I thought that all people should be viewed as equal. I think differently now. I think that people must be seen from the perspective of what makes each person unique. It isn't equality as much as it is uniqueness that should be promoted, I believe.

"Finally," she continued, "you must recall that I am an old woman. I am 78 years of age. I cannot learn new things. I tend to be forgetful. I am now returning to thinking about the big issues in this world and see

things on a more relative basis. I have lived through many changes in my life and am aware that ideas and concepts that felt right in one period do not feel the same in another. One gains new perspectives as the world changes. For example, I thought that poverty was such a serious problem when I was young that I could not imagine how anyone could experience happiness under such conditions. But now I see things differently. I see that people can be happy, whether rich or poor. Different things make different people happy or sad. One cannot generalize. That is the uniqueness of human beings.

"Because I recognize that ideas and thoughts I had in the past have changed, I don't give advice to my grandchildren. I like to listen to what others are saying to them and learn. I'm still learning." With these profound observations, our interview ended.

Mrs. Iwaki is still the open-minded, observant, learning person she was taught to be by her parents; and she is no doubt a model to her grandchildren, just as she was a model to her daughters. This is their inheritance from her. We see in her a strong identification with her parents, especially her father. She internalized his perceptions and values while her mother mirrored her approval of Mrs. Iwaki's work habits and independent thinking. Both gave her the self-confidence to maintain her uniqueness and non-conformist ideas in the face of the Japanese society that even today does not view interpersonal relations, non-conformism, and individualism as Mrs. Iwaki does. She has inner strengths and convictions that permit her to adapt to such crises as war and serious illnesses without sacrificing her sense of cohesiveness. Also, she has maintained a flexible approach to how she views society. While she still retains her compassion for the poor, she is able to individualize people and not merely place them in categories. She impressed us as a person who has achieved the present stage of old age with a wisdom and integrity that offers younger generations a model that we hope they will emulate.

At this time, Mrs. Iwaki is assuming a more passive stance and is still in the process of learning to accept the role of widowhood, a role most women dread and unconsciously start preparing for during middle age. Therefore, she is savoring the memories of her life with her husband, forgetting, at the moment, some of the frustrations she may have experienced living with such an individualist. Surely, when he was off exploring waterwheels in the midst of a rebellion, she was more than worried,

she was likely angry that he went to such a dangerous place.

What is most interesting in reviewing Mrs. Iwaki's presentation of her life review is the fact that she is one of very few women who spoke in considerable detail about her husband. Most gave brief statements and few details, thus making it difficult to learn about their personalities. She is an exception. She and her husband had similar intellectual interests; they selected each other to marry because of that and waited patiently for years for his parents' consent. She was emotionally supportive of him throughout his efforts to avoid business involvements in favor of intellectual and philosophical activities, even when finances were tight. Furthermore, she admired his curious, active mind and encouraged him in his post-retirement endeavors. It is easy to imagine the conversations they had on these various subjects. She was proud of him and let him know it. Although he is dead for only one year, she expresses her grief through devotion and respect.

Interestingly, at the same time Mrs. Iwaki describes herself and her husband as being essentially free thinkers above the dictates of social rigidities and traditions, nevertheless, both were respectful of parental wishes and concerns. They were not rebels within the family. Even though they were determined to marry each other, they respected the traditional need for family acceptance.

While Mrs. Iwaki did not have a significant career of her own due to the War and later her physical condition, she is an independent thinker, a humanist, and a philosopher. Her interests range from psychology, linguistics, and philosophy to religion. If we had had more time to talk, other subjects would have emerged. She has confronted adversity, such as war and illness, through reliance on her family support system. Neither she nor her husband gave up their belief in a peaceful world. She is not parochial in her thinking although she does not reject her country and culture. But she transcends the immediate environment as she identifies herself on a more universal plane. That she is able to individualize people and respect and promote their uniqueness in the Japanese society that emphasizes group values and conformity makes her unique. At 78, her mind is keen, and her views are more modern than most younger people's. She has inner resources and a positive view of herself and her family, and she projects this onto the people in her environment. She combines warmth, high intellect, and a determination to achieve what is essential for the survival of humankind, namely *peace*.

Chapter 15

❧

Mrs. Sakurada:
A Battered
Wife

Diminutive Mrs. Sakurada greeted us shyly with a broad smile, a low bow, and a firm handshake. Dressed in a blue and white woven woolen kimono, she presented herself like a typical elderly traditional Japanese woman. Her short grey hair, parted in the middle and brushed off her forehead, accentuated her broad face, broad nose, and frequent smiles. By observing her constant wringing of her very large, arthritic hands and long fingers, we could see how tense she was about the interview. Only later did we learn that her senior center counselor, who introduced us, stayed for the entire interview at Mrs. Sakurada's request because of her insecurity. Eighty-two year old Mrs. Sakurada had consented to be interviewed only if her counselor was present. Actually, she never once looked to her for assistance or support, and, as the interview proceeded, she shared her life events without appearing tense or upset. Her story depicted the life of a woman who can best be described as having emotional endurance, tenacity, patience, and pathos.

Mrs. Sakurada keeps the senior center supplied with plants that she grows as a serious hobby. Her good fortune is to live across the street from the center in a small old-fashioned house, and that makes it possible for her to come daily to the rehabilitation services in the center. She has "a circulation problem connected with my heart, and I find that the massage machine in the center helps." Also, because walking is laborious for her, living across from the center is a blessing. Ever since it opened four months ago, she comes every day, and she no longer has to visit her doctor regularly. Otherwise, her health is fine, she assured us.

When asked if she had many friends at the center, she replied that she does not have time to participate in any activities or to cultivate friendships.

"I spend most of my time at home sewing Japanese kimonos for customers. I have so many orders that people have to wait a long time before I can fill them. Also, I own a sock store to which I used to go every day; now my daughter and son-in-law run the business. I live with them and my three grandchildren. Two of my grandchildren work, and my granddaughter is studying at Tsuda University. My daughter works hard caring for the family, preparing meals, and working in the sock

shop. She is only a junior high school graduate.

"I have two other daughters, both married. One lives in Mitaka, and she and her husband have a florist shop. My other daughter lives in Itabashi section of Tokyo, and she and her husband have a business making clothing labels and other such items for businesses."

When we commented that she apparently has a hard working family, she asserted that, "I have worked hard all of my life. When I was a child, I was one of seven children, two girls and five boys. I was the third child, but being the first girl I had to help with the family chores, cooking, cleaning, and bringing water from the well. My brothers never helped, and they and my sister continued schooling through junior high school, while I left after the eighth grade because my parents needed me to work at home. In those days, very few people went to high school, especially those in rural areas. Only very special and rich people sent their children for a high school education. But I am proud of my record! I lived two kilometers from the school and walked every day without a single absence in eight years. And when I came home, I immediately had to start all the household chores. It was late before I could do my homework.

"I grew up in Nerima-ku, now part of Tokyo, and not far from this center. Then, it was a rural area. I was a country girl. My nephew still lives in our family house, but the farm was divided among my brothers, sister, and me. My mother ran the farm. It wasn't large, and, therefore, she didn't ask her children to help raise the vegetables and flowers. My father was a school teacher and later had a florist shop.

"I inherited my mother's love of plants that she inherited from her father. Some of my brothers and sisters became florists, and my second daughter would only consider marrying a man who was a florist. I guess it runs in the family.

"I used to visit my childhood home frequently, but since my brother died, I go only three times a year. My sister is dead, as are two of my brothers. My older brother, who is 86 years old, is a florist in Izu Peninsula, and another brother has a greenhouse. I used to see my brothers a great deal, but now it is too difficult. For example, my younger brother needs help walking and has to be brought to my house by his son. He, too, is a florist.

"I had a difficult childhood. I was always busy working, preparing meals, making snacks, and drawing the bath water. By age 15, I sewed so

well that I began making kimonos for women in the neighborhood. I was too busy to be either happy or sad. It was work, work, and more work!

"At age 22, I married. Seven years later, I divorced and then married again. Now, I am a widow; my husband died 15 years ago. My parents arranged both marriages. My first husband was a relative, a widower with a young child. He was an awful husband, a womanizer. He fell in love with many women. He was that kind of man, and I had my troubles. I was married for seven years, but when he made my girl friend, who lived next door, pregnant, I gave up! It was too much for me to put up with that kind of behavior when their baby was born.

"My parents refused to allow me to move back home. In those days, it was shameful for a woman to be divorced. I had to find a way to support myself and, therefore, took a live-in job working for a family in Denenchofu, a wealthy section of Tokyo, until one year later my parents told me that they had found another husband for me."

With laughter, not of mirth but of sadness and irony, she described the second husband. "He was a heavy drinker. He could carry a barrel of sake around with him and drink from it. I was astonished how much he could consume. I had been told that he was a drinker, but I thought that if no girls attracted him, I could somehow manage. It didn't work out that way, and I had an unhappy life.

"My husband owned a sock manufacturing shop. We had seven employees; five of them lived with us. Later, we had fifteen women making socks on the machines. I worked hard at the shop every day collecting threads and threading the machines, then rushing home to cook for the five employees and my family. After that, I would sew for myself.

"When my husband was slightly drunk, he would ask me to go to kabuki theatre with him in Asakusa. I enjoyed that very much. But when he was very drunk, he would beat me. This happened many times. I decided that I would have to endure it this time. I could not divorce again. I had several children and knew that I could not get help from my parents. They had been unsympathetic when I divorced my first husband and told me to find a job away from them. Because of this, I had to leave my first child, a son, with my first husband. I had no way of caring for him while supporting myself. I didn't see my son again until both my husbands died. After that, we were free to see each other. He

visits me occasionally now, I am happy to report.

"I thought that I had to endure the beatings and the hard life and told myself that it was my punishment for leaving my son with his father, for deserting him. It was a harsh way to live, but I felt that I had no choice.

"My husband was about 13 years older than I, and had had several previous marriages, although no children. I was his third wife. He was a short-tempered man, especially when he had too much alcohol. He divorced his second wife, then remarried her, and then divorced her again. It was a relief after he died. I continued to live with my two unmarried daughters and, later, with my oldest daughter when she married."

We were interested in learning how the older Japanese women had coped with such disasters as the Earthquake of 1923 and World War II. Mrs. Sakurada described these experiences.

"I was 20 years old at the time of the Earthquake, alone in my father's shop that was located next to a small river. Suddenly, the river became volatile and overflowed. The second floor of the shop seemed to be moving. I was bewildered and frightened and couldn't figure out what was going on. I decided to run to find my father. Actually, there wasn't much damage to the shop, and fortunately, our house wasn't harmed. We were lucky.

"During World War II, we tried to remain in Tokyo but had to leave our house because we lived next to a railroad track, a bombing target. I went to stay in Itabashi near the factory. We tried to move the machinery to a safe place, but ultimately, our house and the factory were bombed, and we lost everything. My sister lived in Nagano Prefecture, north of Tokyo; my youngest daughter and I went to live with her, while my two older daughters evacuated to the countryside with their schools. My husband went north to Niigata where he was born. After two and a half years, he called us to return to Tokyo, having rebuilt the house and factory and obtained some machinery. Again, we were manufacturing socks. That was in 1948.

"We did have trouble getting food during the War in Tokyo, but I didn't have a hard a time because I was in a mountainous area. We had several good neighbors who helped us, and we did not have to travel searching for food like the city people. I borrowed a small plot of land in the mountains where I grew vegetables. That helped a great deal. Also,

I assisted my neighbors weed their gardens and sewed for them. Thus, the food they gave me was not really a gift."

In looking back on her adult life, Mrs. Sakurada could not recall any happy or sad events. "I have been so occupied with managing my life and managing my family that I can't recall anything special. This is the happiest time of my life. I am free and not hurting or being hurt any more. I have good eyes and can do my needlework to get pocket money. I can support myself. I enjoy raising plants. Sewing and growing plants give me something to do. I have always worked. But now, at this age, I work because I want to work and not because I am pressured."

In response to our inquiry about thoughts about life that she could share with others, she answered, "I am not worthy of giving advice. Working is natural for me. I can't waste time just for enjoyment. Because I had good health, I could overcome the many trials in my life. As for the differences between my childhood and children's lives in the present, I learned as a child never to complain about the food I had to eat, even the leftovers. Today, children complain if they have leftovers. They are surrounded by too much food and waste it. I wouldn't tell them that because they wouldn't listen to such comments. Even if I tried to tell them, they would say that I am still living in the past, that things are different today. But I think that the values are so different now, that I worry about the future." With these words, she ended her life review.

Anyone listening to Mrs. Sakurada would be impressed with the two themes of her life, work and endurance. Her generation of women expected this. Whether they considered beatings to be usual is not known, but it is very likely that a considerable number suffered that indignity. Wife abuse, unfortunately, is found in every country, and Japan is no exception. Alcoholism, as one cause of wife beatings, is common. In Mrs. Sakurada's case, her husband appeared to have a severe character disorder that combined with alcohol was combustive. Today, there is increasing sympathy in some countries for the battered wife, with shelters available if the abuse becomes unbearable and she must flee. In Mrs. Sakurada's generation, families were more concerned with public opinion about a divorce in the family than with their daughters' suffering and even beatings. Then there were no shelters. Society did not consider wife beating a criminal act. Endurance, especially by women, was emphasized in Japanese culture. That had profound effects

on their lives. Some women were dominated by their mothers-in-law and were emotionally abused and had to endure; some were sold into prostitution by their families; and many were devalued because they were women. Their self-images reflected feelings of inferiority, passivity, repression, and unworthiness. Even today, a number of the older women we interviewed could not imagine anyone being interested in their observations and opinions. Mrs. Sakurada is no exception. She defied society once by obtaining a divorce but, having been hurt and defeated by her family's refusal to support her, learned that in order to survive she had to develop defenses that made it possible for her to cope with an abusive husband and an uncaring environment.

Rural women and those from poor families, in particular, had to work especially hard in the pre-war society. Poor farm girls frequently were forced to work in textile mills for pitiful wages and under terrible conditions. The daughters-in-law of all classes were expected to work hard in their husband's home after marriage. Mrs. Sakurada accepted her second marriage without protest because she did not expect life to be kind although she had hoped for something better. She had learned that it was the plight of women to work and endure. She learned that so well that now, when it is no longer necessary, she cannot live any other way. Work is an obsession and earning pocket money is an excuse. In her case, she does not allow herself to make friends outside the family by insisting that she must work. Fortunately, the family does offer her the security she needs, and family relationships appear to be supportive and sympathetic.

Mrs. Sakurada never expressed anger or resentment about her parents' attitudes. They found her two very undesirable husbands which contributed to her sense of unworthiness; they prevented her from raising her own child; they withdrew her from school sooner than her siblings and demanded more work from her than from them. Yet, she never once uttered a word of complaint to us against them. She was resigned to life as it was when she recognized that they did not sympathize with her. The divorce was her only rebellion, and it did her no good. She rationalizes to this day that the beatings she received at the hands of her second husband was her punishment for "deserting" her son. This made it possible for her to cope with her husband's rage.

Like many women in her generation, Mrs. Sakurada showed great strength in enduring an unhappy marriage. It was not masochism but

her rationalization that she was guilty of doing something bad and, therefore, should be punished. She did not once question the attitude of society toward divorce and toward the fact that, in that era, the father and not the mother kept a child when there was a divorce.

"This is the happiest time of my life," said Mrs. Sakurada. A number of the elderly interviewees uttered the same sentiment. In the United States, such comments are rarely, if ever, heard. Widowhood in old age is seen in the United States as a lonely time under any circumstances, especially if the woman is increasingly constricted physically. In contrast, many women we interviewed in Japan, like Mrs. Sakurada, found old age satisfactory because they no longer had excessive work demands; they had buried their husbands and had come into their own; they felt free; and they were cared for by their family. Mrs. Sakurada feels freed from the burdens that she confronted previously, and economic problems, too, are behind her. Some elderly Japanese widows we met use their new freedom to travel, to write poetry, and to make new friends. But Mrs. Sakurada was so oppressed by her tyrannical husband and uncaring parents that she never had time to develop relationships outside the family. She is comfortable only within the confines of her immediate family. She lives in a narrow world, but, having suffered innumerable humiliations from the time of her first marriage to the death of her second husband, what is most important to her is that she now has peace of mind. For her, old age is a welcome stage of life.

Chapter 16

&

Mrs. Minato:
An Abandoned
Rural
Woman

When Mrs. Minato entered the visiting room of this small country hospital in the mountains of Northern Japan, her tensions and stress were evident immediately. She looked bewildered and distressed. She was not certain that it was she we were to interview, even though the social worker had prepared her in advance. She wore old slacks and a loose blouse that did not match. She appeared older than her 76 years as she approached us. Her white hair had not been combed in days and tufts stood upright, adding to her disturbed appearance. Dr. K., a Japanese missionary physician who spoke fair English, volunteered to interpret. This was his first experience with such an interview. The hospital social worker introduced us to Mrs. Minato, and she acknowledged our presence. She even began to smile a bit and appeared to be receptive to our questions.

Mrs. Minato has been in the hospital for three months because of a urinary infection. Although she still has some symptoms, she is ready for discharge. Now, she is facing a crisis that causes her social worker and physician to be very concerned. Her daughter-in-law, who lives in Mrs. Minato's home with her five children, has announced that she does not want her to return. She did not discuss this directly with Mrs. Minato, but communicated with the social worker instead who, in turn, had to break the news to Mrs. Minato. Where will she go? What is her future? She has lived in this rural town for 57 years. She has no one to whom to turn. She has no place to go. At 76 years of age, she does not know how to plan. She feels abandoned, rejected, and bewildered. She was a picture of pathos, and one could only feel empathy and sorrow to see her anguish.

Questioning Mrs. Minato, unlike all of the other women, was difficult. She was so preoccupied with her problems that her answers were not always coherent or to the point. She confused places, times, and dates. She could not recall simple facts and events, and some of her remarks were incoherent. It was difficult to determine if her anxiety about her situation was so pervasive that she could not concentrate, if she was severely depressed, if she had limited intelligence, or if all three factors were simultaneously in place. For example, when asked where she lived

when not in the hospital, she answered "Nagoya." It then became apparent, upon further inquiry, that she came from Nagoya to her present home over fifty years ago to be married.

Mrs. Minato had six children, but when asked about them she could speak only of her oldest son. The others live far away and are married was all we could learn. It was impossible to determine whether she hears from them. Her oldest son, age 55, has abandoned his family, and she views herself as having been abandoned, too. No one knows where he is, and her daughter-in- law is now divorced from him. They used to fight a great deal, mostly because her daughter-in-law insisted upon spending too much money, according to Mrs. Minato. As the oldest son, he inherited the farm after his father's death caused by a stroke 27 years ago. Unfortunately, she and her son had problems running it, and soon they had to sell most of the land. "Since my son left there is no one to farm so everything is sold except the house." What Mrs. Minato did not say was that she is now being evicted from the only thing she thought she possessed. In fact, at no time did Mrs. Minato allow herself to share her dilemma with us. In talking about her daughter-in-law, she stressed only her greed for money. Beyond this, she said nothing more about the situation. The social worker informed us of the problems before we interviewed Mrs. Minato. At the present time, the daughter-in-law has a job earning what Mrs. Minato thinks is a considerable amount of money. Mrs. Minato is living on a pension and, therefore, is not dependent upon her financially.

Mrs. Minato described how she was left daily to care for the five grandchildren when she lived with her daughter-in-law, but, since her hospitalization, the oldest granddaughter, age 16, is in charge of the younger children. The youngest is five years old. During the day, Mrs. Minato had no problems when her daughter-in-law was at work. "We did not have to face each other." She did not say what it was like at night.

The oldest grandchild comes to visit weekly. But, in the three months during which Mrs. Minato has been in the hospital, her daughter-in-law has been there twice. At this point, there was little more she would say. She looked helpless and sad as she made laconic comments in response to our further inquiries.

Because Mrs. Minato reported that she came to this small town from Nagoya, we asked her if she had any problems adjusting to living in the

country after coming from a big city. She could not understand this question. She came here because she loved her husband, she said, and the concept of adjustment meant nothing to her. She explained that she was working near Nagoya during the War as a weaver in a textile company. She was employed there about five or six years, until she left to marry. She met her husband at her factory. He came from this country town and was working near Nagoya until they married. Then they returned to his farm. She, too, came from a farm she reported and laughed loudly in response to our comment, "So you came from a farm, and you returned to a farm." Needless to say, she worked hard on the farm with her husband. Farming in northern Japan is different from in Kyushu in terms of the weather, the variety of crops, the cultivation requirements, and the terrain, she observed. She knew nothing about growing apples and raising rice and vegetables in northern climates. After this, she became so vague that there was no point to pursuing this period of her life further.

With some encouragement, she finally shared a little information about her early life. She was the oldest of five girls and one boy in a poor farm family in Kyushu, and she worked long hours farming as well as helping to care for her brother and sisters. After eight years of schooling, she decided to leave home to work in a factory near Nagoya to earn money in order to help her family. Because the Sino-Japanese War was raging, it was easy to get a job. She liked working and had no problems when bombings took place because the factory was not in the heart of Nagoya.

When asked about happy or sad memories from the past, Mrs. Minato could think of no happy ones. But, she fleetingly referred to her sadness about not returning home when her father died, "even though I left my family by my own will." She, also, commented that life has been difficult because of early widowhood, care of children and grandchildren, and now abandonment in old age.

It was very clear by this time that she did not want to share any more information about herself or her present situation. When we empathized with her about what a hard life she had and how hard she has worked to this day, her only comment was, "I am used to it. I have always worked. I have worked all my life. I'm used to it." She then muttered, "I try to keep my problems to myself. I keep my own secrets. They are private thoughts." This was said more with resignation and hopelessness than

with anger or hostility. It was a statement of fact. She assured us that she did not think seriously about most things. "I try not to give too much thought to my troubles."

Being in the hospital now is very upsetting. "I'm getting fat doing nothing in the hospital." However, she observed that she really wants to do nothing. With this, Mrs. Minato made clear, as she slapped her leg vigorously, that she considered the interview finished. She could say no more. "I could not help you very much," she commented when we assured her that she had been very helpful. With that, she left the room escorted by the social worker.

The social worker reported, upon return, that she is in the process of exploring Mrs. Minato's eligibility for an old age home owned by the local government. This has not been discussed with Mrs. Minato as yet because she does not want to give her hope that she will be admitted if there is no room or if she is not eligible. In the meantime, Mrs. Minato remains in limbo.

Among the women we interviewed, Mrs. Minato was the most inarticulate, the most troubled, and the least capable of finding her own solutions. She is in the midst of a crisis and feels vulnerable, having no social or familial support network to whom she may turn for help. She impressed us with her aloneness and being forsaken by all her children, so much so that one wonders what her relationships were with them. She may be choosing not to let them know of her present plight, or she may have no communications with them. She passively accepted staying with a daughter-in-law she did not like, enduring such a relationship because the alternative would have been to leave, and she had nowhere to go. Given her pension as her sole income, she cannot afford to find new quarters. She has had a very limited life. Poverty, hard work, and losses are the themes she repeated in the interview. Currently, she is depressed, helpless, and completely dependent upon the good will of her hospital social worker. Without her help, she will be homeless. Depression, accompanied by stress, anxiety, and anger are overwhelming her. Whatever capacity she may have had in the past to cope with adversity and crises is no longer present. Her limitations are more apparent than whatever strengths she may have. Insufficient education, inadequate relationships, and few reported successes make it impossible for her to confront the tasks ahead. She is no doubt pondering what she will do with the rest of her life after this rejection and these feelings of utter

abandonment. She is struggling with anger and despair. It is difficult to predict how long she can keep these under control given the narcissistic injury of being excluded from her home of over 50 years. It is no wonder that she is frantic and distraught.

Not everyone learns to cope successfully in adverse situations. Mrs. Minato is, unfortunately, a woman whose emotional and possible intellectual limitations have left her vulnerable and alone. Neither the past nor the present, were particularly happy, and the future looks bleak. What could be worse than feeling abandoned, friendless, and homeless in old age?

Chapter 17

≈

Mrs. Saka:
Strong
and Smart

A s Mrs. Saka entered the room, it was immediately apparent that she is a woman in command of herself and her situation. She has an air of self-assurance and sophistication as she relates to people. Dressed in a smart beige and black dress, hair well-groomed, and with a secure and serious manner, she quickly grasped the purpose of the interview. When we admired her dress, she explained that older Japanese women should wear muted colors, shibui, she called them, because they go well with their grey hair and tan skin. Although 83 years old, Mrs. Saka has very few grey hairs or wrinkles on her face. Probably, she is dyeing her hair, a practice common among older men and women in Japan.

Mrs. Saka is active in the senior center chorus. At her home, she conducts ikebana or flower arrangement classes for which she gets paid.

"It is a hobby that I learned in 1952 for relaxation. I was so busy then that I decided I needed this for relaxation. I've been studying and teaching it ever since and enjoy it immensely. At the time I started to study ikebana, I was caring for my two sons and three student boarders. I would make lunch for them, and, when they went off to school, I dashed to my class. I boarded the students until they graduated and found jobs. They were like sons.

"I had to make a living after my husband died. I was 37 years old at the time. He was an army surgeon stationed in the southern part of China where there were many battles. It was in the midst of the Sino-Japanese War. I had many ideas about different businesses, but none of them worked out. I explored manufacturing judo uniforms because one of my relatives was in that business. But without the help of a husband, I could not get recognition or credit. I then tried managing a taxi company. But that, too, was a failure. I did not know enough about automobile mechanics. So I gave that up. I made plans for two other businesses. I tried to start a nursery school, and, after that, I thought of establishing a public bath which I could run alone. But, by this time, I became fearful of losing what little money I had and the land I inherited from my husband. I had to preserve the land in order to avoid feeling penniless.

"After my husband died, I was responsible for my mother-in-law and

three children, two sons and a daughter. My mother-in-law cared for my children while I went out to work first in a maternity home; but her caring for them ended when my mother-in-law died seven years later. At the same time, my daughter had tuberculosis having developed it during the War when her classroom evacuated to the countryside to escape bombings, and she eventually died of this disease.

"After their deaths, I realized that I had to stay home to care for my children. I decided to farm the land that I owned in this area (close to the center of Tokyo). For four years, I farmed and even raised wheat with no machinery. This was during the American Occupation. The previous War years and those following were very difficult. Food was scarce. During the War, I would go to Kanagawa Prefecture, adjacent to Tokyo, in search of food. My family lived there. Frequently, on the way there would be bombings, and I would have to search for shelter. But I desperately needed the food for my children. After I started farming, I did everything by hand. By the end of the day, my hands were rough, sore, and red. I even made and sold udon (Japanese noodles) from my hand grown wheat. Living on the farm was different in those days. It was in an isolated and desolate place. I did not like it. So many houses were burned and abandoned. You could even see Mt. Fuji from my house.

"Yes, my house was burned, too. I lived there for five years until the bombs destroyed it. Let me explain. My husband owned his hospital, but I could not run it without him. Therefore, I sold it and with the money bought the land and built the house. I lived there with my mother-in-law and three children." This was explained with much laughter.

"My husband died in 1940. While he was still alive, I had an income, but, after that, I had to earn a living. All the banks were closed, and I felt stressed and pressured. That was when I first went to work in the maternity home. I had to walk a considerable distance because there was no public transportation. My mother-in-law died seven years after my husband, as did my daughter. I was left with my two sons to care for. Life was difficult, but we managed."

We inquired about her family. "My father was a doctor, and I had five brothers and three sisters. We were a big family. One brother died during the War, and my sister died by accident. She had an operation and was healing very well, when a nurse, by error, made her drink

alcohol. At age 18, she died of a heart attack. I was the third child in the family. Three of my brothers and two sisters are still alive, and I see them often. We are all healthy. Of course, I am especially close to my sons. My oldest son is an engineer, and the second son is vice-president of the Nagoya branch of a large oil company. My oldest son is divorced, and he kept his three children. They were two, three, and seven years of age when the divorce occurred. He and his wife had very different personalities and could not get along with each other. So I ended up caring for the children after the divorce. It was my second family.

"In the past, when I was growing up, there were not as many divorces as there are in my children's and grandchildren's generations. Women endured every kind of condition once they married. When I talk with the present generation, I see many changes. They think about themselves first and not about others. Sometimes I talk with them about it. I thought that, as they grew older, they would understand me. But instead, they say that their friends act and believe as they do, and it merely confirms their points of view. They just don't agree with me. Their life is so different from when I was growing up. They are so free. I would have liked to have had such freedom. I would have liked to work to make a contribution to society. Now, I just teach ikebana and sing in the chorus. I like music. In fact, if I had been free in the past to make choices, I would have gone into the field of music and orchestra studies. Also, I would have traveled outside Japan. Japanese people do not really know the world beyond our shores. I was in Hawaii and Canada ten years ago and would have done much more traveling if it had been possible. The world outside Japan is so big, so open, so wide, and so different. I found everything in Japan small."

We inquired about Mrs. Saka's schooling. "I went to a jogakko for five years. We received no special training although my school was the forerunner of the Japan Women's University a number of years later. There was nothing left for us to do when we graduated in that era, except to get married. Actually, I did not marry for several years because my mother was very ill. She was bedridden for twenty-five years. Therefore, I stayed home after graduation and nursed her. I had a home helper to do the heavy work, but I had considerable domestic responsibilities. And I cared for my new-born brother. My mother had a spinal disease after the birth of the last baby. Some of the older children were not living at home at the time. They went to school in Tokyo although our

family lived in Kanagawa Prefecture. They stayed with my aunt in Tokyo.

"My brothers went to a university, and my sisters graduated from jogakko. This was the typical pattern of education for upper-middle class children.

"At twenty-three, a go-between introduced me to my husband. I had rejected other men because I did not want to marry an army officer. Then, what happened you already know. Ironically, because he was a doctor, he was drafted into the army a number of years after we married, and, in less than a year, he was dead in the battlefield in southern China. We had been married 14 years at the time that I was left a widow with three children, ages 6, 9, and 11. We were scattered at the time. My mother-in-law and one child had been evacuated from Tokyo; my daughter was evacuated to the countryside with her entire classroom; and my oldest son and I remained in Tokyo. Life was fragmented and so difficult.

"As I look back on my life, the happiest times were when I was a school girl and had many happy hours playing with friends. Even though the school was strict, it was interesting and a challenge. For example, in biology class we went fishing in the river and then observed the fish through a microscope." Mrs. Saka was a good student and acknowledged enjoying her studies.

"I would have liked to have gone on to college. I am interested in what goes on in the world and would have liked to have made a contribution. During the War, I joined a feminist group to learn more about society. I particularly felt that it was important to bring peace to the world and to build a better society, but, unfortunately, we haven't achieved this yet. There is not enough equality among people. Politicians today think too much about themselves and not enough about the people."

"You should be in the Diet," we observed. At that she laughed and agreed. "I wanted to be. I should have studied more, especially about politics."

To learn more about how Mrs. Saka copes under extreme stress, we asked if she had experienced the 1923 Earthquake. So many Japanese women then, for the first time, discovered their organizational and administrative abilities.

"I was twenty years old when the Earthquake occurred. I was standing near my sick mother. The house shook; medicine bottles fell off the

shelf; the fences around our house were destroyed. Fortunately, the house remained standing. I was so frightened that I felt as if I had lost consciousness. I should have taken my mother to a safe place, but instead I stood frozen next to her. When it was over, we were told immediately to evacuate to the mountains because there might be strong tidal waves. We did. Upon returning, we learned that many people who had hidden in the okura (a storage building) were trapped when it collapsed. I saw a baby whose finger had been caught on the fence and his mother, in trying to force it off, severed the finger. The baby cried all night."

We asked if there were other recollections or thoughts that she would like to share with us because we could see that she is a woman who has broad interests and thinks and feels deeply about society.

"Yes, I feel happy that older people's lives are easier today than in the past. Then, women were too restrained and were kept primarily in their homes. Now, I find it interesting to see so many come to this senior center and take advantage of the many activities. The past image of women was one of loneliness and non-involvement with people other than the family. Now, they express what they used to repress in the past. I come to this center often.

"I had many responsibilities raising my children. I was careful not to allow them to feel lonely, nor to take the wrong paths. Now, my grandchildren are over twenty years of age, and I am free. I am taking advantage of this and doing what I like. I read many books, mostly novels and Japanese classical literature. I also practice calligraphy. Most of all, I like to talk to my grandchildren about music and politics. They have different opinions from mine; I am more conservative, and they are more socialistic. I think that politicians should worry more about the nation and less about themselves. My grandchildren tell me that that type of person does not become a politician."

We asked what kind of life she thought she would have had if her husband had lived.

"We would have run the hospital together. I would have helped him. And when not engaged in the hospital, I would have occupied myself with creative activities."

We commented that, in spite of her many trials or maybe because of them, she had proven that she was a very resourceful, creative person, and should feel considerable satisfaction.

"I feel contented and relieved. Now is the time to think about myself because my children and grandchildren are old enough to assume their own responsibilities. I feel that Buddha always protects me." With those thoughts, the interview ended.

Mrs. Saka's life history is a repetition of what we constantly heard among women her age. She adds, however, the uniqueness of her intelligence and dignity. Brought up in an educated family (her father was a doctor) it was not surprising she was matched with a doctor in marriage. She and her sisters had a proper middle class Japanese education, and she learned to be a "good wife and wise mother." As a good wife, she expected to help her husband in his hospital, and, as a wise mother, she planned to supervise her children's education and upbringing. She was not prepared to support her family and to take full responsibility in such an undertaking. Girls in Japan were not expected to do this in spite of the fact that before the War many men died in early middle age. Mrs. Saka was trained "to endure" and "to fulfill obligations" and did so in caring for her ill mother and infant brother. However, she called upon this experience later when confronted with early widowhood and immense obligations in the midst of the War.

What made Mrs. Saka unusual was her intense desire to operate her own business, particularly at a time when women rarely undertook such enterprises. Her independence, determination, and self-confidence in face of the many obstacles she encountered and the failures she endured, are singular. But, unfortunately, she was not educated to run businesses, and the Japanese society did not make it possible to do so. For example, she could not get bank loans and had no business training. Although she had a strong family support system, she had to solve her problems without their financial assistance. She recognized her serious educational and business limitations realistically and found modest, hardworking ways of earning a living to support her family. She was not too proud to operate a farm and to take in boarders.

Just like other Japanese women during the War, Mrs. Saka described her efforts to find food for her family, to dodge bombs, to build a new home when her old one burned, and to confront the deaths of her husband, mother-in-law, and daughter. It is not the numbness of grief and mourning, but the resilience of character that she portrays as she describes the cumulative tragic events that weaker women anywhere would find difficult to surmount. Crises and stress occupied a great

portion of her life from the illness of her mother and her responsibilities nursing her and the newborn baby to the divorce of her son and her need to care for her grandchildren and the multiplicity of War events in between. She had tremendous strengths and adaptability as she coped with these many life crises. Some might say that she is an example of a typical older Japanese woman, but she appears to have greater internal resources and recuperative powers than most.

Rather than become depressed, withdraw socially because of her labors, focus only on the day-to-day minutiae, and feel sorry or even martyred because of her plight, she carried on her daily activities and sought relaxation and stimulation in her ikebana studies in order to cope with her stresses. This activity, along with her family support system, helped her tolerate her trials and tragedies. As is true for many women her age, she recounts them today with a smile, aware that she has the endurance and the capacity to survive.

Her stable character, her ability to maintain close relationships, and her intelligence have made it possible for her to allow herself to enjoy the freedom old age has brought to her. Finally, today she can engage in the interests and activities that past obligations and responsibilities had not permitted. Rather than seeking only parochial activities, she has the breadth of vision to want to see the world far from the shores of Japan. Also, within her country, she looks beyond her home, family, and neighborhood and is interested in politics. In her generation, very few women had such interests and sophistication. Thus, although she describes herself as "conservative," she grew through the years into a very modern woman who sees herself as part of the world and who does not cling to tradition to avoid present-day complexities. She has strong convictions, a philosophy of life, a value system, and the capacity for growth. While she is representative of the traditional woman's ikigai, concepts of sacrifice, endurance, and hardship, she is also a forerunner in advocating greater freedom, greater education, and social responsibility for women.

Chapter 18

❧

Mrs. Takahara:
Born to
Teach

Eighty-four year old Mrs. Takahara met us at the door of her home. This short, stocky, smiling woman was eager to show us her garden, a hobby that takes up much of her time and energy. The variety of flowers and shrubs reflected great care in selection, imagination, and attention. At once, she stated that she hopes, at her age, for continued good health in order to be able to continue to garden.

She was dressed in a very attractive brown and white dress. When complimented, she told us that she bought it for this occasion. She has been looking forward eagerly to this interview. Her round, hardly wrinkled face was full of smiles as she guided us into her home. Her grey hair was carefully concealed by a black wig.

Mrs. Takahara announced that she keeps busy every day with her many hobbies. Water color painting, calligraphy, poetry writing, and daily walks, in addition to gardening, occupy her time happily and maintain her health. She is content with life at this point. Her son and daughter-in-law returned to Japan to live with her recently, and they share the newly enlarged, very attractive house. Now that she is not alone, she is especially happy. She explained that her sister lived with her until her death five years ago at age 94. Since then, it was lonely living alone. She and her sister, a retired missionary, had shared her home for 25 years.

Several themes emerged in Mrs. Takahara's life review: the importance of good health, the supportiveness of religion, the importance of relationships, and the love of teaching children. She particularly described very happy and fruitful years teaching; when times were hard, such as during the War, her pupils were a great comfort. Her friends and family, too, were helpful during crises, but it was the children who meant a great deal to her. She repeated this numerous times with earnestness and conviction, wanting to be certain that we understood the depth of her feelings about her former pupils. However, she sees herself as fortunate, also, because she has so many friends and family. Life would have been very difficult without them all of these years.

Mrs. Takahara was born in Meiji 37 (1905), the eighth of ten children, on a farm in a prefecture north of Tokyo. She had eight sisters and one

brother. She came from an unusual family, she announced; her father's attitude was unique, especially for a man in that era. He believed that his daughters, as well as his son, should have a good education, should be professionals, and should be capable of being independent. Hence, all of her sisters and she became either teachers or missionaries. Even though teaching was the favored profession for girls in Japan at that period, most families did not press their daughters to make it a career because they expected them to marry. Ordinarily, once married, they would not work outside the home. She was grateful for her father's foresight, especially when she found herself a widow with a young child because, having a profession, she could support herself and her child. However, her father was traditional in continuing the custom of having his oldest, and, in this case only, son, inherit the farm. Fortunately, none of the sisters objected.

Her childhood on the farm was a happy one, with many siblings who doted on her and a rural environment in which she could enjoy nature. "I was brought up in a free atmosphere in every way." All this she attributed to her liberal father and her equally unusual mother.

"My mother was a Christian. There were not many in Japan at that time. Although my father did not join the church, he thought that children should have strong religious principles and beliefs. All my sisters and my brother became Christians. My mother's uncle was a missionary who traveled around Japan converting people. Mother belonged to the Salvation Army as did my sisters. I recall many Sunday mornings when a minister offered a sermon in our kitchen, and we sang hymns. Toward the end of his life, father also converted, but mother never pushed him into it."

We agreed that Mrs. Takahara did have an unusual childhood, being brought up in an atmosphere that was very stimulating and promoted independence, values, a worldly view, and philosophical insights. Even today, few families offer such an environment.

"My mother was not the only one to encourage my religious interests. As I was growing up, two of my sisters were already missionaries, and they had a strong influence on me. All my life, at every turning point, religion has been a comfort and support." We asked about her only brother. "Because he was the only boy in the family, my sisters and I treasured him. He never acted spoiled, and he grew up as a clever, good boy. We were proud of him and respected him as a fine person."

Mrs. Takahara did not intend to marry because she loved teaching and planned to devote her entire professional life to it. She studied at a teacher's college in a town fairly close to home. After several years of teaching in her home town, she was invited to teach at her college. Her career started at age 18 and continued for 45 years, until she retired.

After six years in the countryside, she decided that it was time to go to Tokyo. When there, she considered briefly becoming a missionary like her sisters. However, when she was invited to visit a school and heard the voices of the children, she knew that she could not leave them. She was so determined to remain in her career that she decided never to marry because she was certain that a Japanese husband would insist that she give up her profession. That usually happened to the teachers she knew. Nevertheless, after her 30th birthday, she changed her mind and accepted a marriage offer from her cousin's cousin.

"I thought of the whole life ahead of me and decided that I should marry. I knew him as I was growing up. When he assured me that he would never expect me to sacrifice my career, I agreed to marry. I felt that he understood me, which was important."

Mrs. Takahara's marriage did not last long. When her son was four years old, her husband, an engineer with the Japanese Railroad, was sent by the Japanese Army to Burma to build a railroad. Three days before the War ended, he was killed.

"I was left with a pension from the Japanese Railroad and a young child to raise. I was fortunate to have my teaching position and the support of my sisters. Unfortunately, my son does not remember his father. He has only his picture as evidence that he did have a father."

During the War, Mrs. Takahara taught in the neighborhood in which she now lives. She owned her home. As the War intensified, she, her sister, and her son were evacuated with her entire class to a ryokan, a small inn, in the mountains some distance north of Tokyo.

"I hired a cook and janitor, and my work was cut out for me. It was a heavy responsibility. Evacuating children with their teacher to the countryside was a common practice. Their parents stayed behind in Tokyo. My son was cared for by my sister in a rented house near the ryokan, but I was with him every day. We remained there for over two years.

"Returning to Tokyo was a shock. My house was burned to the ground. Fortunately, I did not lose my furniture because I had left it at

my parents' home in the countryside. My son and I stayed with my sister at the missionary hospital for six months. Then, we moved to a cottage next door to another sister. Later, I rebuilt my house and moved back.

"Fortunately, I am an optimist. My situation was difficult. I had such heavy responsibilities. But I thought of my school children and did not allow myself to ponder about how hard life was. I went to school every morning. The children were so cute. I loved them, just as I loved my son. My sister observed how happy I looked when I went to school to teach. I did not feel as if I had any troubles. Fortunately, I was healthy, as was my son, so I never had to lose time from school to take care of him.

"I remember vividly one episode with my son's teacher. When he went to school, he always looked so happy that the teacher did not know that he lost his father in the War. When she read his record and learned that his father was dead, she was astonished. She called him to her and sympathetically asked if he missed his father. To her surprise, he happily responded that it could not be helped, that his father died for his country, and that his mother worked doubly hard to be mother and father to him. He assured her that he never feels lonely. His teacher was so moved by this conversation that she called me to school to tell me about it."

Mrs. Takahara returned to her favorite theme. Teaching was the right profession for her.

"The moment I entered the school, when I said 'good morning' to the children and they said 'good morning' to me, I forgot all about home. I thought only of my work and my pupils. When I returned home, it was different. Then, I would concentrate on my son, and I would tell him about the children I taught. After a while, he knew so much about them, he would ask about individual children. It was a pleasant, sharing experience."

Eventually, Mrs. Takahara's son went to Tokyo University and then received a scholarship to study in the United States. Unfortunately for her, he was offered several fine positions and remained abroad for many years although he visited her frequently.

"I always encouraged him to be self-reliant, and he learned that lesson well. I'm not really surprised that he was independent. People often ask me why I let my only son go so far away, and I reply that each person has his own life to live. I have mine, and he has his. I should not put

myself in his way, nor force him to stay at my side. I recall that when I was teaching, some of the girls' parents would cry because their daughters would marry and live far away. I always told them that I had let my son go. He observed my way of living; that taught him how to manage his own life. He has done it well. Now, in my old age, he is back. But I did not force him to return. He came because he wanted to." She said these last words with great joy.

Mrs. Takahara then reflected on her present life. "I am at the point in life when I am beginning to look within myself. I am no longer thinking about what contributions I should make to the world. I think deeply about everything. I'm fortunate to have good health and rely upon religion. God is important in my life. But, when I go to church, I leave action to the young people. Now, what is important is who I am and not what I do.

"The first student I taught is now 70 years old. When in school, I devoted so much of myself to teaching that I gave from the bottom of my heart, and the children responded to my feelings. The teachers today tell me that children are different and that the relationship between teachers and pupils and among teachers has changed. Many things are different in present day society along with the changes in parents and children. Teachers are no longer respected as they were in the past. People think that they are freer now, but I don't think that they are really free.

"Now that I think of it, I did not just teach. I learned from the children as well. As the children grew, I grew with them We learned from each other. Through our communications we all grew."

As our interview ended and we thanked Mrs. Takahara for sharing so much of her rich experiences and thoughts with us, she, in turn stated, "I thank you for giving me an opportunity to review my life. I thank God that I'm living so happily. I feel that each day is precious." With that, she presented us with a book of poetry that she has published. It was a fitting ending to our conversation with this thoughtful, intelligent, and stimulating lady.

Being a teacher, a Christian, and a rural-born woman made Mrs. Takahara a particularly important elderly woman to interview. Careers in elementary school teaching and nursing were the only professions open to women in pre-war Japan. Most did not remain until retirement unless unmarried. But Mrs. Takahara was among the exceptions. We

were, also, able to learn the influence and role of Christianity in the lives of some Japanese women. Finally, we could observe the influence of a rural upbringing through her deep love of nature and gardening.

When Mrs. Takahara described her parents appreciatively as being unusual, she was not exaggerating. Elizabeth Knipe Mouer comments, in <u>Women in Changing Japan</u> (Lebra, Paulson, Powers eds., 1976), "Few questioned the traditional belief that men are superior to women (danson johi)," consequently daughters were not expected to be as well educated as sons. Mrs. Takahara's father's message on education for women and independence, which he gave to his nine daughters and his son, reflected a stance that was non-traditional in that era when most women received only six years of compulsory schooling and only the upper class girls attended a jogakko, at which they were taught primarily domestic sciences and literature in order to make them "good wives and wise mothers" (Mouer, p. 158). It is remarkable that Mrs. Takahara was encouraged to enter the teaching profession without the expectation that it was merely a step toward marriage and motherhood. There were families who tried to hide from others that their daughters were determined to secure a higher education and pursue a career (Mouer, p. 162). If a daughter was singled out favorably for her "high ability, disciplined mind, and tenacious spirit," she was considered the unusual family member (Mouer, p. 180). The fact that, in Mrs. Takahara's family, nine daughters received that encouragement indicates the remarkably stimulating, enlightened, and permissive environment in which she was reared. In selecting teaching as a profession, Mrs. Takahara was not seeking to break new grounds or to be a pioneer. Nevertheless, her determination to be independent, unmarried, and have a profession in a period when most women prepared only for marriage and motherhood, marked her as a non-traditionalist. She does not deny this. She was able to communicate her values to her only son and could philosophically accept his being separated from her for many years. Others were critical of her, and she could acknowledge that, while she would have liked him to be available to her after the death of the sister who lived with her, she had transmitted to him the spirit of independence that she had in herself.

Perhaps, in thinking about Mrs. Takahara's life history, what is most striking is the remarkable mutual support system she and her family evolved. The ten siblings retained relationships and loyalties to each other that were extraordinary. Through peace and war, they were avail-

able to one another. Although each sister had her profession and the brother had his farm, they were helpful to each other during all crises. Thus, Mrs. Takahara's capacity for independence and professional involvement was made possible because she could turn for assistance and nurturing when needed. But, what was just as important, she could economically support herself and her son. She did not have to become dependent. Her support network also made it possible for her to allow her only son to take advantage of educational and professional opportunities abroad, and she could feel satisfied that she could manage comfortably. His return, now that the numerous sisters are dead, is more important and urgent at this time than if she had pressed him in the past.

Perhaps one of the most important aspects of Mrs. Takahara's ability to cope so well is her capacity to form and retain relationships. She saw both parents and several older sisters as ego ideals and sought to emulate them. She readily internalized and reflected the values they instilled in her. Furthermore, her closeness to her parents, her sisters, and her brother gave her an early start in experiencing the satisfactions that come from warm and giving relationships. She was able to extend this into marriage, motherhood, and professional life. The children she taught became so important to her that she could shut out all other concerns when she entered the classroom. She could immerse herself in her work and her pupils. She could be available to them and to their parents, thus achieving tremendous emotional fulfillment. No doubt she became an important idealized figure to many of those children, and the reciprocal nature of these associations met the needs she and they had and enjoyed. This capacity to form outside relationships prevented her from becoming overdependent upon family, including her son, and, therefore, allowed her to be flexible in the demands she might have made on them. It also permitted her to realize her full potential. She did not confront the extreme loneliness and depression many women experience when losses occur because there were others ready to give to her, just as she gave to them. She used activity and relationships to avoid the emptiness people who experience losses usually report.

Christianity, too, has served as a support and has given her strength during crises, as well as in everyday life. She could confront adversities and deaths philosophically, finding comfort in this way. Furthermore, religion meant service to others; it meant caring, loving, and relatedness. It, also, empowered her to act on her convictions, and to develop her

own identity.

How did Mrs. Takahara cope as a widow and during crises? Through activities, through immersing herself in her profession and her pupils, and through her extensive support system, she could accept changes and losses without complaints and regression. And when she retired, she could turn her creative energies to developing and enjoying hobbies that she had not had time for in her earlier days. Even retirement was not experienced as a serious loss. During these years, she has had good health and an optimistic outlook. This, too, contributed to her ability to move relatively smoothly from one stage of life to another. Elderly people, in particular, dread the possibility of illnesses, operations, pain, and frailty in old age. She has been spared these problems thus far and is conscious of the need for exercise, good nutrition, and bodily care.

Now, in her 80s, Mrs. Takahara may indulge in healthy narcissistic preoccupations to maintain her self-esteem. She is conscious of her clothes and fashions, of her appearance, and of her body. She is, in addition, keenly aware of her inner thoughts and feelings and admits that, to the extent that she does not maintain her previous numerous community commitments, she is withdrawing into herself. This disengagement in no way disturbs her. It is a sound move that gives her time to contemplate and to engage in her poetry writing and watercolor painting. She is currently working on another book of poetry. In reviewing her life, Mrs. Takahara expresses a sense of accomplishment and satisfaction. While she regrets the societal changes that reflect a shift in traditional values of respect for teachers and older people, she has not experienced these personally and understands that there are reasons for these changes. Now that she feels that she will be cared for in her last years, she is content.

Chapter 19

❧

Mrs. Mase:
A Westernized
Traditionalist

Mrs. Mase is a woman much admired by both Japanese and American women in Tokyo. This diminutive, slender 85 year old woman, dignified in appearance and demeanor, wears her grey hair piled high, adding to her height and bearing. She is as comfortable in a well-tailored Western-style suit as she is in a colorful Japanese kimono. As one of the founders and a current active member of the Japanese-American Women's College Club, she is well-known to the intellectual Japanese and American women of Tokyo. She is called upon frequently to chair committees and give talks to numerous groups. When not busy with her social interests, she travels to foreign countries. At 85, Mrs. Mase leads a full life, uses public transportation, and lives in her own home near the heart of Tokyo. Mrs. Mase's English is formal and perfect, without an accent, and it is only when listening to her ideas and thoughts does one become aware of how Japanese she feels and thinks. She enjoys sharing her life story with others and thoroughly appreciates the interest shown in her.

A graduate of the class of 1924 of Wellesley College, Mrs. Mase is very much aware that she has had a unique life, having experienced the American jazz age and its rah-rah extravaganzas in the 1920s, and then having wed into a very conservative, rural, Japanese, traditional family. At the same time, as an adult she lived abroad as the wife of a diplomat, thus retaining her cosmopolitan interests and outlook.

Her life has been full of contrasts. Most of her growing-up years were spent in the U.S.A., but her adult life was divided into segments consisting of a conservative Japanese environment, the Japanese diplomatic society, War-time Japan, the American Occupation, the rebuilding of Japanese industries, and, finally, personally serving as a bridge between Japan and the U.S.A. She claims to have enjoyed the freedom of American society, yet she embraced Japanese traditional life obediently and voluntarily. She loved the life of a diplomat's wife in the U.S.A. and its sociability and glamour, and, at the same time, accepted the constraints and rigidly defined status of a Japanese traditional wife. She had not anticipated becoming a career woman, particularly since Japanese women did not have many career choices in the 1920s and 1930s, yet, in

the 1940s, she embarked upon several careers unique for women in Japanese society, that of a college instructor, a businesswoman, and, lastly, an administrator and organizer. She loved every moment of her several careers, but, when asked about careers for young Japanese women, she thought that they should not try to compete with men. Her life is one that could be envied by Japanese feminists and could be looked upon as a model, but her philosophy is decidedly not that of a feminist.

Mrs. Mase is one of six children of a father in the import-export business and an ambitious mother, well-educated by English-speaking missionaries. As her father's business was San Francisco-based and her mother was very determined to raise her children to have an American education, when Mrs. Mase was a pre-schooler, her mother bought a house in Oakland, California and moved there with her several young children. But life was not as smooth as she had anticipated. There was serious discrimination against Orientals in California. Her mother was informed by the public school principal that Oriental children "were not eligible" for an American education. "So my mother gathered her children and moved back to Japan to live with her parents in Kanazawa, a beautiful, traditional, castle city still reflecting samurai influences." By this time, Mrs. Mase was seven years old.

"I received my elementary education in Kanazawa and consider that this was the most important influence contributing to my feeling culturally very Japanese. Ages 7 to 12 are a very impressionable period in a child's life. Some of my siblings are very Japanese, and others are very American. I am very Japanese. Although I was educated in an American college, I remained the most Japanese of my siblings. I prefer Japanese food, like to wear Japanese clothes, and feel very Japanese." All of this was stated with a perfect American accent from a woman who looked so trim, smart, and comfortable in her Western dress.

Upon returning to the U.S.A. with all her children, again her mother discovered that discrimination had not disappeared in California. "So, she said to my father, 'There must be a good school somewhere in the U.S. where my children can get a good education.' And she left her children in California, while she traveled to many places in the U.S. in search of a good school system. Among the places she went to was Princeton, New Jersey, because she knew a minister there. She liked the community attitudes and the schools and returned to California to pick up her children to move us there. Father would visit us once a year. We

had a wonderful education in Princeton. Then, one brother went to Princeton University, another to Amherst College, another to Stanford University, and I went to Wellesley College. My sister completed her education in Dana Hall (a girl's private high school), and only my youngest sister went to college in Japan."

We observed that her mother was a remarkable manager and decision-maker. "That is true in many Japanese families. My father was very busy making a living for his growing family, and my mother took responsibility for raising the family. She was a good manager. My father was very willing to live this way. He had no chance to get an education, having come from a propertied family in Kyushu that had lost its money. Therefore, he had not received an advanced education. He was very eager for his children to be well educated. He was willing to work hard, make money, and turn it over to my mother. He asked himself, if Japanese children were given the same privileges as Western children, would there be any difference in their accomplishments. So he wanted all of his children to be educated in the U.S.A.

"Our government did the same thing at the beginning of the Meiji era. When a Japanese diplomat went to the U.S.A. to negotiate a treaty with the American government to make Japan more equal internationally, there were over 130 students aboard the ship. Among them were five little Japanese girls, ages seven to fifteen. The government wanted to learn whether, if young Japanese children were given the same opportunities as American children and went to the same schools, they would do as well as the American children. The girls were placed with American families and went to American schools. Two became ill and eventually had to return home. Three remained. Two graduated from Vassar College; one became the valedictorian of her class. One returned home, and later came back to the U.S.A. to study for a doctoral degree in Bryn Mawr College. Later, she founded Tsuda University. One of the Vassar girls married the Minister of War and later became a princess. She was a leader in women's patriotic work during the war with China in 1894-1895. Another married an admiral and helped introduce Western musical education into Japan. These three women proved that there was no difference between Japanese and American children. It is only a question of exposure.

"In college, I majored in sociology and economics, of all things. Japanese families considered it was something to be ashamed of, and you did

not talk about it. My mother was embarrassed. In Japan, when a girl is to be married, the family writes a bio-data sheet. No man would marry a girl with a degree in sociology and economics, my mother feared. I started first to major in mathematics, but my mother stopped that! I then sought something lady-like, so I took economics and sociology." Mrs. Mase was laughing at this point.

"In Japan, you don't meet the eligible gentlemen when you wish to marry. Your friends and acquaintances run around the city with your bio-data sheet, and they, in turn, also appear at your house with packets about eligible gentlemen. Only my mother saw the packets. Father was in America. I was not accustomed to this as I had been abroad and, therefore, I was slow to be interested, let alone make a decision. One day a certain businessman came to say that he had someone for me to marry, a diplomat. Because, in this case, my education was considered a plus rather than a minus, he thought that I would be interested and eligible. The young diplomat had been educated in Cambridge, England. For once my education was not a handicap. It actually could be helpful in his career.

"The first person to see my bio-data sheet was not my future husband. It went to his father. After studying it, he said, `But this girl is born in the year of the tiger; my son is born in the year of the sheep. What shall I do?' He picked up my packet and went to the geomancer (mystical forecaster). My future father-in-law was a superstitious man from the countryside. The geomancer pondered and then observed, `But she is a reclining tiger, and it may be that this tiger can give the necessary push to the gentle sheep.' That settled the whole thing. That is the way things happen in Japan."

We asked how the tiger reacted to meeting the gentle sheep. "In those days, you saw the person you were marrying once; you did not date. He was very good looking and seemed to be a nice person. He was frequently mistaken for a handsome South American. I was not concerned that he was a sheep. I did not even know the story at that time. The two families met and made all the wedding arrangements, and that was how marriages were made in Japan."

We commented that all of this must have been a contrast to life as a student in Wellesley College. "Yes, there I went to theatres, football games, and dated. But I grew up knowing attitudes toward life and marriage were different in Japan. I had been prepared by my parents. I

could have picked a man in the United States, but I was an obedient girl and accepted the Japanese way. Having gone to elementary school in Japan, I had absorbed the Eastern way of thinking and combined it with my Western experiences. I am glad I had both exposures and am grateful that I studied in America. It especially turned out to be fortuitous as my husband died young. As a diplomat assigned to the Japanese Embassy in the United States, he knew what was going on behind the scenes, and told me to prepare for war. He said that things were changing fast. He died shortly after.

"And that is when my Western education was useful. I knew that a woman, if she had to, could do things. I did not have a Japanese diploma, however, and in World War II this was a problem for me. Nor did I have a certificate to teach. During the War things were getting more and more Japanese and anti-American. And that is when Tsuda College came into my life. One of the Tsuda teachers was at Wellesley College when I was there. She called me one day and said, `I hear you are a widow. We need western educated English teachers. All of our American teachers are leaving because of the War.' And from that time until I retired, I led the life of a career woman.

"I was just 40 when this occurred. Yes, I was a young widow. My husband was seven years older. At age 40, women in Japan are freed from child rearing and can start working. That is what happened to me. But the problem was that my specialty was economics, not English. I, therefore, was always one or two days ahead of my class. It was exciting. Until my husband died, I was always following him or my mother-in-law. I learned upon becoming a widow that I could make my own decisions. An entirely different side of me emerged. That was the part of me that became a career woman.

"During the War, the Japanese Army was curious about what was being taught in the colleges. They came to observe me. But the army man could not understand English, and I taught in that language. Patiently, I sat down with the army man and told him what I was teaching. I had to explain Thomas Hardy, Jane Austen, Shakespeare, and others. I needed to help him so that he could submit correct reports. I did not want him to make up anything.

"I have one son who was born in Washington D.C. My husband was with the Japanese Embassy there at the time. Because of that my son is not considered a nisei (a first generation American born to Japanese

parents). Today my son is a businessman."

We asked what it had been like to be the wife of a diplomat. "It was an interesting experience. When I first married, I recall that I was helping serve a group of colleagues my husband was entertaining. I spoke up in response to what one of them was saying. My husband frowned at me, and I knew then that as a Japanese woman, I was not supposed to speak. But in Washington D.C., it was different. There, I had a new view of America. In California, I had experienced discrimination. In Princeton, there was no discrimination, and I was invited to many dances. In Japan, I was trained by my mother-in-law to be a country wife. But in Washington, a diplomat's life was exciting and elegant. At least, that was the case before the Crash (the Great Depression). We went to dinners, parties, and dances, and left calling cards at appropriate times and places. Many women even liked to come to the parties in horse-drawn carriages, and not in Pierce Arrow cars. There were responsibilities, also, being the wife of a diplomat, even though my husband was among the lower ranks because he was so young. I remember one time when the Japanese senior couple could not attend an affair and the last minute we substituted at the dinner. The guest of honor was William Howard Taft (a past American President). He was a huge man, and the whole room shook when he laughed. My husband worried that he would break a chair and sought a big strong one for him. "I was a young girl at the time. Many of my college friends were high in Washington society. I saw a good deal of them. However, the Embassy had its Japanese hierarchy, and we always had to be very careful not to hurt anyone higher up."

I commented on the contrast between the informality of American college life and the formality of Japanese society. "It was not easy. Actually, I was a servant in my in-laws' home. I did everything a servant did. I had to be a good actress. I was taught by my mother-in-law to wash floors, sew kimonos, cook, and clean. One day I overheard my mother-in-law say to my father-in-law that soon they would be able to discharge their servant. I guess I was doing a fairly good job. But, fortunately, my husband's work took us to Tokyo where I was freer, except that, when in diplomatic circles, I had to be very watchful. Before World War II, the diplomatic world was especially very formal.

"I was the one in the marriage who had to do all of the adapting to new ways and new demands. My husband had studied in Cambridge,

and then worked in the Japanese Embassy in London. He, too, had to adapt to many changes in his life. He came from the conservative countryside and felt loyal to his family. He was a very dutiful son and wanted to please his father. I wanted to do nothing that would cross him. I went overboard to adjust to my mother-in-law and to Japanese society and to do nothing that would reflect negatively on my husband. He was caught between a superstitious father, a traditional, provincial mother, and a modern girl. You recall, his father relied upon his geomancer."

Later, I pointed out, she had to readapt to becoming a sensei (teacher), an honored position, when she became a widow. "If I cannot adjust properly to new roles, what good is my education?" she asked.

"Some women might rebel and question why a daughter-in-law has to be a servant. I wonder how women today would feel about that role?" I asked.

"My husband was caught between his mother and wife. Also, I always followed what the geomancer suggested to my father-in-law. I decided that I would conform to what I was expected to do, and, in time, things would change. I did not let my father-in-law know how I felt. If I had, it would have made trouble with my mother-in-law, father-in-law, and my husband. My in-laws thought I was stupid. I didn't know how to sew, cook, or wash floors. My mother-in-law had to teach me everything. I didn't come with the proper training."

In answer to inquiries about her son, Mrs. Mase explained that during the War years he was in high school and had to work in a factory. The War made a vivid impression on him. Life was very confusing. Later he went to Keio University. Children his age lived under a strong authoritarian government, and then suddenly their world changed radically with the American Occupation. She observed, "Character is important, but I noticed that high school children during the War years had a hard time adjusting later to a new way of life." Her son was born in Showa 2, (1928).

Returning to a description of her life as a career woman, Mrs. Mase continued, "I taught for four years in Tsuda College. Then, we lost the War, and the Occupation Forces came in. Behind Tsuda College, an American engineering outfit was set up. One day a soldier-officer came to Tsuda to find an interpreter. The President of Tsuda called me in and told me it was important to go with him. I got into a jeep, in fact a

group of jeeps came just for me. I could have walked, it was so close. Maybe it was to impress us that they sent the jeeps. The first thing that happened was that they showed me dirty clothes piled high. It was in a gymnasium of a boys' school. 'We need a laundry. We need an interpreter to get the laundry equipment.' I was told to get the equipment and set up a laundry. And I was given the lowest rank, because I worked with ordinary G.I.'s. I didn't understand G.I. jargon. I couldn't make them out. I learned it after a while. I requisitioned laborers and found two men who had owned laundries. So after teaching at Tsuda, I was running a laundry!

"An officer asked me suddenly one day if I was a spy. He thought that usually interpreters ask for favors or a change of jobs, he said. Therefore, because I hadn't made any requests, he decided that I must be spying because I was so well educated. He considered my job was inferior and could not understand why I remained in it." She told him that she did have a friend who could help her get a job in Occupation Headquarters, but she would not be comfortable asking for a favor.

"One day several young men whom I had known in the past and who were Waseda University graduates in their 20s, came to see me. They had been in the service during the War. I was asked by these boys to join them in a new business venture. My son was growing up and needed a college education. I didn't want to ask my parents-in law for help. It was a good opportunity. We went into the textile business and sold to the Occupation Forces. I would get orders from the 8th Army or the PX for silk weavings. Then we would get releases to obtain the locked goods.

"I did very well. It was a matter of wits, especially when the world was so topsy-turvy. The boys with whom I worked did very well but had no previous experience. When big companies started competing with us, one eventually invited us to join with them. I knew then that there was no room for a woman in the big zaibatsu-type (large pre-war monopoly) company.

"I joined another group of sharp men in the textile field. I obtained orders for tents, uniforms, and the like. This was during the Korean War. I learned a great deal and memorized army specifications. Again, we did well, and I stayed with them until I became ill in the late 50s.

"I had an unusual operation. They removed one-third of my liver. I, then, had to get my body in condition. However, the medical school did

not expect me to live. Some time later, they sent me a card asking if I was dead or alive. A liver team studying such operations was so surprised to see me alive that they wanted to open me to study my liver, in order to see what had happened. I refused. They wondered if my liver had regrown. At a later time, they did discover that a dog's liver regrew. I had a wonderful doctor who told me his one hour operation was a five hour operation in U.S.A. I was not surprised.

"How I learned I had a liver problem is interesting. I had a friend, who was a high level fortune-teller, able to forecast many things. He said certain people were in tune with him, and I happened to be one of them. When I saw him, well before my marriage, he told me that he felt sorry for me, that my husband would die young, but that I should not worry. I would go into business. I used to see him while I was in business, only just to visit with him. One day he said, `Mrs. Mase, you have a lump. If you do not go to see a doctor soon, it will be serious.' No one had told me that before. I took him seriously, and that is when I had my liver operation. I stopped working for a year. Life was difficult. Food was still scarce, and Japan was still in a state of reorganization and rehabilitation.

"One day, a friend told me that the Fulbright Committee was being established and that they were seeking someone who knew American and Japanese education systems. I knew that I should not return to business and that this was a good opportunity. For eleven years, I was with the Fulbright Committee. I handled American scholars coming to Japan. It was fun working with the American Embassy. And, when I retired from that position, I worked for two more years with the East-West Center. At that time, it was part of the Fulbright program but later was separated and moved to Hawaii. I, also, established the International Experiment-in-Living program in Japan and ran their office. Then, I decided that I had done enough work. My son had been educated, married, and had a job. So I started traveling. I was already past 70. I was old and grey.

"I looked old, but I didn't feel old. Yet, so many of my friends were dying. I felt that I had left them. Yes, I have done other things. For example I helped develop the Japanese Women's College Club, and then helped start the Japanese-American Women's College Club. I enjoy putting things together and getting things moving."

"You spoke of Japanese women informally always being managers.

What about your experiences as a woman business manager, not feeling treated as an equal with men in business if you went into a large company?" we asked

In response, Mrs. Mase stated, "Japanese women are fortunate. In my days, women did not grow up feeling competent about work. Each household had at least three generations. The woman at home watched everything happening and saw to it that the family worked well and things ran smoothly. The woman spent the money and budgeted for the younger people. The Japanese woman was prepared for catastrophes, like torrential rains, earthquakes, and fires. Because of her management, Japanese salaried families had savings and skills to help them during these catastrophes. Unconsciously, Japanese women prepare for these eventualities. American women were not prepared for these eventualities.

"Today's Japanese women can get jobs if they have abilities. But not every woman wants a man's job. Women should not pit themselves against men. They should do what they want for themselves. They do not have to compete with lawyers or with men in big companies. In time, they will be accepted. I am worried about women who have raised their children. In their late 30s they are finished, and from ages 40 to 80 there is much for them to do to develop their interests. These women should get together and decide how to use themselves after they have raised their children.

"First, women should marry; then raise children; and then, with so much intelligence, should find what they can do best. I don't know what to suggest to them. I am out of touch with the business world."

We commented that in Japan many women are closed out from high level jobs and professions, and instead get clerical and low paid jobs. She had been fortunate and had wonderful experiences being a business woman, a career woman. What about the women today?

"Something new will happen in Japan. I am sure women will find means to find themselves. They are well educated. They will do well," was her answer.

Mrs. Mase is a most interesting woman who demonstrates both the passive and aggressive sides of her personality. She is at once obedient and adaptable to the demands of those around her, and, at the same time, given the opportunity, she is a real leader. She clearly appears to have the organizational skills that her mother had, and, when necessary,

the drive to put them to good use like her father. But she is careful not to place herself in an adversarial position. When she was faced with the possibility of discrimination against women by a large Japanese company, a practice still current today, she removed herself rather than confront it or experience rejection. She carefully avoids such situations. She could have defied her mother years ago by majoring in mathematics, or by refusing to have a husband selected for her, but she did not. Part of her wanted to be accepted, obedient, and traditional, but another part of her enjoyed being independent, a leader, and assertive.

In marriage, Mrs. Mase accommodated herself to an especially rigid, narrow, conservative relationship with her in-laws rather than inform them that her American experience was contrary to their style of life. However, she knew that it would not be for long, given her husband's diplomatic career. She could be patient. Patience and adaptability are traits that are particularly prominent in her life. She put up with social expectations and situations that were essentially antithetical to her past experiences because she could anticipate that they would not continue indefinitely, and she would come into her own. Always, it worked out well for her. Thus, she lived peacefully in both an authoritarian environment and in a freer, more democratic milieu. She evolved a pragmatic approach to her life which allowed for success in all endeavors. The contradictions and incongruities remained unacknowledged and, therefore, ignored, likely even denied. She could profess very traditional thinking and advocate that Japanese women not "fight the system." Yet, she lived a life that was not traditional. She held numerous positions that were prestigious and unusual for a Japanese woman, and earned an enviable reputation, a good income, and public admiration. Even in the shadow of her husband and his career, she lived a unique life as a diplomat's wife, and she maintained her American friendships, not as a Japanese woman, but as an American college classmate.

Mrs. Mase may have professed her love of tradition and provincialism, but her long residence and education in a western culture permitted her to move beyond such boundaries and, therefore, enjoy the best of both worlds. She was the richer for it. And she enriched the people with whom she associated. She is a unique woman, comfortable in the East and West. When tradition becomes too rigid, she can escape to the other world. There are very few people who have had such opportunities and have performed as well as she has. In some ways, she is like her

mother who never gave up her Japanese traditional approach to life, yet who, in a most determined way, insisted upon an American education for her children in the best American schools and universities. Perhaps, she was the model for Mrs. Mase's many contradictions and ambivalences.

Chapter 20

ֆ

Mrs. Wakiro:
A Frustrated
Intellectual

W̲e met Mrs. Wakiro at a Catholic nursing home in an attractive area of western Tokyo. Her social worker, a former philosophy instructor, described her as a particularly intelligent woman. She was an interesting but very sad person because of the frustrating life she described. Only after both her mother-in-law and husband died, when she was already old, was she able to pursue interests she longed for before and during her married life.

Mrs. Wakiro uses a wheel chair because walking is extremely difficult. She appears shrunken, with her shoulders rounded and her body implanted rigidly in the chair. Her broad round face alternates between a usually depressive expression and a fleeting smile when she relaxes. She looks her 86 years, and one senses the pathos in her life. Upon speaking to her, one is impressed immediately by how thoughtful, serious, and perceptive she is.

Mrs. Wakiro came to the nursing home two-and-a half years ago. "I was living alone and had trouble walking. During a hospitalization, a friend told me about this nursing home. Because I am a Christian, it interested me. I could no longer live alone because I needed full time assistance. Now, I walk a little with a cane as a result of frequent rehabilitation exercises."

Mrs. Wakiro spoke at first in a halting, withholding manner, listened thoughtfully, and showed little spontaneity. However, when we mentioned that she appeared to understand some English, she perked up, smiled, and became freer. She admitted studying it in college. She, also, used her hands to accompany her animated facial expression. In a burst of energy, she explained that she was married at age 24, lived with her mother-in-law for over 30 years, and had no children.

"My mother-in-law was a great figure; I learned a great deal from her; she made my life rich."

These words became the theme of her life review. She repeated them several times during our session, as if she had frequently rehearsed the lines. She originally gave us the impression that she had lived only with her mother-in-law and without a husband. In reality, she has been widowed since age 69; her husband outlived her mother-in-law by five

years.

Although born in Tokyo, Mrs. Wakiro spent most of her childhood and adolescence in Taiwan, Korea and the city of Kobe in Japan. At that time, Taiwan and Korea were Japanese colonies. Her father was a government bureaucrat engaged in administering those colonies, and she enjoyed moving to interesting places.

Her mother died when she was one year old. A year later, her father married a Japanese woman who had been educated in a German family. She had many progressive ideas about the education of children, especially girls. "I had a happy childhood. After my older sisters went to Tokyo, I remained at home with my mother as an only child. Later a sister and brother were born. It was nice being alone with my second mother. She was eager to educate her children in a way that was different from the usual Japanese education in those days. She learned about child rearing from foreign books and followed their prescriptions. So I was raised with tremendous emphasis on intellectualism and with the enjoyment of a more expansive knowledge base than most Japanese children had. I went to a jogakko, but that was not enough for me. I wanted more because I wanted to study English. My two sisters finished jogakko but did not want to continue their studies."

She gave us a big smile of pleasure as she thought about her love of studying and commented on how much she enjoyed attending Kobe Jogakuin College. "It was at the end of World War I, in 1918. Japan was experiencing wonderful times. I had a happy, enjoyable time during the Taisho Period (1912-1926). That was an era when women had increasing opportunities to get a higher education; some were even going on to college. Mine was a Protestant university at which they had us read the Bible in English. I have since lost most of my ability to speak English, but I can still read English newspapers," she stated proudly.

"I enjoy looking back at my college days in Kobe. During World War I, many famous musicians left Europe for the United States; upon returning home after the War, they traveled through Kobe. Because my college had a good auditorium, they played there. I heard Horowitz and others. These experiences left a life-long impression on me. Although the regular tickets were expensive, as a student, I could hear wonderful music for low prices." Her joyous face as she recalled these events told us a great deal about her and her interests. She still enjoys reminiscing about those experiences. "Because I have no children, these memories are

especially important."

Mrs. Wakiro became somber again as she continued her life review. "Despite my family's stress on a good education for girls, they were very traditional. They wanted me to marry and discontinue my studies. I preferred to finish my education and become a librarian. I loved books and reading and did not plan to marry. I had dreams of getting a higher education and a profession; unfortunately, they were only dreams because I was a woman. I had to leave college at age 23 when my parents found a husband for me. We were introduced by a go-between and saw each other only once or twice before marriage. I had to marry because that was the custom in those days. I had to live with my mother-in-law, a very distinguished lady who had a hard time raising her many children. I was happy to learn from her. Not having children, I had time to learn haiku, a unique form of Japanese poetry. However, my happiest time was when I went to college and was free. After I married and lived with my mother-in-law, I was not free."

We see here that Mrs. Wakiro changed the theme that life was wonderful with her mother-in-law to a theme that life with mother-in-law was very constricting. Her own interests, aspirations, and wishes were laid aside in favor of pleasing mother-in-law around whom the domestic world of the Wakiro family revolved, as she described it.

We learned about Mr. Wakiro only because we asked about him. He graduated from Tokyo University and took a position with the Mitsuibussan Company.

"In those days, it was difficult to get such a good job. Only very well qualified people succeeded. He was fortunate to have this very good position, and we lived in Tokyo. He was a good man; he liked to read, as I did, and we spent many evenings reading."

Mrs. Wakiro's father died of a stomach illness that was poorly diagnosed and incorrectly treated. This happened shortly after her marriage. Now, only her younger sister is alive. She sometimes visits Mrs. Wakiro at the nursing home. The only other relatives are her husband's two nieces to whom she has turned over her estate. They, in turn, handle her financial obligations, such as paying for the nursing home.

Life with mother-in-law preoccupied Mrs. Wakiro for over 30 years. According to Mrs. Wakiro, this older woman was, "weak in body, but strong in will. I admired her and recall learning many things from her, for which I am very grateful. She was warm-hearted, generous, and kind.

But, she was very strict and had a very strong character. There was nothing grey about her. Everything was black or white. She disapproved of me when I was hesitant, and told me so. She wanted direct answers and decisions; everything had to be definite. There was not much I could do except care for her. I was not allowed to go out to work which is what I wanted to do. Therefore, I stayed home, nursed her, read books, wrote essays, kept a diary, and composed haiku. Yes, I have published poetry and recently I wrote a book about the life history of my mother-in-law. I made a limited edition and gave it to friends and relatives."

When asked if there were any other significant things about her early married years, she laughingly commented that, "I lived with my mother-in-law from the beginning of my marriage and was not free to travel with my husband. His work involved considerable travel. I would have liked to have gone with him, but I had to stay home with her instead. After my mother-in-law's death, I did not travel with my husband because he was so busy. It was actually not until my husband died that I could travel, and then I did with my friends."

To our comment that despite her closeness to mother-in-law, she might regret not having lived the kind of life she wanted for herself, she responded with a positiveness and definiteness that was firm and sorrowful. "Yes, that is right! After I was alone, I felt much freer." And in answer to our inquiry if she wished that she had children, she replied in the same manner, "No. My mother-in-law was strict, and I did not want to have children." She did not say more, and we did not pursue the topic.

After she became a widow, Mrs. Wakiro found herself alone in a large house and decided to rent rooms to four or five students. "That was enjoyable," she observed with a big smile. She found them interesting people. One received his Ph.D., she recalls. "I took care of these hard-working students and still get letters from some of them. They write me when they get married and about their careers. One still writes to me at the nursing home." She spoke enthusiastically, as if they were her children.

Freedom, after the death of her husband, permitted her to travel whenever she wished because she cultivated friends with whom to go places, enjoy sightseeing, and write haiku.

"My mother-in-law died somewhat over 20 years ago, and five years

later my husband died. After that I was free."

Until Mrs. Wakiro's health failed her, she led a rather active life. Now, all this has changed, and she is in this nursing home until she dies. This she said with resignation and no apparent regrets.

Because Mrs. Wakiro kept returning obsessively to the subject of mother-in-law, which was the central focus of her entire marriage, we had to retrace steps to learn of other experiences during those years. We inquired about her life during World War II and the bombings in Tokyo as well as the food shortages everyone suffered.

"We did not have to evacuate because there was very little bombing in our area. But some of our relatives' homes were ruined, and they came to stay at our house. We had to find food for them as well as for ourselves. It was difficult. I took several of my kimonos to farmers to exchange for vegetables. I had to go considerable distances to find food. Farmers acquired fine items and became the richest people at that time in Japan."

In contrasting the past with the present, Mrs. Wakiro is impressed with the many changes that have taken place in Japan in her life time. "Today, we are surrounded by many objects, too many, in fact. The past was better. If you have too much available, you are not aware of how precious things are. You do not appreciate what you have." However, in thinking about herself she stated, "In recalling my life, particularly since coming to this nursing home, I think I have lost my sense of being thankful. I have plenty and must be careful as I look back on my life. I must be grateful for all I get here. They offer me many services and take care of me because I have no children to help me. I have visitors, my neighbors and nieces. My neighbors and I became good friends after my husband's death, and it was with them I traveled."

In the nursing home, Mrs. Wakiro has made no friends. She talks with people, but they are not really friends. However, she occupies herself with the many programs the home offers such as calligraphy, painting, music, and handwork. She continues to read voraciously. Fortunately her sight is good. Currently she is reading religious books on life and death, studying some Catholic writers on this subject.

"I read difficult books. At this moment, I am reading an especially difficult one written by a professor at Sophia University. I want to continue my studies and readings for the rest of my life which will not be for very long. I don't want to waste my life; I want the remaining

days to be meaningful. So I read and think."

We, in turn, supported Mrs. Wakiro wish, acknowledging the importance of keeping her mind alert and developing her own philosophy, one that comes from within her and not just what she has read. She was touched as she said, "Thank you for saying so." Unfortunately, she has not found anyone in the home to talk with about these profound thoughts. "I wish I could talk to someone to share my thinking." She looked sad and so alone as she spoke these words, and we, in response, urged her to discuss the philosophy book with the social worker in this home who had studied and taught philosophy. Mrs. Wakiro's last words to us were, "I want to cherish the few years I have left. They are important. I am grateful to the people here and hope to live happily for the rest of my life in this home."

Mrs. Wakiro had a number of losses in her life that are revealed in her present reflections and that had a lasting effect on her. She evokes sympathy as one listens to her slow, deliberate, and depressive speech. At one year of age, she lost her mother. She did not have her step-mother to herself as long as she would have wished and needed, considering how young she was at the time. Furthermore, probably because of the birth of her two younger siblings, she had to share her step-mother with them before she was psychologically ready. She lost her wish to make her own decisions about her studies, career, and dream of becoming a librarian. Her desires were ignored in favor of a marriage she did not want. She presents her marriage as a loss of freedom. As she describes it, she even lost her ability to make decisions and felt constricted, fearful, and overwhelmed by her mother-in-law. She claims that she never wanted children and one may speculate why she did not have any. This, too, was a loss because she could not experience motherhood. Interestingly, several years after the death of her mother-in-law and husband, she tried to compensate by mothering students who were intellectually her equal.

Mrs. Wakiro never had sufficient opportunities to truly assert herself. Fulfillment came only in old age, after the demise of her husband and mother-in-law. She still rationalizes her relationship with mother-in-law as she obsesses about what a wonderful person she was. She cannot admit to herself the depth of anger she very likely felt toward this infirm but domineering woman. It appears that she had to free herself of the guilt engendered by these feelings by writing a book about her. Clearly,

her husband did not relieve her of the burdens of caring for his mother. He took for granted that this was her responsibility. In the Japanese society of that era, this was a way of life and women were resigned to their daughter-in-law role. Takie Sugiyama Lebra, the famous Japanese anthropologist, refers to the "general obsession with the in-law relationship" found in many Japanese marriages. In her interviews with women, the respondents "tended to call my attention immediately to how much they suffered under severe mothers-in-law or, conversely, how lucky they were to have nice in-laws" (Lebra, 1984, p. 141). Lebra states further that, "Underlying all these demands (made by mother-in-law on her daughter-in-law) was the imperative of compliance with the senior supervisor" (p. 144). Mrs. Wakiro presents a picture of a typical mother-in-law syndrome which she endured for over 30 years. She is not the only elderly woman with whom we talked who referred to her years after the death of her husband and mother-in-law as a time when they could pursue activities long not permitted. Many women openly stated that they achieved freedom in old age. Mrs. Wakiro is one of these women. She never gave up her wish to study and develop the intellectualism her step-mother cultivated in her as a child. Now, as she is preparing for the final life experience, confrontation with death, she is approaching it in the same manner, looking to books to help her.

The Japanese culture stresses that women are expected to endure stoically whatever life presents them. They are trained in self-discipline, patience, and devotion. To depart from this ideal of womanhood, "in Japanese society often is a feat of heroic proportions" (Lebra, Paulson, and Power, 1976, p. 303). Mrs. Wakiro is a fine example of the Japanese woman of the past era who could not follow her own life designs, who endured a life limited by her total devotion to her mother-in-law and obliteration of her own wishes, and who showed the self-discipline that made her an exemplary ideal Japanese woman. Only in old age was she able to resume her girlhood dreams, but it was too late to pursue her many interests and to follow her personal wishes to involve herself in her ambition to become a professional librarian. She is now content immersing herself in her books, her writing, and religion. She is preparing herself for death with the same patience and endurance that she was forced to experience from the day of her marriage. She is well prepared.

Chapter 21

❧

Mrs. Kaga:
A Lady
of Action

We were particularly pleased to interview Mrs. Kaga, whom we met at a senior center, because she had combined a nursing career with marriage and raising a family before World War II. We were eager to learn how she managed to do this in the Japanese culture where professional women, especially in her generation, had considerable difficulties in being accepted as well as in balancing the demands of family and career. Even today, pursuing a professional career, in contrast to working at an ordinary job, is difficult, and many well-educated women do not remain in long-term professional work (Lebra, 1984, p.229).

Mrs. Kaga was one of the most active, dynamic, kinetic, and expressive women we interviewed. Her conduct reflected her enthusiasm and eagerness to talk with us. At 89, she is very much aware of her appearance, her body posture, especially her straight back, and, most important, how others react to her outspoken manner. She is not only articulate but also demonstrates with gestures and action what she is describing and accompanies her movements with engaging laughter. She is aware that she can be entertaining and dramatic and enjoys the attention she elicits. She came eagerly to the interview, prepared to be responsive and enjoy it. The center staff had described her as "a strong character." She had decided opinions on many subjects including the need for elderly women to exercise their bodies. For greater emphasis several times during the interview she demonstrated her daily exercises.

In appearance, Mrs. Kaga has a lively face, full of expression. Her high forehead and straight, short, grey hair brushed off her face add to her vigorous, erect body and give her a striking appearance. She presents herself in an assertive manner, very much aware of her impact on people. She commented laughingly that she often frightens others by her directness. Her clothes are old, simple, and neat, but it is evident that she does not spend much money on herself.

Mrs. Kaga lives in Tokyo outside the geographic area of the senior center where we interviewed her. Technically, she should not be attending this center. However, in her usual persuasive manner, she was able to induce the authorities to allow her to participate in the Japanese dance class once a week. She hopes to return to live in this area in a few

months when a rental apartment will be ready for occupancy. She lived here previously, in fact, since 1951. For the past 26 years, she has been a widow living alone.

Born shortly before the turn of the century, Mrs. Kaga was the fourth of six children; she had three sisters and two brothers. The family, including her father's parents, lived together in a village near Nagoya. Her grandfather held an important position as the shoya or headman of the village, and, therefore, was close to the daimyo, the feudal lord who controlled a huge estate and who in turn was responsible to the shogun. That was during the Tokugawa era (1615-1865) and into the Meiji Restoration (1865-1912). Her grandfather managed his own land, supervised the farmers for the daimyo, governed the village, and collected the taxes. Being only the second son, her father did not inherit that honorific position and, instead, busied himself with gardening and playing go, a favorite game of Japanese men. He also had the honor of serving one of the most important daimyos under the Shogun of the Tokugawa clan.

Mrs. Kaga's family believed in education for all their children and sent them to public school. After that, each was expected to select specialized training. Her two brothers became potters, and her younger sister studied sewing. She did not speak of her other two sisters. When Mrs. Kaga decided to study nursing, she came to Tokyo to enroll in the Red Cross Hospital Nursing School. Her reason for choosing nursing is best expressed in her own words.

"I became a nurse because I was very weak. When I was a young child, my parents were told by a doctor that I would not live long. Because of this, I decided that I had to take care of myself, and, therefore, I picked nursing as the proper career.

"My parents did not pamper me. They dressed me like a boy and placed me in the garden where grass grows. I picked the grass, played in the mud, and became healthy. Within the earth, there is energy, and I absorbed it from the soil and from the sunshine because I was outdoors so much. I grew from the energy of the light of the sun and the roots in the earth."

We could not learn from her the nature of the medical problem that justified such an ominous prognosis, only that treatment "in the usual way" would do her no good. That is why the doctor prescribed the outdoors. "So my parents raised me like a boy. My sisters were dressed in beautiful kimonos, but I wore my brothers' clothes and was raised like

my brothers." She enjoyed this special status and identified with her brothers. When her brothers' friends fought with them, she would hit the boys. With much laughter, she described how she frightened the boys by showing them her rash (erysipelas) to deter them from striking her.

She repeatedly referred to herself as having a poor, weak body. Because of that, not only was she raised in this unusual manner, but she decided that she would not marry. "And if I were to live alone, I had to learn to know how to take care of myself. So I decided to become a nurse."

Even when she eventually decided to marry, her selection of a husband was dominated by what she perceives as her physical weakness.

"I did not think of marriage because I was weak, and if a weak person marries, family life will not be well organized. But then I thought, who will help me and bury me when I am old? My parents were dead. So I decided to marry. I had many men interested in me. But, because of my weak health, I had to be careful not to destroy my family by choosing the wrong type of husband."

She selected her husband from among her many suitors because he was weak! In doing so, she thought that, at the least, they could understand each other. She also had another reason. "If I was lying in bed weak, and if he was strong, he would go out to play around and I would be left home alone." Therefore, a weak man was preferable!

Mr. Kaga was a manager of a branch bank; she claims that he retired because of poor health. Nevertheless, he made a good living for her and their two daughters. She wed at age 30, and at 63, she became a widow when her husband died of a brain hemorrhage.

At this point, we observed that she went into a profession that required considerable strength. She replied, "I cannot rely upon doctors. I have to take care of my own health. I am still weak and must exercise." With this, Mrs. Kaga demonstrated her innumerable facial exercises to avoid cataracts, exercises to keep her back firm and straight, and exercises to keep her knees and other parts of her body from deteriorating. "I wake up at 5:30 a.m. every day to exercise for at least one hour. It is no good to exercise for ten minutes."

Mrs. Kaga's parents died when she was in her early 20s; first, her father died of a brain hemorrhage and her mother of lung disease several years after Mrs. Kaga finished her studies. For that reason, Mrs. Kaga took responsibility for her younger sister's education, paying her tuition

to study sewing in Tokyo. "Sewing was a good way for a woman to make a living," she explained.

Mrs. Kaga had a great deal to say about her own career.

"Being at the Red Cross Hospital, I was called upon whenever any serious events occurred such as the Earthquake of 1923 and, a number of years later, the Sino-Japanese War. At that time, I went into the battle-field. I was in China for six years serving as a Red Cross nurse. I cared for both Japanese and Chinese soldiers equally. It wasn't a case of the enemy and the Japanese. Every human being is the same so, as a nurse, my job was to care for all people. I wore my uniform every day except when bathing. I was busy caring for soldiers. There was no time even to eat lunch when a battle was taking place. Fortunately, it was not like that all the time.

"I was happy when the patients got well. I was sad when soldiers died. When they died, I prayed that God would care for them so that they could go to heaven. When I had to look after a patient who was dying, it was a very sad experience. Generally, it was in the midst of the battlefield, but we had to bury him properly. We would dig a hole, put wooden planks on the ground, and then burn the dead. Seeing all of this in front of my eyes was a sad, shocking experience. It was real hell!"

We commented that she was a real survivor and asked her to recollect other events about that period. She could only add that her hearing was impaired because a bomb exploded near her during one of the battles.

Mrs. Kaga had a long career. She started training after completing secondary school and worked until retirement age. During that period, she served in China, returned to Japan, married, had two children, and continued her career at several large Tokyo hospitals, retiring after having been head nurse in the Red Cross Hospital.

When asked how she had time to bring up her two daughters in a way she thought was proper, she replied, "It is the duty of every human being to care for her children. And, if you have a job, you must do it." She had only two children because she wanted them to go to a university and, therefore, she could not afford to have more than two.

"If I had wanted to have more children, I would have had to marry a millionaire. It's nonsense to raise children for your own joy. If you are a responsible parent, you have to plan and think carefully, especially if you want them to go to a university."

Both daughters worked for the American Army of Occupation after

their university studies and were offered jobs in the U.S.A. eventually, which they declined. The older daughter, when she married, went with her husband to his business assignment in the United States and later to Canada. However, when the company ordered them to return to Japan, they were not prepared to give up their big house and garden. Instead, her son-in-law changed jobs in order to stay in Canada. Mrs. Kaga visited them last year, and they traveled together through parts of the United States and Canada. She enjoyed it and showed us pictures of her trip. She writes frequently to her daughter.

The younger daughter married a company man in Tokyo. With a decided change of tone and facial expression, Mrs. Kaga commented that daughter died ten years ago.

"I cried for one year. I really wanted to die also. When she was alive, she visited me frequently, but now my grandchildren don't visit much. I feel so lonely."

We observed that it is very hard for a mother when an adult child dies. Her immediate response to this sensitive subject was to jump up, then to lie on the floor to demonstrate the exercises people should do to keep healthy. When her anxiety was under control, she returned to talk about her daughter.

"I was sad and wanted to die. But, I could not die, of course, so I thought that I should protect myself by exercising. Before, I used to exercise in a military style. But when you get old, you need different exercises, ones that are less vigorous. You have to be conscious of your age and must protect your back by lying on it when exercising so that you don't fall."

Whenever the subject of death was broached, Mrs. Kaga demonstrated her exercises. We observed that she had two serious losses, her husband 26 years ago and her daughter 10 years ago, and that it took strength to handle her grief. She responded, "I think that man is born alone and dies alone. When a baby is born, the parents care for it. But when you die, you are not certain that someone will take care of you. It's each person's last duty to prepare for death." Mrs. Kaga married to have children who would bury her when she died. Unspoken now is the fact that her surviving daughter is in Canada and not quickly available and that it was Mrs. Kaga who had to bury her other daughter. When we commented that we all have to think of such things when we get old, she responded by demonstrating exercises and massages to keep her body

healthy and alive. She sits straight, she pointed out, so that "all nutrition can go through the body." When she rides the bus, she taps people on the shoulder to remind them to sit straight. Laughing, she acknowledged that they react with surprise.

Mrs. Kaga spends many hours each week going to four senior centers in order to attend their dance classes. She is remarkably graceful, but, for her, dance may be viewed as another form of exercise which she pursues obsessively. She demonstrated a few movements in a most elegant manner.

When we asked Mrs. Kaga if she had evolved a philosophy of life, given her many experiences, she could not answer directly. She does not think in conceptual terms. Her life has been action-oriented from birth and, hopefully, will remain this way until her death. Even though she is 89 years of age, she continues her activities in order to maintain her health and to avoid the doctor's prediction of an early death. Her preoccupation with health and exercises on the one hand, and her frequent exposure to death in her professional life appear to be incongruous, phobic and counterphobic. Her response to our question ultimately was, "I think that everyday life is important. Food is important to keep in good shape. You have to be careful about what you eat, and you must have an upright life so that everything will go smoothly. It is important to walk and not dawdle." And when she was asked what advice she would give to younger people, her final words were, "The important thing is that mothers should instruct their children; present day mothers are different from those of the past. Today mothers do not care how their children's hair looks. Some look like a bird's nest." Hence, her advice is that parents must be educated and concerned about their children's health and appearance.

Mrs. Kaga was a stimulating and entertaining woman to interview. Many of her actions were dramatic, unexpected, and unpredictable. Her responses were frequently delayed as she sought to control her anxiety when sensitive subjects arose. She uses exhibitionism and humor to defend herself when depressive feelings are aroused. There is a frantic quality in many of her actions, indeed, in her entire life pattern. She is still running in many directions to avoid the fears of death, weakness, and loneliness. She is counterphobic in exposing herself to dangerous situations which require strength and stamina in order to prove to herself she can survive. Currently, she is narcissistically preoccupied with

her body and still sees herself as entitled to be treated differently from other people, just as when she was as a child. She enjoys shocking others and asserting her ideas. She is not a typical Japanese woman, yet she clings to traditional Japanese tenets.

Mrs. Kaga stands high, straight, and strong, serving as a bridge between the past and the present with respect to women. Although she cannot conceptualize how her life has been a model for present day women, she is very proud of her achievements. She represents the paradox seen in Japan today in which women are still expected to lead a life based on past traditions while, at the same time, forced by present changes to assume responsibilities that are the antithesis of the past. She was born during the Meiji Restoration when women, while permitted an education on a secondary school level, were not encouraged to have careers other than as elementary school teachers or nurses. But they were expected, upon marriage, to give up their professions, particularly after bearing children. Mrs. Kaga had no intention to marry, which was also a deviation from societal dictates, and purposely embarked upon a nursing career with the intention of being independent. But she went beyond the usual nursing career by enrolling in the Red Cross which led her into the battlefields of China without nationalistic overtones. She is a modern woman who has made her own decisions in most areas of her life. She carefully planned her life in selecting and pursuing her career, in choosing her husband, and in determining the number of children she could afford. As chief nurse in several large hospitals, she did not shrink from leadership and daily made many important decisions. By Japanese standards, she is unlike the average woman who is expected to be strong within the family, deferential to men, and unassertive in the community. Yet, self-assertion would appear to be a trait from childhood, and, in adult years, it was her way of life and ingrained in her personality.

Mrs. Kaga attributes her unusual upbringing, so different from her sisters', to the physical weakness she supposedly had as a child. Her identification with her brothers and her parents' permission to be free of the usual feminine restraints, stood her in good stead throughout her career, her marriage, and her widowhood. Even though devastated by the death of her younger daughter and the lack of relatedness of her grandchildren, she is able to cope with living alone and to control her depressive feelings. Her emphasis on exercise and her concentration on her physical well-being reflect this same assertive, positive, and deter-

mined approach to life.

The theme of physical weakness, which Mrs. Kaga repeated throughout the interview, reflects her perennially paradoxical and conflicted state. The weaker she feels, the more she has to fight to counteract it; and the stronger she becomes, the more vulnerable she feels she may become. She entered a profession in which weakness is unacceptable; she exposed herself to dangers on the battlefield most men and women would do anything to escape; she selected a weak husband to avoid being dominated or abandoned by a strong male; and she organized and planned her life carefully in order to assure herself that she was in control. Yet, she protests she still feels weak!

Mrs. Kaga is more at home in modern Japan with its substantially increased freedom of expression and reduced repression of women. If these changes had not occurred and feudalistic traditions had continued, she would have been the non-conformist par excellence. Her strength lies in her sense of organization and her ability to adapt effectively in a wide variety of circumstances, such as war, physical problems, medical institutions, widowhood, and loss of family members. She comes on strong with people to avoid appearing weak. This is her continuous battle.

In observing her frenetic quality as she dashes day after day from one senior center to another ostensibly to study dance, she would appear to be having a difficult time at this moment in maintaining her defenses. She is lonely. She is 89 and, therefore, confronting the possibility of frailty, inability to care for herself, and having no family to care for her in the event of illness and death. She is trying desperately to control her anxiety.

Mrs. Kaga presents today's women with a legacy through her example of an adaptable, strong, assertive woman who could combine career, marriage, and motherhood. This type of woman is in the process of emerging in Japan in spite of the continuing emphasis in women's education on "the good wife and wise mother" dictum from the Meiji era's ideal of womanhood. Independence, assertiveness, personal satisfaction, and individual development are qualities that have yet to be recognized as virtues. Nevertheless, as women are moving into the work place increasingly and as they are living longer and, therefore, confronting widowhood, some of the traits modeled by Mrs. Kaga may become more acceptable. It is hoped that the present generation of women will find

in her life story a demonstration of the vitality and determination that are urgently needed for women to develop more fully as they take their place in modern society and live to a ripe old age.

Chapter 22

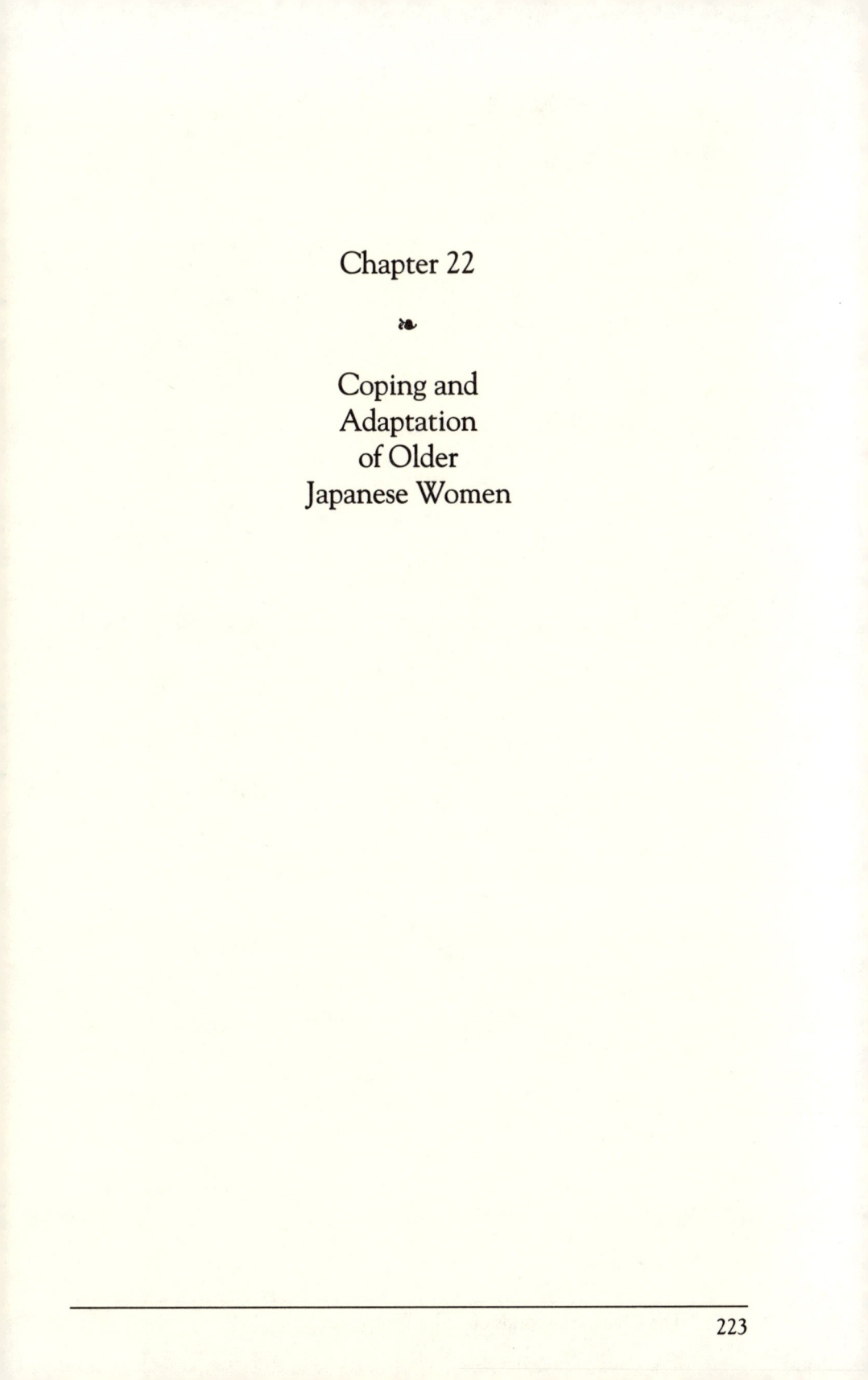

Coping and
Adaptation
of Older
Japanese Women

A life review is merely a key step in a process of confirming one's identity and defining the meaning of one's life. Although that is true at any age, it is particularly the case in old age. That review is more than a chronological log of a person's life events. More importantly and precisely, it is the person's effort to capture a unique sense of self, to make a final assertion of one's humanness and identity, and, to a very major extent, summarize how one has coped with life's vicissitudes. For some older people, it is also a declaration of a philosophy of life.

However, the listener often contributes to the richness of a life review. That is done both by validating what is being shared and by providing external stimuli and insights into the facts disclosed. For example, the listener discovers how the person has grown and developed, what has contributed to the particular personality formation, and, equally important, how the person has adapted to, and coped with the many changes and events everyone experiences during a lifetime.

People cope differently with the basic life milestones. These include primarily childhood and adolescence, young adulthood and marriage, parenthood, midlife, and the achievement of old age. In addition, there are many unique experiences such as occupation, status, accomplishments, traumas, losses, deaths, roles, relocations, wars, and peace that also challenge a person's coping abilities. Each person approaches these events, demands, and related problems in a highly individualized way. This is true even in Japan where the culture is essentially group-oriented and mandates stricter social conformity than in the United States. Individualism is neither encouraged nor favored in Japan. Nevertheless, as Japanese people move through the life cycle under the identical cultural umbrella, each person copes and adapts uniquely in confronting the inevitable changes in the progression from one stage of life to another and to life events (Breytspraak, 1984; Coelho, Hamburg, Adams, 1974).

As older people recall their life experiences, they think back about a number of significant facts, events, and people. Those include their upbringing, their parents, their siblings and schooling, their marriage and parenthood, their occupations, their lives after their children left home and married, their retirement, and their old age. Special events,

such as relocations, widowhood and other losses, care of in-laws, disabilities and health problems, earthquakes, wars, and post-war events loom large (Mathews, 1979).

As they recount these events, they find that patterns and themes in their lives surface. They are sometimes astonished by what they perceive, as if they are undergoing revelations. This experience can lead the more philosophical and thoughtful among them to search for deeper meanings in their lives and to assert their life values. We observed this among a number of the older Japanese women, especially as they objected to war and as they criticized the values represented by the present affluence that they perceive as waste.

In this study, it was possible to appreciate their individuality and character development as we played the role of the life review listener. We explored their adaptive and coping capacities in following their life stories. It was particularly revealing to analyze the strategies they adopted in the face of many devastating events that very likely destroyed weaker people. These include experiencing divorce and widowhood; being the sole wage earner while caring for children and mothers-in-law; nursing ill spouses, parents, and in-laws under extremely trying circumstances; unhappy marriages; surviving wartime bombings, evacuations, and food shortages; returning to war-ravaged Japan from Manchuria and China after Japan's defeat; being physically handicapped; being institutionalized; and suffering personal abuse. It is only because of their insights that we could understand them and appreciate who they were and what in their personalities made it possible for them to cope, adapt, and survive.

The women in this study of adaptation and coping were not selected because they had special histories. In fact, only one had a business executive and public service career that was unusual for a Japanese woman in that era, and only two had the unique experience of growing up in a foreign country. A few had successful positions in their family businesses, however. Several had successful professional careers acceptable for women in the Japanese culture, namely teaching, nutrition, and nursing.

The women were selected primarily because they were willing to share their life reviews with us. With one exception, they did not consider themselves unusual, and they did not see themselves as a select group. Most were middle class, but a number came from very poor families; several were very well educated, but most had a relatively lim-

ited education. Two were single, most had been married, and many were widowed for a number of years. Two were divorced. Several of those who had married were childless, but most were mothers of from one to five children. They came originally from the countryside as well as from the city. But all, when they were young adults, coped with life in a militaristic and authoritarian nation that had a feudalistic disregard for women's rights. After the War, this changed to a considerable extent although even today the Japanese admit women are capable of achieving a higher status than is as yet permitted. Most important, the elderly women lived through an extended war period when women were expected to assume responsibilities for which they had no education and preparation, and they did very well. Finally, they weathered the transition from autocracy to democracy and from the narrowly prescribed societal constraints on women's lives to broadened opportunities.

The older women have lived through profound historical changes that have required tremendous adaptive capacities. Some readily adopted the new values brought about by post-war democracy and the American Occupation. Others still clung to the pre-war ways, being fearful and resistant to giving up the traditions they found comfortable for unpredictable, unfamiliar, and individualistic values. And some, without much thought, passively accepted whatever was necessary to survive.

Before summarizing how these Japanese women adapted to changes in their lives, it is important to define the concepts of adaptation, coping, mastery, and defenses. Adaptation refers to strategies of dealing with problems that arise either every day or in unusual situations, ranging from mild frustrations to complex predicaments. Coping refers to adaptation under relatively difficult, acute situations and dislocations that depart from usual patterns and require new behavior. The problems that trigger adaptation generally cause discomfort, anxiety, despair, guilt, shame, and grief (White, 1974). Coping involves actions taken to avoid being harmed by life's strains in order to prevent, avoid, or control emotional distress (Pearlin and Schooler, 1978). Mastery is the exertion of cognitive and manipulative efforts to solve complex problems without excessive anxiety and frustration. Finally, a person seeks defenses to respond to perceived danger and anxiety when necessary to avoid becoming so overwhelmed that it is not possible to function and solve the problem adequately (White, 1974).

People who lack the ability to accept change, to make accommoda-

tions to new situations, and to confront crises and strains that inevitably occur during a lifetime are fated to lead very troubled, even chaotic lives. Rigidity, disorganization, constriction, withdrawal, seclusion, and poor reality testing may result. There is no such thing as a frustration-free or conflict-free life. Problems inevitably arise — some foreseen, but many unanticipated, and people must be able either to compromise or to cope by adopting innovative behaviors and ways to handle new situations. Doing so requires some autonomy or freedom to act, cognitive abilities to perform problem-solving, and information processing to carry through solutions. Coping also requires the type of personality that is not over-whelmed by crises, has internal stability, and can sufficiently control anxiety to be able to act rationally and planfully. In other words, people who cope successfully have the capacity for adaptation to novel situations in an ever-changing world.

"Adaptive behavior involves the simultaneous management of at least three variables: securing adequate information, maintaining satisfactory internal conditions, and keeping some degree of autonomy" (White, 1974, p. 58). White observes that studies in coping reveal that persistence, the will to live, courage, and heroism are as much part of human nature as the retreats, evasions, and petty impulse gratifications found in the behavior of people who have poor adaptive abilities (p. 64).

Under stress or during emotional upsets resulting from life's problems, successful coping and adaptation generally involve three types of responses: (1) responses that modify the situation; (2) responses that control the meaning of the problem by changing it from something negative to something positive; and (3) responses that convert the stresses from unavoidable hardships into "moral virtue, using such defenses as denial, passive acceptance, withdrawal, magical thinking, blind faith, and avoidance" (Pearlin and Schooler, 1978, p.7).

People cope with stress in a wide variety of ways. Some react with strong emotions; some are controlled and reflective; some show passive forbearance; some become self assertive; some demonstrate strength and determination; some express helplessness and resignation; finally, a number express optimistic faith (Pearlin and Schooler, p. 7). Success in coping is measured by how well it prevents hardships from resulting in emotional stress and disintegration. A variety of coping mechanisms must be present in one's life repertoire because the attributes needed to confront stresses in marriage and family life are different from those

needed in community and occupational situations.

Problems in family relations increase particularly during periods of social change. Then, one finds more violence, suicides, protests, and disruptions. Thus, a turbulent urban environment reveals increased social pathology leading to new values and new adaptive norms. Family problems become, as a result, indicators of social and institutional changes. These observations were especially evident in this study as the older Japanese women reviewed their lives, their joys, and their tragedies and losses during World War II and in the immediate post-war period. Most of these women had to work to help support their family and themselves. Many of them had become widows and, therefore, had to assume added roles and burdens. Several divorced their husbands. Others admitted enduring unhappy marriages and expressed relief when their husbands and in-laws died. Finally, the adaptation to the single family unit in contrast to the multigeneration family presented other problems.

Generally, as we have seen, during the War, the women shouldered burdens admirably and maintained their families alone remarkably well under severely trying and hazardous conditions. This was described by the women at great length in the preceding chapters.

In any discussion of coping and adaptation, a reference must be made to the internationally recognized crisis studies of Gerald Caplan. He was interested in how people react to serious life events and in their abilities to master emotional stresses at those times. In crises, they have to mobilize their resources to change the environment, reduce their feelings of threat, find alternative sources for satisfaction, and solve their problems. Under stress, people feel more vulnerable and must find means within themselves to muster their resources. However, each person also assesses each situation in terms of a unique, culturally determined perspective, set of values, and tradition (Caplan, 1981). While in crises people must work through their feelings, assemble their inner resources, and focus on goals and methods for problem resolution, Caplan comments that a social support system is extremely helpful in the process. In a society that is centered on the family, it becomes a source of stress-relief and support. This, indeed, is what we saw in most of our interviews. Where family supports were missing, and there were several such cases, unhappiness, heightened anxiety, withdrawal, or tragic resignation were found.

In analyzing the coping capacities of the women interviewed, a num-

ber of factors must be noted with regard to the timing of the changes and events necessitating adaptation. They include personality and life style, age, life situation, environment, important events like war, economics, and disasters, family, and the fit between inner resources, community services, and social support systems. Further, we must take note of mental status at the time of stress, the accumulation of losses and multiplicity of crises, evidence of self-esteem, morale, and social and psychological functioning. Each woman's perception of crucial events, beliefs, values, and culture also contributed to her coping abilities at the times of stress. Finally, physical disabilities inevitably influence her ability to tolerate and cope with crises.

To evaluate the coping capacities of the interviewees, we learned how they generally handled stress and the accompanying tensions. Some were tense when confronting new situations and reacted both physically and emotionally. Others tried to avoid acknowledging their problems, and a number tackled solutions logically and selectively. A few saw the crises as challenges to be confronted, mastered, and even resolved creatively. Some used denial, and others rationalized a bad situation by fatalistically saying it was God's will or that they deserved to be punished. Most, with the assistance of their family support system, mastered very serious situations. Some were over-dependent and insisted upon being cared for.

In reviewing the personalities, one could predict their coping patterns even as they described their early life. Those who were independent and assertive reported innumerable situations, however serious, in which they successfully found new ways of adapting to the unanticipated. Miss Katase, always self-reliant, when she realized she would not marry, sought a profession that would be satisfying in itself and meet her need to help people. She became a nutritionist. Mrs. Takahara, brought up in a household that emphasized independence, when confronted with evacuation from Tokyo, assembled her young students, found a ryokan in the mountains, and with the help of a janitor and her sister for over two years, continued to teach. Mrs. Nakai, held by the Chinese Communist Army for eight years, became a leader among her colleagues, eagerly learned new skills, and upon her return to Japan established her own business. Mrs. Mase, widowed just as the War began, became a college teacher and later a business executive and community leader. The successful women described themselves as independent and re-

sourceful young people. Clearly, their basic personalities permitted them to cope with the trying times they faced as adults during the War.

Institutionalization in old age presents an especially difficult coping challenge. Three of the women were in nursing homes. All were bound to the wheelchair, had no hope for recovery, and were confronted with the prospect of living in the home until death. There the similarities end. Mrs. Wakiro was depressed, resigned, and preparing for her death by reading deeply philosophical religious books. Her adult life had been one of resignation to caring for and being dominated by her mother-in-law and never being able to pursue the career that she had dreamed about in college. Miss Yabe, in contrast, was enjoying her new home after 20 years of life in a hospital. Because of her crippled condition and life-long illness, her family had virtually abandoned her. The elderly residents offered her the mothering she had not received growing up. Passivity and aggression were two themes in her life, and this was evident in her adaptation in the nursing home. Mrs. Akino, reared in severe poverty, had always tried to accept her trials with equanimity. Even her marriage was trying, and only after her husband's death did she start enjoying her life. Suddenly, at age 70, she lost the use of her legs, and now found herself in a nursing home. Accustomed to hardship, she accepted her present disability, made friends with residents, participated in activities, read, and enjoyed the arts and crafts.

Mrs. Saka, in her late 70s, offered an excellent example of a woman who saw herself as an independent person and in control. She coped remarkably well after her young physician husband died in the Sino-Japanese War. She was forced to support her three children and mother-in-law. She tried to be an entrepreneur several times, but was unsuccessful until she farmed and later ran a boarding house for students. Her tenacity and determination were remarkable. Nevertheless, each effort was a challenge in which she grew and coped. In old age, she enjoys talking politics with her grandchildren and wishes she was young enough to run for a political office.

Mrs. Kato described an indulged childhood, and in adulthood demonstrated a dependent personality. At each life crisis, she coped by relying on her mother, her in-laws, her husband, or her eldest son and daughter-in-law. Born to wealth, she expected to be cared for. During World War II, she evacuated to western Japan to stay in the countryside with her in-laws. Her husband, a highly cultured man, was very protective of

her and made few demands. Now, she is depressed because her husband suffers from Alzheimer's Disease. "He was the smart one. Who would have predicted that he would deteriorate and that I would remain mentally healthy. I'm exhausted watching him. I couldn't do it without my daughter-in-law and my son, the doctor." Mrs. Kato is fortunate because she has a strong family support system. She admits that without their loyalty and assistance, she could never manage.

Probably the most traditional and conservative woman we interviewed was Mrs. Hara, in her mid-70s, who lived with her daughter's family in a very modern home. This competent woman had adapted to many trying circumstances, but she always expected others to help solve her problems. Today, she spends most of her time doing church work and teaching the tea ceremony. Her wealthy father insisted girls should learn only to be teachers, which career she pursued until at age 22 she married. Her husband, also from a well-to-do family, worked in Indonesia, and there she learned to adapt to a foreign culture and to a more primitive, isolated life. Her most important task was to educate her three daughters. During the War, she returned to Japan and relied upon her husband's company to find her housing, to evacuate her to safe quarters when the bombing became dangerous, and to help her obtain food. She never sought a paying job. She clings to tradition and asserts that, "Women should assume only women's roles, teaching, marriage, and care of children, and should be the strength behind the men. Women have more freedom now, but should not try to do work men can do." The changes in Japan during her life time do not seem to have affected her.

In contrast, Mrs. Ishii, age 94, successfully coped with more changes and crises in life than most women. She had no extensive support system, insufficient education, and expected to work hard. She described herself as always taking the initiative when confronted with a problem. At age 21, she left the cold north to come to Tokyo. She worked on a cattle farm and eventually married her employer. She recalled the Earthquake of 1923 when their house was destroyed and they had to camp out. At age 39, she found herself a widow caring for five children and her mother-in-law. Undaunted, she continued to run the farm and sewed at night to support her family. When she could no longer manage financially, she sold the farm and took a job. During the War, she was evacuated to a mountainous area where, again, she found employment. Her children eventually married, and today she lives next

door to her youngest son about to retire. Each day, she walks to the senior center where she brings sweets to share with new friends. "I don't participate in the activities. I just like to sit and talk to people. This is the happiest time of my life. I have no responsibilities, and no demands are made on me. I do what I feel like doing, and I am happy." At no time did she complain or voice any regrets. She accepted the fact that she confronted an extraordinary number of difficulties. She saw hard work as the expected way of life. That she had survived to be 94, physically well, and happy mattered most.

Mrs. Minato, too, came from a farm family and worked hard. However, she is a passive woman who accepted whatever life brought to her. She rarely made her own decisions. Relationships were never deep. Resignation and fatalism characterized her outlook all her life. When we met her in the hospital, she was not coping well. Abandoned by her son, unwanted by her daughter-in-law, ignored by her five other children, and told that she could not return to live with her daughter-in-law, Mrs. Minato was stunned, dazed, confused, depressed, and helpless. At 76, with only a small pension, she had nowhere to go, no family support system to help her, and no knowledge of resources. The hospital social workers were trying to help her. She coped by accepting their suggestions unquestioningly, just as all her life she had done with her family, her husband, and her children.

Each of the twenty-seven women had a unique coping repertoire. Most of them were remarkably adaptable in the face of the innumerable upheavals and severe traumas they endured. That was revealed in their capacity to survive earthquakes and wars, hard labor, and, for a number, poverty. They lived through the changed post-war social and economic scene with its western character. Now, in old age, as we see from their vignettes and interviews, they continue to confront life with the same patterns they developed early in their lives. Some are depressed because of problems presented by old age, some are still seeking for what they did not have in their youth, and others are facing old age wiser and less troubled.

The previous chapters record more fully, primarily in their own words and with substantial commentary by the interviewer, the life experiences of seventeen of the twenty-seven women interviewed. For some, old age is the best time in their lives. For a number it is a burden. Some regret that their lives were so directed that they had little control. They would

have liked more autonomy and more choices. They envy young women today who are free to seek a university education. A few preferred past traditions to the present freedoms. A number were apprehensive about the future which is not surprising given their ages. They were fearful about being a burden to their children as they grow older. Others feared that their children would not want to help them if they became frail and disabled. On the other hand, many expected their children to care for them until they die. However, with few exceptions, women interviewed coped remarkably well up to this time. But, a number of them, when they allowed themselves to think aloud, worried whether they could cope with physical or mental deterioration. Elderly, the world over, not just the Japanese, voice this concern. Given the longevity we now witness, and in spite of the Japanese culture that expects families to care for their aged parents, few aged want to be a burden. And those who coped and adapted best in their lifetimes, want this least of all.

Chapter 23

ₐ

Some Closing
Thoughts About
Japanese and
American Elderly
Women

In the preceding twenty-two chapters, we described the lives of 27 Japanese elderly women, as they were revealed by the life review process. We made the stories of most of them live by letting them speak for themselves. While seventeen are quoted almost verbatim in individual chapters, ten are referred to in the other chapters. We tried to present them in the straightforward manner in which they presented themselves. In the process, we heard their living histories, their values, their tales, their thoughts, their fears, their struggles, their failures, their successes, and their hopes.

The oldest women's lives spanned three eras starting with the Meiji Restoration and the beginnings of industrialization, westernization, modern militarism, and expansionism. That was followed by the more democratic but short Taisho period, and, then, the unusually lengthy, most recent, and constantly changing Showa epoch of military and authoritarian rule, wars, invasions, expansion, defeat, occupation, regeneration, and democratization. The remaining question to be considered now is how did the lives of these Japanese older women compare with their cohort in the U.S.A.? Because an American social work professor interviewed them with the collaboration of a Japanese psychologist, Japanese as well as Americans should be curious about this.

It is easy to dismiss this question by reflecting, "Of course, their lives were different from those of Americans because they experienced a very different culture; they lived on a relatively small island rather than on a huge land mass; their country was so devastated at the end of its last war that its older people pray 'Never again,' in contrast to a country that had not had a war on its own soil since the mid-1800s, and that had never been bombed." However, the answer is much more complex and requires a more lengthy analysis.

Actually, elderly women in Japan and in the U.S.A. share many of the same basic experiences. The elderly in both countries have been subject to innumerable, radical and rapid social and economic changes. They have adapted to new technologies, new political, economic, and social forces, wars, and new evolving philosophies. The impacts of these pressures and changes are universal. For some women, they have pro-

duced a sense of challenge, exhilaration, stimulation, and fulfillment. Many have accepted and adapted to whatever came their way with few questions while a few have been left feeling helpless, despairing, apathetic, or fatalistic.

Life cycle experiences are similar in both countries: infancy, childhood and education, young adulthood and marriage and children, middle age with growing children, old age and grandparenthood, retirement, and ultimately, death. In their late years, they confront the same aging problems of declining health, concern for their future and fear of being a burden to their children, increasing longevity, economic and housing problems, and deaths of spouses, siblings, and friends. It is the cultural environment and historical events that place differing significance and expectations on how the life cycle is lived and perceived.

No matter how much we may generalize with confidence based on historical and cultural indicators, individuals in both countries react to external events in terms of their own past experiences and unique personalities and not only because of cultural determinism. Therefore, the comparison of the lives of women in these two countries can only be valid in a broad sense. Each individual life history reveals, for example, similarities in dreams and aspirations and in reactions to joys and disasters. Are there many similarities? Are there many differences? The answer is "yes" to both questions and is already evident in their comments.

Perhaps the most conspicuous difference between the two groups is their philosophical orientations. Generally, Americans — men and women, old and young — live in a society in which individualism and independence is stressed and competition is expected (Lowy, 1988). They have the American dream of upward mobility and accumulation of the materials of this technological age. In recent years, Japanese have created their own materialistic dream, similar to that of the Americans. However, individualism still remains frowned upon and the group, be it the family, the colleagues at work, or the Japanese society at large, is pivotal in their life course and decisions. They cling closer than Americans to the family and their groups, especially work associates, for their identity. They are still extremely sensitive and responsive to group pressures, group demands, and cultural dictates. Being unique, standing out, taking leadership, appearing conspicuous or aggressive, and ignoring family and community criticism are not their way of life (Vogel, 1971; Christopher, 1983). These patterns of behavior, so pervasive in the past

that they were deemed to be a national trait, still persist among the aged. Even the young who want to shed them thus far have not been able to do so significantly.

Another difference between the two elderly groups is the tremendous variation of the cultural and ethnic backgrounds in the U.S.A., in contrast to the apparent homogeneity in Japan. The Japanese rarely intermarry with Caucasians or even with other Asians. Their backgrounds vary merely with regard to the prefectures of origin, urban versus rural birthplaces, and social class differences. With few exceptions, they are simultaneously Buddhists and Shintoists, but not likely to be religious in the American sense of church attendance. A few are Christians. Very few were born abroad.

The American elderly present a completely different picture. Although many today are native born, large numbers migrated to the United States from everywhere in the world, including Japan. Even if they are American born, their parents, grandparents, or great-grandparents came from abroad. When Japan was struggling to modernize during the Meiji Restoration, millions of Europeans were flooding onto the American continent annually. And once in the U.S.A., they did not necessarily set down roots in one place. Because the country is large, transportation easy, and opportunities available in innumerable places, people did not hesitate to migrate repeatedly. Americans are a mobile people and there is room to move. Family members are scattered around the country. Thus, while the Japanese migrated from the countryside to the cities and some migrated from Japan to other countries, the U.S.A. was the haven for people from all over the world who brought with them their own languages, cultures, religions, values, and dreams. However, most of their children did not necessarily maintain their parents' culture but adopted the New World's culture. With the exception of the American Indians, everyone has ancestry elsewhere. As a result, it is not surprising that diversity, differences, individuality, separation from one's roots, and a dualistic identity to one's country of ancestry and to the United States are common among elderly in America. Listen to the life review of an American 90 year old woman, even one born in the U.S.A., and you will not be able to anticipate and predict what she will recount in contrast to the Japanese. Because the elderly in the U.S.A. represent most of the races, religions, and ethnic groups in the world, each group needs to be studied separately to be understood. This is not the case in

Japan.

A considerable number of older American women are widowed, poor, and living only on their social security income. In fact, to be old, a woman, and Black or Hispanic, it is more than likely that she will be found living at or below the poverty line. In contrast, in Japan, many live with their children and have pensions, however small, and, therefore, poverty is not as serious a problem.

Tradition is most important in the lives of the Japanese older folks, while American elders, if they were born abroad and came to the U.S.A. as children or young adults, had to adapt to the American society and maintain a loose relationship to their country of origin (with the exception of the Hispanics who maintain close ties to their neighboring country-of-origin and the more recent Southeast Asians). Many elders who migrated to the U.S.A. years ago came because they sought a new life and new identity or to escape political and economic oppression. They wished to shed the old world. Yet, paradoxically, there is a growing tremendous awareness of ethnic origins in the U.S.A.; ethnic neighborhoods persist, and the "melting pot" concept has been proven a myth. Diversity, not sameness, characterizes the U.S.A.

While the Japanese elderly women were neither prepared nor educated to cope with change and upheaval, their American counterparts consider that to be a way of life. In reviewing the lives of the 27 women, we noted that they found themselves socially and educationally unprepared for the changes resulting from the nationalism and militarism of the 1930s and 1940s. They looked within themselves to find the capability to survive, especially during the wars. Their individual capacities and their apparently inherent organizational skills made this possible. If 27 random interviews were conducted among American elderly who were not economic, political or war refugees, one would guess that their lives probably would contain fewer radical changes, hazards, and traumas than their Japanese cohort.

The Japanese historical events shook up the traditional women's roles and lives because all economic groups were forced to work outside the home due either to early widowhood or the wars. In contrast, the lives of the Americans who grew up in an atmosphere that anticipates change, actually contained less obvious historical traumas. American working class and professional women were working outside the home long before World War II. However, it was World War II that drew the major-

ity of women in all socio-economic groups in both countries in droves from their homes to the factories and offices. With the end of the War, many had no wish to return to their former homemaker roles.

If one asks an American older non-refugee woman what was the most upsetting historical event she lived through, she is likely to mention the Great Depression. In contrast, the Japanese older woman will recount personal hardships in wars, bombings, evacuation, and adaptation to westernization and modernization.

Takie Lebra (1984) observed that because of the innumerable changes in their lives, "Older women (in Japan) come to appreciate, in retrospect, the traditional structure under which they lived harsh lives" (p. 299). This attitude is still strong. For example, Mrs. Mase, who had the most exposure to the West, having attended high school and college in the U.S.A., insisted that she preferred Japanese ways and traditional women's roles. Interestingly and ironically, the Japanese women we interviewed, although they expressed appreciation and envy of the numerous educational opportunities young women have today and a preference for their freedoms, cling to the traditional concepts of femininity and the woman's roles. Yet, almost all had been forced to depart from these roles and had been effective in their new capacities.

Studies in both countries reveal that the family is the focus and core of the lives of elderly women. Their families are supportive; neither Japanese nor American adult children are abandoning their parents (Cambell and Brody, 1985). Filial responsibility is not being ignored. But it is manifested differently in Japan from the U.S.A. (Sodei, 1987 Seoul speech; Sodei, 1987 St. Louis speech). There, many more elderly live with their families, as much as 60 percent (Maeda, 1983). In the U.S.A., elderly are more likely to live in their own homes but within easy reach of at least one of their children. Only 12 percent married elders and 17 percent single, widowed, or divorced elders live with their children (Shanas, 1980). Donow observes, "Both generations want independence, and both crave closeness" in the U.S.A. (1990, p. 486).

The women in the family are the caregivers to frail elderly in both countries. However, in Japan, the daughter-in-law is still the one most likely to care for her in-laws, whereas in the U.S.A., the daughter reaches out to her parents (Akiyama, Antonucci, Campbell, 1990). The Japanese culture, while it is still in transition from the feudalistic ie system, has not changed appreciably in its expectations that the oldest son will

assume responsibility for his aged parents. This, of course, places the actual burden on the daughter-in-law. However, the relationship between the mother-in-law and daughter-in-law may be changing because the aged parents rarely move into the son's home at age 60 as was the case in the past, nor does the oldest son take his bride into his parents' home, as was traditional. More elderly remain in their own homes well into their 70s, until one is widowed or no longer self-sufficient. Increasingly, daughters-in-law are resenting the responsibility and are discouraging their in-laws from moving into their homes. Ambivalence is more openly acknowledged (Mori, 1979; Koyano, 1989; Donow, 1990; Tobin, 1987), but this does not mean that there is a revival of the legend and myth of obasute, meaning "discarding granny" (Donow, 1990).

In Japan today, the nuclear family is established upon marriage, and the multi-generation family is formed many years later if at all. Thus, the former subservience of the daughter-in-law to the mother-in-law, when they lived under the same roof from the time of the oldest son's marriage, is less prevalent although it has not entirely disappeared (Akiyama, Antonucci, Campbell, 1988). Mrs. Mase and Mrs. Wakiro, both in their mid-80s, described very well the relationship that started at the beginning of their marriages when they were literally servants to their in-laws. However, in contrast, we saw the changes that have occurred when Mrs. Watari, in her late 60s, described her daughter-in-law's rejection of her to the extent of forcing her son to build her a tiny house next door to the large house they shared and to separate them with a huge fence. She sees her grandchild only when the daughter-in-law permits. Today, most of the intergenerational relationships in Japan are unlikely to be either of these extremes.

However, in present day Japan cultural patterns and practices are at odds. The oldest son is still venerated and preferred by the elderly, but daughters are being turned to increasingly. The legal abolition of the ie system, the popularity of the nuclear family, and the reduced size of the family led to this development. Most families have at most two children and, therefore, many seniors may have only daughters. In that case, the families usually adopt the husband of their oldest daughter, a practice that goes back in history. Many young women are not eager to marry eldest sons, and one observed to us that when she considered marriage, she asked the following questions about her suitor, "Is he handsome? Can he make a good living? Is he the second son?" A current study of

the reciprocal relationship between generations found that where the daughter-in-law was not caring for the mother-in-law, the daughter maintained a very close helping relationship (Akiyama, Antonucci, Campbell, 1990). However, in one of the families we interviewed, the two daughters, after caring for their ailing mother, demanded that their oldest brother and his wife assume this task. His wife was furious and resolved that if her mother-in-law would become ill, she would send her to a nursing home.

In both countries, while the responsibility for the care of the aged remains a family duty, it is becoming more difficult to retain this practice for a number of reasons. Elderly live much longer; urban housing remains small and constricted; and the life style of the dual-working couples makes it impractical or too arduous to care for an ailing parent. Thus, in both countries, family hardships and ambivalence force the community social institutions to create support services to help families and elderly (Asano, Saito, 1988; Freed, 1990; Maeda, Teshima, Sugisawa, Asakura, 1989). In both countries, the aged say, "I don't want to be a burden to my children when I become disabled and old." Lebra (1979) heard this frequently when she interviewed aged Japanese women, as did we. The attitudes and concerns in the two countries are not as different as they purport to be in this respect despite culture and traditions.

However, when we consider suicide among elderly women, the situation in Japan is different from the U.S.A. in that their rate is second only to late adolescents and is the second highest in the world (Lebra et al, 1976, p. 263; Lebra, 1979). Sister Rose Marie Cecchini (Lebra et al, 1976, pp. 263-297) attributes this to role conflict, persistent religio-cultural factors, and role disintegration. Furthermore, she found that they are acutely aware of their dependence (and helplessness if their health is failing), particularly when they become widowed. They, also, may feel very isolated even when living with the family. Asano, Maeda, and Shimizu found socio-economic factors had a substantial impact on the social isolation of the aged (1984). Christopher (1983) expands this observation. "... in their scheme of things, suicide can be the ultimate form of imposing guilt in others" (p.73). Suicide among American elderly women, while not as high as in Japan, nevertheless is the highest of any age group in the U.S.A. according to Kermis (1986, p. 200-203). Given the high rate of depression among elderly women, this is not a surprise, especially because women's greater longevity brings with it in-

creasingly poor health. However, other American authorities disagree with Kermis and stress the fact that white aged men have the higher suicide rate (Lowy, 1989, p. 180; Payne, 1975, pp. 292-293; Zarit, 1980, pp. 227-233). Zarit states that, "Among white women and nonwhites, suicide rates are lower at all ages, and are generally somewhat lower after 65 than in middle age. . . . Similar increases in age in suicides of men are found in virtually all Western countries" (p. 227).

The role concepts and role ideals of Japanese and American older women have few similarities. Both ordinarily grew up with the expectation of marrying and having children. Being a wife and mother were not rejected. But the similarities end there. Japanese women were (and still are) induced to believe that being a wife and mother are their most important roles in life. Educating the children in post-war Japan is their mandate, and they are held responsible by the family and society if their children are not successful. Their dual roles of wife and mother are not only traditional, but are frequently performed to exclude the husband from serious involvement. In post-war Japan, the women are, also, monopolizing the management of money (Vogel, 1971). Despite the changes brought about by higher education for women, employment of women outside the home, modernization, and westernization, the traditional role concept of the ideal wife and mother persists. Some analysts even describe the Japanese family of today as matriarchal within the home, and patriarchal only in the outside world (Lebra, 1984; Christopher, 1984).

The feminine role is viewed more broadly in the United States. Roles are not as clearly defined, and the suffragette tradition stresses equality and individual autonomy rather than gender role differences. That is not to say that no women in the United States agree with the Japanese view, any more than that there are no women in Japan who prefer the American feminist attitudes. In Japan, some women are moving slowly toward a more Western feminist view, while in the United States there are women who are protesting that the equality they seek is still elusive, and there are women who prefer the traditional role. The history of the Japanese women in the eras in which our interviewees grew up records that some women did rebel (Robin-Mowry, 1983), but their effectiveness was limited, they encountered innumerable road blocks and resistances. They still have an uphill battle. In contrast, today the feminist movement in the United States is well organized, political,

articulate, and, interestingly, has many leaders over the age of 60. While a number of the Japanese women we interviewed had traditional views about women's roles, many either approved of, or were envious of the young women in Japan who are receiving a higher education and have greater opportunities than they had.

Women enjoy very different seniority roles in Japan than in the U.S.A. Takie Lebra observes that, as women reach their seniority roles in Japan, they can become dominant in the family (1984, p. 299). In contrast, in the U.S.A., feminine seniority is not stressed or valued despite Erik Erikson's comments about wisdom in old age (1963).

The general concept of the role of women in Japan is more strictly and narrowly defined than in U.S.A. (Vogel, 1989). The more feminist-oriented women in Japan resent this, but the average Japanese woman has lived with it so long that she accepts it. The wife and mother role is dominant in her life, and she prefers her dominance in the domestic sphere (Vogel, 1963; Christopher, 1984). Remaining single is still frowned upon, and, at the same time, it is not easy for a married woman to choose a highly demanding career. If she does achieve a high status, the cooperation of her husband is essential, but not necessarily forthcoming. When these elderly women were growing up, a career was secondary and marriage demanded. Only two who were interviewed remained unmarried, one because of the War and lack of eligible men and the other because of her physical handicaps. Lebra observed that women over the marriageable age were willing to marry without love, and, after marriage, the husbands and wives would have nothing in common. Sometimes, however, after retirement, they might find that they had developed an affection over the years (Lebra, 1984, p. 300). Mrs. Watari described her marriage in these terms. This occurred in the lives of a number of the women we interviewed. However, interestingly, only a few interviewees spoke a great deal about their husbands. They concentrated on their own lives and own thoughts.

Primarily, in Japan, men were expected to have role specialization in their careers, but women were supposed to have only generalized roles, and these were considered inferior. In our interviews, the women who coped most successfully during life crises were those with careers or those who worked in businesses with their husbands and, therefore, became specialized. However, Lebra comments that whenever the husband and wife were equal, they would not allow this to be observed by the outside

world (1984, p. 301). She holds that the Japanese continue to be more asymmetrical than Americans in gender role expectations, and to accept males as being smarter, more competent, and more foresighted. Women in the United States generally reject role division and the concept of gender inferiority. Women have always interacted more freely with men. The historical frontier spirit portrays women in an active rather than in the passive role that the division of labor theory implies. Also, women who were immigrants in the U.S.A. had to work to help the family income.

American and Japanese elders contrast conspicuously in their political activities on their own behalf. Great numbers of American elderly are organized in lobbying groups to assure that they will receive government social and economic entitlements. These groups are led by elderly, many of them women. Similar organizations do not exist in Japan.

In contrast to the American concept of marriage offering companionship and equality, the Japanese marriage and family are described as vertical, i.e., the mother relates primarily to her children, her parents, and her in-laws, and the husband remains essentially on the side lines. This is particularly the case of the salary man class in the cities (Nakane, 1970; Vogel, 1963; Lebra et al, 1976). Takeo Doi (1971) believes that this vertical relationship makes the husband-father-son very dependent. From birth, the sons, especially the oldest son, are shown preference by the mother, can do no wrong, and receive special treatment and better education. Throughout life, the dependent relationship is fostered. Doi refers to it as amae. Even the mentor relationship concept, so common in Japan, is an extension of amae. A man's entire career may be dependent upon a mentor. Thus, the emphasis on dependence takes two directions: the man is encouraged from birth to be dependent upon the mother, which he might transfer to the wife later, and the woman from birth is encouraged to be dependent upon her family, and in old age upon her oldest son. This stress on dependence in relationships is very prominent in Japan. In the U.S.A., dependence is discouraged. Separation-individuation development is considered the norm. Thus, the elderly American woman does not assume that as a widow she will automatically move into her child's home. Whereas, even though a growing number of Japanese aged widows do live alone, most are living with their children.

In both countries, healthy elderly women are active in the commu-

nity. A number of Japanese women are taking courses at "elder universities," they are encountered everywhere in the community, and many are still working or volunteering. They are living longer and expecting the community, not just their children, to offer them better health services, pensions, senior centers, home care services, social services, senior housing, and nursing homes. They use their pensions to maintain greater independence from their children, at least, financially. They are traveling abroad in large groups. They are joining social and cultural organizations. They are flocking to classes in flower arranging, tea ceremony, traditional dancing, calligraphy, and haiku (poetry). The Americans, too, are heavily involved in the arts and crafts as well as in volunteer work and attending classes in elder hostels, "evergreen" universities, and adult education centers. They are traveling widely. When illness and frailty occur, children are relied upon to help with care and planning (Maeda, Nobuo, 1989). Those who can afford to are joining retirement communities. Interestingly enough, the Japanese government is encouraging this, too, even suggesting places in the U.S.A., Spain, and other sites.

In both countries, women are outliving men and pursuing interests outside the home to keep occupied and alert. In the U.S.A., these activities are generally co-educational. Today, this is becoming the case in Japan, also. One of the women commented to us that she liked it better this way. She can bowl and play pool in the senior center with men as well as women. "It was unheard of in my childhood."

The changes of the last 45 years in the lives of Japanese older women have brought them closer to experiencing a world similar to their American cohort. They examine change from the time of their birth, some as far back as the 1890s, and not just from the end of World War II. They recall that as children they worked very hard in the family. When they became adults, many helped their husbands in the family businesses or farms. Very few were idle. Only those whose families encouraged higher education, especially in women's professions of teaching and nursing, could gain a higher status and greater security on their own. This was evident among those we interviewed. Some Japanese women were recognized in the arts and literature (women authors go back to the Heian period beginning 794 A.D.), but most were subject to many constraints and social dictates that stressed only domesticity and family involvement, endurance, submissiveness, and self-sacrifice, but rejected intellectual pursuits. Unfortunately, early widowhood left many women vulnerable,

defenseless, and insecure. Only the "Meiji matriarchs," a small educated group, were able to speak up and demand a change in the status of women. Other women suffered in silence. The present offers many older women in Japan the leisure to pursue interests they missed in earlier years. A number asserted to us, as if it was a big secret, that the best time of their life is the present now that there are fewer constraints and burdens of family care and earning a living. It is less likely that American women, brought up in a society in which youth and not old age are valued, would point to old age as the best time of life. However, Takie Lebra observed that Japanese older women might envy the freedoms and informalities of the lives of their American cohort, but many American older women ". . . do not look as contented as the latter (Japanese). Some of them indeed have declared to me that women are much better off in other societies including Japan" (1984, p. 315). Perhaps the grass always looks green elsewhere.

More complaints of loneliness are verbalized by American women, especially widows (Lopata, 1978), than are recorded in Japan, where so many live with a family member. In the U.S.A., so few do. However, one cannot ignore the fact that many Japanese elderly are isolated within their homes, and the suicide rate among the older women is high (Maeda, 1983).

Finally, comparisons should not be stretched too far. Older women in both countries have confronted enormous changes in their lives — social, economic, physical, political, demographic, and cultural. Their endurance and adaptability are evident. In this small book, we have documented what some Japanese older women are saying, how they view their lives, and how they coped under traumatic conditions. A comparable volume should be written about American women. But, it is very clear that, while women are generally considered "guardians of their country's domestic well-being and they become as well the architects of social change" (Robin-Mowry, p.309), their lives have been in a constant state of transformation, and many are still trying to control and adapt to those changes. In Japan, the younger women would like to remove the barriers in the work place as American women have done although not successfully as yet on the highest levels. But others are content to retain their monopoly within the family and live an internal matriarchal system and an external patriarchal one. The changes will come more slowly in Japan, but each generation is making its own efforts, as did the grand-

mothers we interviewed. External events and societal conditions will also influence the process. It is the older women in Japan, taking advantage of the opening of the community to women, that made possible the new status of women in their country. While in the U.S.A., the women's movement, sparked by the grandmothers of this generation, is constantly challenged by the same traditional and conservative forces that make progress difficult in Japan. In both countries, the traditional and progressive forces will likely continue to be articulate in pressing their points of view.

Nevertheless, in spite of the push and pull in the world of women, this small study of a group of Japanese older women demonstrates dramatically that women, confronted with adversities and trials, can cope, change, adapt, and survive, and that they do not have to hide in their homes feeling helpless. If they wish to, they can challenge themselves and their societies. The older women in both countries have proven this, and for this we are grateful.

Bibliography

Akiyama, Hirako; Antonucci, Toni; Campbell, Ruth (1990), "Exchange and Reciprocity Among Two Generations of Japanese and American Women," in Sokolovsky, Jay (ed.). The Cultural Context of Aging. New York: Bergin and Garvey Publishers.

Ariyoshi, Sawako (1984 English translation). The Twilight Years. Tokyo: Kodansha International.

Asano, Hitoshi; Maeda, Daisaku; Shimizu, Yutaka; (1984), "Social Isolation of the Impaired Elderly in Japan," Journal of Gerontological Social Work, Vol. 6, No. 4.

Asano, Hitoshi, Saito, Chizuru (1988) , "Social Service Delivery and Social Work Practice for Japanese Elders," Journal of Gerontological Social Work, Vol. 12, No. 1/2.

Austin, Lewis (ed.) (1976). Japan: The Paradox of Progress,New Haven, CT: Yale University Press.

Breytaspraak, Linda (1984). The Development of Self in Later Life. Boston: Little Brown and Company.

Butler, Robert (1963), "The Life Review: An Interpretation of Reminiscence in the Aged," Psychiatry, Journal for the Study of Interpersonal Process, Vol. 26, No. 1. Reprinted in Neugarten, Bernice (ed.) (1968). Middle Age and Aging. Chicago: University of Chicago Press.

Campbell, Ruth (1985), "The Reciprocal Relationships Within Japanese Families," Unpublished paper. 13th Meeting of the International Gerontological Society, New York City, July 1985.

Campbell, Ruth; Brody, Elaine (1985) "Women's Changing Roles and Help to the Elderly: Attitudes of Women in the US and Japan," The Gerontologist, Vol. 25, No. 6.

Caplan, Gerald (1981), "Mastery of Stress: Psychosocial Aspects," American Journal of Psychiatry, Vol. 138, No. 4.

Carlson, Christie (1984), "Reminiscing: Toward Achieving Ego Integrity in Old Age," Social Casework, Vol. 65, No. 2.

Cecchini, Sister Rose Marie (1976), "Women and Suicide," in Lebra, Joyce; Paulson, Joy; Powers, Elizabeth. Women in Changing Japan, Stanford, CA.: Stanford University Press.

Christopher, Robert (1983). The Japanese Mind. New York: Fawcett Columbine.

Coehl, George; Hamburg, David; Adams, John (1974). Coping and Adaptation. New York: Basic Books.

Coleman, Peter (1986). Ageing and Reminiscence Processes. New York: John Wiley and Sons.

Coleman, Peter (1974), "Measuring Reminiscence Characteristics from Conversation as Adaptive Features of Old Age," International Journal of Aging and Human Development, Vol. 5, No. 3.

Cressy, Earl Herbert (1955). Daughters of Changing Japan. Westport, CT.: Greenwood Press.

Doi, Takeo (1985). The Anatomy of Self. New York: Kodansha International.

Donow, Herbert (1990), "Two Approaches to the Care of an Elder Parent: A Study of Robert Anderson's 'I Never Sang for My Father' and Sawako Ariyoshi's 'The Twilight Years,'" The Gerontologist, Vol. 30, No. 4.

Erikson, Erik (1963). Childhood and Society. New York: W.W. Norton.

Frankl, Victor (1963). Man's Search for Meaning. New York: Pocket Books.

Freed, Anne (1990), "How Japanese Families Cope with Fragile Elderly," Journal of Gerontological Social Work, Vol. 15-1/2.

Freed, Anne (1988), "Interviewing Through an Interpreter," Social Work Journal, Vol. 33, No. 4.

Kaminsky, Marc (1978), "Pictures from the Past: The Use of Reminiscence in Casework with the Elderly," Journal of Gerontological Social Work," Vol. 1, No. 1.

Kermis, Marguerite (1986). Mental Health in Late Life: The Adaptive Process. Boston/Monterey: Jones and Bartlett Publishers, Inc.

Kiefer, Christie (1990), "The Elderly in Modern Japan: Elite, Victims, or Plural Players," in Sokolovsky, Jay (ed.). The Cultural Context of Aging. New York: Bergin and Garvey Publishers.

Koyano, Waturu (1989), "Japanese Attitudes Toward the Elderly: A Review of Research Findings," Journal of Cross-Cultural Gerontology, Vol. 4, No. 4.

Lebra, Joyce; Paulson, Joy; Powers, elizabeth, (1976). Women in Changing Japan. Stanford, California: Stanford University Press.

Lebra, Takie Sugiyama (1976). The Japanese Pattern of Behavior. Honolulu, Hawaii: University of Hawaii.

Lebra, Takie Sugiyama (1979), "The Dilemma and Strategies of Aging Among Contemporary Japanese Women," Ethnology, Vol. 18, No. 4.

Lebra, Takie Sugiyama (1984). Japanese Women: Constraint and Fulfillment. Honolulu, Hawaii: University of Hawaii.

Lewis, Charles (1971), "Reminiscing and Self-Concept in Old Age," Journal of Gerontology, Vol. 26, No. 2.

Lewis, Myrna; Butler, Robert (1974), "Life Review Through Therapy," Geriatrics, November.

Lieberman, Morton; Tobin, Sheldon (1983). The Experience of Aging: Stress, Coping, and Survivial. New York: Basic Books.

Liton, Judith; Olstein, Sara (1969), "Therapeutic Aspects of Reminiscence," Social Casework, Vol. 50. No. 5.

Long, Susan Orpett (1987). Family Change in the Life Course in Japan. Ithaca, New York: East Asia Study Program, Cornell University.

Lopata, Helen (1978), "Widowhood in America: An Overview," in Seltzer, Mildred; Corbett, Sherry; Atchley, Robert (eds.), Social Problems of Aging Readings. Belmont, CA: Wadsworth Press.

Lowy, Louis (1979). Social Work with the Aging. New York: Harper and Row, Publishers.

Lowy, Louis (1988), "Independence and Dependence in Aging: A New Balance," Journal of Gerontological Social Work, vol. 13 3/4.

Maeda, Daisaku (1983), "Family Care in Japan," The Gerontologist, Vol. 23, No. 6.

Maeda, Daisaku; Teshima, K.; Sugisawa, H.; Asakura, Yokiko (1989), "Aging and Health in Japan," Journal of Cross-Cultural Gerontology, Vol. 4, No. 2.

Maeda, Nobuo (1989), "Long-Term Care for the Elderly in Japan," in Schwab, Teresa. Caring in an Aging World. New York: McGraw Hill Information Services.

Matthews, Sarah (1979). The Social World of Old Women. Beverly Hills, CA: Sage Publications.

Mishima, Sumie Seo (1953). The Broader Way: A Woman's Life in the New Japan. New York: John Day Co.

Mori, Mikio (1979), "Service to the Aged in Japan," in Teigher, Morton; Thursz, Daniel; Vigilante, Joseph. Reaching the Aged. Beverly Hills, CA.: Sage Publications.

Mourer, Elizabeth Knipe (1978), "Women in Teaching," in Lebra, Joyce; Paulson, Joy; Powers, Elizabeth (eds.). Women in Changing Japan. Stanford, CA.: Stanford University Press.

Nakane, Chie (1973). Japanese Society. Tokyo: Charles Tuttle Co.

Payne, Edmund C. (1975), "Depression and Suicide," in Howells, John (ed.). Modern Perspectives in the Pscyhiatry of Old Age. New York: Brunner/ Mazel Publishers.

Pearlin, Leonard; Schooler, Carmi (1978), "The Structure of Coping," Journal of Health and Social Behavior, Vol. 19, March.

Pharr, Susan (1976), The Japanese Woman: Evolving View of Progress. New Haven, CT.: Yale University Press.

Plath, David (1980). Long Engagements: Maturity in Modern Japan. Palo Alto, CA.: Stanford University Press.

Plath, David (1972), "Japan: The After Years," in Cowgill, D.; Holmes, L. (eds.). Aging and Modernization. New York: Appleton-Century-Croft.

Robins-Mowry, Dorothy (1983). The Hidden Sun. Boulder, CO: Westview Press.

Shanes, Ethel (1980), "Older People and Their Families: The New Pioneers," Journal of Marriage and the Family, Vol. 42.

Sodei, Takako (1987), "Family Care for Frail Elders in Japan." Unpublished speech, George Warren Brown School of Social Work, Washington University, St. Louis, Missouri.

Sodei, Takako (1987), "The Effect of Industrialization and Modernization on Filial Responsibility Toward Aging Parents: A Comparative Study Based on a Survey in Tokyo, Seoul, and Taipei" Unpublished speech given in Seoul, Korea.

Shimer, Dorothy (ed.) (1982). Rice Bowl Women. New York: New American Library.

Sugimoto, Etsu Inagaki (1966). A Daughter of a Samuri. Rutland, VT. and Tokyo, Charles Tuttle Co.

Tanaka, Yukiko; Hanson, Elizabeth (1982). This Kind of Woman. New York: Putnam Co.

Tobin, J. (1987), "The American Idealization of Old Age in Japan," The Gerontologist, Vol. 27.

Vogel, Ezra (1971). Japan's New Middle Class. Berkeley, CA: University of California Press. 2nd Edition.

Vogel, Suzanne (1989). "Some Reflections on Changing Strains in the Housewife/Mother Role," Mental Health, Tokyo, No. 57.

White, Robert (1974), "Strategies of Adaptation: An Attempt at Systematic Description," in Coelho, George; Hamburg, David; Adams, John. Coping and Adapting. New York: Basic Books.

Zarit, Steven H. (1980). Aging and Mental Disorders. New York: The Free Press.